D1596521

THE EPITHETS IN HOMER

THE EPITHETS IN HOMER

IN HOMER

A STUDY IN POETIC VALUES

PAOLO VIVANTE

YALE UNIVERSITY PRESS
NEW HAVEN AND LONDON

Designed by Sally Harris
and set in IBM Press Roman type.
Printed in the United States of America by
Edwards Brothers Inc., Ann Arbor, Mich.

Library of Congress Cataloging in Publication Data

Vivante, Paolo.
    The epithets in Homer.

    Includes bibliographical references and index.
    1. Homer—Style. 2. Greek language—Epithets.
I. Title.
PA4037.V48   883'.01   82–4856
ISBN 0–300–02708–7   AACR2

10 9 8 7 6 5 4 3 2 1

CONTENTS

PART III: THEORIES OF THE EPITHET

PREFACE

I deal in these pages with a principle of imaginative focus as characteristic of poetic expression. Homer's noun-epithet phrases illustrate it continually by arresting the image of a thing in the fleeting passage of action. Around these phrases clusters the large body of discourse which brings out ideas of relation: cause and effect, reciprocity, narrative connection, swift transition, descriptive pointedness. We may thus distinguish a purely representational moment on the one hand and a relational one on the other. The epithets generally belong to the former; and they tend to be dropped out when the latter prevails. These two modes, however, constantly interpenetrate each other, giving rise to innumerable complexities. What I do is to explore some of these complexities and draw conclusions which contain, I believe, a clear core of truth, though some of their details might be questioned.

My concern is to discover a truly poetic reason for the occurrence of the epithets. By *poetic* I mean here intrinsic to the value of the expression, intimately pertinent to the expressed object and to the moment of its emergence, quite apart from any external frame of reference. This is not to say, of course, that ideas of relation may not be poetical; but then the focus shifts to comprehend the terms of the relation and a broader identity occurs. The relation itself, in other words, becomes a point of focus and it requires a different form of expression.

My view of the Homeric epithets thus points to one comprehensive view of poetry. It is time, I think, to dwell on similarities and common essences rather than on differences. There is one concept of poetry which emerges through infinitely varied manifestations. If Homer's epithets seem peculiar, it is only that they do in their own particular way what poetry does in any age or place.

What stands out is a sense of potentialities embedded in the language, a mode of perception bodied out in words, poetic tendencies rather than rules. I could have pursued the same aesthetic and linguistic ideas by studying any other element of the language. If I have chosen the epithets, it is because they have lent themselves most to theories which banish Homer from the world of thought by positing a peremptory differentiation between "literary poetry" and "oral poetry."

It will be objected that I am letting my own judgment take the place of those historical considerations which led to the theory of "oral poetry." "How so?" I may be asked. "How explain a single poet using a phraseology so recurrent, so systematic, so adapted to versification? Is not the source to be sought in tradition, in predetermined formulas orally transmitted?"

Such objections hardly touch the gist of my argument. Whatever origin we assign to Homer's expressions, they carry within them the measure of their own worth, and it is this intrinsic value with which I am chiefly concerned. I may object in turn: "Why did these formulas come into being in the first place and attain such currency? What kind of excellence, what felicity made them so vital?" Or, more particularly, from the viewpoint of meter, "Did not these formulas condition the hexameter as well as being conditioned by it, an expressive value precipitating both at one and the same time?" Or, again, from the viewpoint of meaning, "Why 'formula'? Should we not rather speak of form in the fullest sense, in that some significant instance of life is embodied in self-contained expression?"

Such questions are most relevant, even from a historical point of view. Any research in the formation of a poetic language cannot avoid the question of what poetic value underlies that language. It is quite inadequate merely to invoke social and cultural habits, thus confusing the work with its outward conditions. We might as well study a political constitution without inquiring into the idea of justice or a religion without concerning ourselves with the nature of its god. Any phenomenon would become a matter of custom and ritual. Any momentous development or achievement requires some overriding idea to bring it about and impart to tradition a new direction. The historian should take into account such a compelling cause and make room for it in time and place.

The idea of an expressive value thus throws light on the composition of the poems. Homer's expression is a *causa sui*, not a means to an end. We should find within it the reason and justification of its emergence. It was a sense of its poetic value which fashioned it and established it. Growth and success, in other words, were ultimately due to the effectiveness of a poetic principle —to truth in the expression, adequacy of representation, and a consequent applicability in the broadest sense. The phases of composition were thus all one with the varying degrees in which the formative stress might be powerful enough to reduce and assimilate the material.

What was, more precisely, this poetic principle or expressive value in Homer? I try to define it in the present work insofar as the noun-epithet phrases may offer some glimpse.* Most generally we may say that it consisted in rendering any narrative theme in the concrete aspects of its realization—as succeeding moments of movement and rest, pulses and pauses of life. Hence a dynamic juxtaposition of sentence to sentence, of scene to scene—a pattern, or a form of thought, pursued on a widening scale in such a way as to encompass any complex human event in the same concrete outline. A general action seen in the vital continuity of single acts, time realized in its consecutive creative moments, narrative actualized and dramatized—all this implied no less than a radical transfomation in the very ways of perception.

In this light we must reconstrue the historical background. However we may view the personality of Homer, we must recognize that there *was* a poetic intelligence at work, that there *was* a point of intensified activity and a full consciousness of what was being achieved. This is to say that we must reckon with the intellectual climate of the age. The poet and his listener were at one in a moment of poetic awareness, and this relation was not the mere interplay which exists between a performer and his audience. The interest lay in the mode of delivery, quite apart from any particular subject matter. What stood uppermost was a most vital style: things visualized both in their solidity and transience, at once the stillness of form and the swiftness of movement.

Here was a breaking point in the tradition, an intellectual and artistic movement reaching its acme. Such an intense experience could not be drawn out at length; a long elaboration would have weakened it. I thus imagine that the creative period was much shorter than is commonly assumed, not necessarily longer than three generations. Here was time for a new poetic function to reveal itself, for a vast linguistic material to be drawn into the representation of action in the Homeric sense. In tracing sequences of lifelike, self-developing acts, even the most antiquated formula found its place and vital role.

The initial effect must have been at once pervasive, magnetic. We may realize this if we look at the composition of the poems as style decisively penetrating the material. See how the repetitions of the same phrase or typical scene are but literal instances of an intuited measure which is rehearsed upon a variety of matter—from the battle scenes, say, to the encounters in Hades. Rather than inveterate craft we have here a touch so firm and so pliant as to become a mode of thought. Can such a sense of things be traditional?

The alternative view, which magnifies the tradition, seems far less plausible. It presents Homer as the spokesman for opaque generations of bards succeeding one another through long, nameless centuries. The formulas float, as it were, over a no-man's-land—compositional elements at anyone's disposal, aids to versification and performance. No focus here on any poetic idea, no

---

*The translations of passages from the *Iliad* and the *Odyssey* are my own. They are intended to bring out the value of the epithets.

hint of the intellectual side of art or of those mental dispositions which must be present even in the meanest singer. We are left with the pale concept of oral techniques—or, at best, mere skill, talent, taste. My view, on the other hand, has the advantage of removing us from this neutral ground: Homer's forms of expression regarded as the realization of a poetic ideal. Even the classifier of formulas might find something to gain in perceiving some added worth in his classification.

PART I: THE EPITHETS AND POETRY

1. QUALITIES AND IDENTITIES

1

Grammatical usage, as well as Scholasticism, has accustomed us to think of substantives as separate from their attributes. They are solid, permanent, whereas what we impute to them is alterable, elusive, arbitrary. We thus have primary elements and their secondary modifications: a subject and its predicates, objective data and their qualities. The very terms *adjective, epithet* convey the idea of something supplementary, adventitious. They imply that things are identified first and qualified later, as if qualities were not part and parcel of their identities.

Such a view has a solid logic of its own. It provides us with basic classifications. We cannot help using its terms. But it is valid only for the purposes of a descriptive analysis. Language itself tells us otherwise, by hardly differentiating the inflection of nouns from that of adjectives. And our aesthetic sense here concurs. For when we perceive anything with unusual vividness, what strikes us is a characterizing quality rather than an obvious, specific figure. A tree, for instance, may appear as a shimmering mass of color, and in this qualitative impression we discover anew the identity of a tree.

This is always the case in moments of fresh perception. We do not take things for granted; we do not merely mention them and use their names for some ulterior purpose. No, we realize them. We naturally dwell on their identity. They come imbued with the qualities which give each its distinction. There seems to be, in such moments, a perfect coincidence between the perceived object and the vague, fluid, unlimited world of values which are pertinent to it. Whatever we may envisage, the process and the outcome are the same: implicit qualities center at a point of focus, and a mental image arises which charms or repels us or subtly strikes us with its sensuous appeal.

We are all aware of such an experience, even though we seldom put it into words. This happens in instants of extreme lucidity, when we look at a familiar object as if it were for the first time, and our visualization is at the same time cognition, insight, awareness of values. It would be hard, of course, to give any example. It may be best to be quite plain and draw from instances of common speech, reading into them as much as we can. Take such a phrase as "dear friend" or "glorious sunshine." Consider it, trying to recover, if possible, the full value of the words so used. It will then be not a cliché but the expression of a basic feeling or idea. There is here a positive, natural extension of what we mean by "friend" or "sun." The adjectives do not serve to describe, instruct, explain: they simply dwell on the meaning itself, working up the identity of the thing in question. Designation, impression, value judgment are all merged into a single form of expression.

Here is a basic enunciation of meaning. What we say is not prompted merely by a practical need of communication, but by a creative disposition to perceive and express things in the name of their own intrinsic value. It might, of course, be objected that in the examples just quoted the adjectives "dear" and "glorious" are quite dispensable, that the names "friend" and "sun" are by themselves capable of suggesting these qualities. But this confirms my point. A mere name, when used in its pregnant value, is in itself resonant; and if adjectives are added to it in this perceptive sense, they simply elicit values which are implicitly there. In such instances the adjective but confirms the substantive idea in that the name is not a mere matter of fact designation, in that it is not used merely for an ulterior purpose.

All this points to poetic moments of ordinary speech. What is it we do whenever we spontaneously express something for whatever it is worth without prejudice or external motive—outside the immediate necessity of begging, asking, obtaining, denying, granting, commanding, deciding whatever we may have in view? What is it we do in such cases if it be not to dwell for a moment on the intrinsic value of what we perceive or think—whether we happily characterize anything or formulate an idea which we have in mind? Even when we plead or argue, we are most eloquent and poetic whenever the immediate point of contest recedes and we dwell on the worth of our cause in itself and by itself. It is then that we strike fully upon the object of perception or thought, isolating it, enhancing it, universalizing it by bringing it out in full light quite apart from any plan or calculation. Whether we use nouns with their adjectives or any figure of speech, what we do is to focus on a principle of identity—that is to say, on the nature of a thing insofar as that thing is both objectively determined and a source of intuited values.

2

It is in poetry that expression of this kind is attested most richly. Since nouns and epithets are my main topic, let me start by quoting this passage from Emerson's journals:

In poetry, Nature bears the whole expense. In prose, there must be concatenation, a mass of facts, and a method. 'T is very costly; only a capitalist

can take hold of it; but in poetry, the mere enumeration of natural objects
suffices. Nay, Tennyson is a poet, because he has said, "the stammering
thunder," or "the wrinkled sea beneath him crawls"; and Longfellow, "the
plunging wave".[1]

What does Emerson mean here by "enumeration"? Not, obviously, counting
or numbering a series of items, but so to present things that they each stand
out in their own right. This is why he says that in poetry Nature bears the
whole expense. To the extent that natural objects stand out in themselves, nature is given full scope. What we find is nature's resourcefulness, things rendered in their native color or form, and not a laborious, systematic treatment
which compresses the objects of experience in order to prove its own valid-
ity. The poet thus names an object and, in the very act, exposes it, lets out the
secret of its spell. Subjectively perceived, wondered at, realized, such an
object is transfigured into an image and set forth in relief. We may, therefore,
elaborate a little on Emerson's concept of enumeration. It means bodying
forth, disclosing an identity, naming in the fullest sense. It implies a contemplative moment of representation. The reader or the listener is here at one
with the poet. We make the poet's image our own. It speaks for itself, it is self-
existent.

Emerson's quotations might be paralleled by many others of a similar nature. The poetic use of adjectives is singularly appropriate. Rather than describing or particularizing for any arbitrary purpose, they enhance the nature
of a thing, giving it a richer reality. Take, for instance, Keats's

> White hawthorn and the pastoral eglantine;
> Fast fading violets cover'd up in leaves;
> And mid-May's eldest child,
> The coming musk-rose, full of dewy wine,
> The murmurous haunt of flies on summer eves.

What is the purpose of the adjectives? Certainly not to explain the peculiar-
ities of these plants nor to bring out any particular point. We might again
say, with Emerson, that Keats simply enumerates. He sets before us points of
focus. We see qualities solidifying into things and things extenuating into
qualities. Botanical names and qualifications would merely instruct us. And a
mere effect of color or atmosphere would not be convincing. As it is, the
imaginary place suddenly comes alive. The words are concrete, evocative. The
delightful sensations of an April woodland night seem to find a name and a
native spot.

5

3

A characteristic of the poetic expressions mentioned above is that they are in themselves memorable. This is true even of such noun-epithet phrases as those cited by Emerson. They have a haunting, suggestive quality, even though they are cut off from the sentence to which they belong. They can thus stand by themselves and still be meaningful. For they constitute images, in the sense I have tried to outline; and it is the property of such images to be self-contained, clear-cut, significant within their contours.

There is an ultimate, existential reason for such independent force in an image, even in a solitary image expressed by a mere name or noun-epithet phrase. The reason lies in the fact that a qualitative identity stands revealed. Some vital spot, something imaginatively as well as objectively true is brought out and isolated from the tangled web of existence. I find what I wish to convey well expressed by Max Eastman. Referring to what he calls "the selective poetic name," he writes:

> It guides the attention to a focus. And this service, though it may seem slight in the proposal, is in fact very great, and for the majority indispensable to the acute realization of anything. Even to that lucky few who are by nature awake when their eyes are open, the living word is no superfluity. He who can speak it, who can sometimes catch the humour of their sensibility and crystallize it upon a point, is as dear to them as he is tedious who can neither select a focus nor remain silent, but spreads adjectives all over the face of nature.[2]

Or again:

> For words make the world grow—not, I think, because they express a feeling, . . . but because they give to the feeling locality and distinct body.[3]

A poetic image thus ultimately draws its strength from nature itself, and this strength gives it its self-existence, its autonomous status. Though of course it must have a certain context, though it must always be possible to trace it back to some definite occasion, though it may presuppose much mental activity, yet it naturally detaches itself from its background and its weighty motivations are silently implied in a pure relevance of form. Take again the verses of Keats quoted above. That imagery of plants and flowers, those simple names with their epithets and appositions, have of course their place in the train of thought which governs the "Ode to a Nightingale," and the ode itself has in turn its place in the life of the poet and in the history of literature. At the same time, however, the passage could be appreciated by itself, even if it were an anonymous fragment. For this fusion of sound and meaning centers upon an element of existence, identifies it, brings it out at one stroke. It is important, in this respect, that the adjectives and qualifying words do not have any narrative or other pointed connection with the rest of the poem but are only bound with it by deeper undercurrents of meaning. We are drawn to an existential quality and not to any particular topic.

4

Obviously we are going here far beyond the theme of nouns and epithets. That qualitative identity which they touch upon is the object of poetic expression as a whole. Parts or figures of speech are but details of the craft. We cannot do justice to them as elements of poetic technique unless we form some idea of what they are all about. Even at the risk of falling into generalities, we must so broaden the concept of poetic expression as to feel and understand what it is that makes the representation of anything "poetic," in whatever age, in whatever literary genre, whether in verse or prose.

I submit that this common poetic element lies in the sense of qualitative identity which we have seen most simply expressed in a mere name or noun-epithet phrase. Take any single poetic passage or poem, and you will find that, on a far more complex scale, it achieves the same thing. Insofar as it is really poetic, it so presents a material object or event or idea as to expose it in its own right—in its full actuality, in its deep and transparent identity. And, as a consequence, anything so exposed will stand for a moment isolated in its own vantage point, as much as possible liberated from the chain of cause and effect, from the complication of circumstances, from the distraction of fastidious descriptive details.

It may be objected that any material object has its environment, any event its cause and effects, any idea its pertinence to a given situation, and that a poet—especially a dramatic or epic poet—must take these things into due account. The answer is that any such environment, cause, effect, pertinence will, if poetically treated, become a point of focus in its turn: it will be seen for its own sake, as a spot given full exposure, as a moment freshly realized, as something existing through its own virtuality. The plot, on the other hand, will grow out of each occasion seen in its own self-relevance; the general picture out of each feature seen in its own significant outline; the message, if there is one, from an idea understood and experienced for all it is worth in a moment of insight. The poetry, in any case, resides in the degree of realization. Something intensely felt and lucidly perceived passes into the transfiguring substance of words—into a form which heightens its identity by simply focusing on its baffling existence.

5

Let us test this principle of qualitative identity upon significant passages of poetry. Take *Hamlet* 1.4.39ff. Seeing his father's ghost, Hamlet says,

> Angels and ministers of grace defend us!
> Be thou a spirit of health or goblin damned,
> Bring with thee airs from heaven or blasts from hell,
> Be thy intents wicked or charitable,
> Thou com'st in such a questionable shape
> That I will speak to thee. I'll call thee Hamlet,
> King, father, royal Dane. O, answer me!
> Let me not burst in ignorance, but tell
> Why thy canoniz'd bones, hearsed in death,
> Have burst their cerements; why the sepulchre
> Wherein we saw thee quietly enurn'd
> Hath op'd his ponderous and marble jaws
> To cast thee up again. What may this mean
> That thou, dead corse, again in complete steel
> Revisits thus the glimpses of the moon,
> Making night hideous, and we fools of nature
> So horridly to shake our disposition
> With thoughts beyond the reaches of our souls?
> Say, why is this? wherefore? what should we do?

What is it that makes the passage so impressive—and quite apart from its place in the drama, quite apart from Hamlet as a character? The diction plays of course an important part. What is it then in the diction—in the diction as expression of what is seen, felt, thought? It is that the expression dwells entirely upon the sheer presence of the ghost. We have no descriptive account of the beholder's feelings or of the ghost's appearance or of the circumstances. No, again and again the speaker returns to the phenomenon itself. His own emotions but enhance the questionable shape. What matters is its nature, its presence. There is, therefore, a self-contained movement. We are not carried forward as in a narrative or an argument. We linger, rather, on the reality laid out before us. No sooner is it shown in one perspective than we return to it; and every turn means a deepening identity.

Each clause seems to bear out this point. The bare statement "I'll call thee Hamlet,/King, father, royal Dane" strikes the same note as any of the wondering apostrophes. The questions are thus realizations of what is perceived. They contain their own answer. The experience and the wonder, the object and its mystery are all one. What matters is the ghost itself, the penetrating touch which gives it existence at that moment. Hence the power of the imagery: how final are those bones, how perpetually significant of life on the planet are those glimpses of the moon.

We might very well make similar remarks about the scene between Odysseus and Anticleia's ghost in *Od.* 11.210-24. Odysseus' cry

> Is this but a shadow, did bright Persephone send it
> yet further to deepen my pain . . .?

wells up from his futile embrace, and at once brings out the sense of what is there in all its poignancy. No other is Anticleia's reply:

> Oh my child, amongst all men the most hapless,
> it is not Persephone daughter of Zeus that deceives you,
> but this is the nature of mortals, whenever one dies;
> no longer the sinews can hold the flesh and the bones,
> but the flame's strong fury all subdues
> whenever the spirit leaves the white bones,
> and the soul like a dream in flight is lifted away.
> But strive thou quick to the light. . . .

Anticleia's statement, though intended as an explanation, is again a pure rendering of the thing itself as it is imagined to be. It does not dogmatize. It does not exhaust or diminish the mystery. Nor does it go into any detail. Rather it simply conjures up the image of the soul. Anticleia's words might thus be presented in the form of a question and not of a reply, as part of Odysseus' wonder: "Is this the nature of mortals . . . ?"

Hence, in both passages, the strong sense of realization: in Homer, Persephone's deception which is no deception at all, and in Shakespeare, "fools of nature." Also the same bare recognition occurs in "white bones" and "bones hearsed in death"; and, on the other hand, the same elemental sense of existence: the dear light of day from which Anticleia is excluded and back to which she urges Odysseus, the glimpses of the moon which Hamlet's ghost revisits as a stranger. But the points of resemblance can hardly be analyzed. What gives to both passages their self-contained strength is the fact that they both present a ghost without taking it for granted, that they strike directly upon its nature or identity, thus dwelling for a moment upon a deep, existential theme and not merely upon a plot.

6

The same is true of single lyrics—high keynotes arising from that vast field of associations which, like an unwritten or unspoken epic, constitutes a poet's inner life.

What always stands out is a center which expands as far as it can remain

9

true to itself. Poems as different from each other as, say, Spenser's *Epithalamion* and Shelley's "To a Skylark" have this common characteristic in that they dwell again and again on the same thing, imparting to it precision of contour and infinity of suggestion. At times, as in Blake's "Tyger! Tyger! burning bright," the focus is sharper, harder, but equally significant. The object becomes a thought, the thought an object, so fused that we could not tell which comes first. But no particular object is required as a point of support. It may be the very drift of thought which, turning upon itself, finds its focus and form. This is especially so in much modern poetry, as in Dylan Thomas's "The force that through the green fuse drives the flower." Thomas himself gives us a cue, speaking of his poems as "fugues of sound expressing some lyrical impulse, some spiritual doubt or conviction, some dimly-realized truth I must try to reach and realize." [4] The term *fugue* is here revealing: an effect as encompassing as that of point and counterpoint.

There is no need, however, to seek outstanding examples. Countless high points in prose or verse show this concentration of expression in whatever way. Even a sally or a conceit may exemplify it. In what does its felicity consist? It is a sharp edge, a sudden climax which gives delight even if we do not care for its ulterior purpose. Figures of speech have the same quality: a new focus displacing the matter-of-fact designation of things. "Such figures are but forms of amplification, ornamentation," the rhetorician might retort; and, in so doing, he would be begging the question. For we should attempt to recapture the original value of a so-called figure—some vital kernel of meaning identified, isolated, exposed in its own right.

This expressive principle is thus naturally poetic, nonrhetorical. It holds its own ground. Simple and broad as it is, it asserts itself regardless of subject matter. "Yes," it may be objected, "so broad and simple that it is hardly a principle at all, merely pointing to the fact of expressing a certain meaning." Indeed, I may reply, here lies the burden of the question. The act of expressing a meaning cannot be taken lightly. It must give us pause. If appreciated in its fullness, it implies nothing less than realization. When we really express something we do not merely communicate what we wish: the object of perception or thought stands out in its own identity removed from the hackneyed world of things taken for granted or accepted as common currency.

7

We may find confirmation of these reflections if we consider our own response to a work of art. What is it that strikes us first and foremost? Is it not some such point of focus or qualitative identity? This is so especially in regard to a composition of vast dimensions. For our imaginative understanding is naturally selective. It isolates certain instances out of the vast material which lies open to it; and these instances, we may assume, cannot but be a very positive element in the artist's work. Here lies our only source of immediate concrete knowledge. By such knowledge I mean a sense of how expression is realized in relation to the thing expressed—of how any object in nature is brought into poetic representation; and this vivid knowledge is reached most directly by focusing, as the artist must have done, on those vantage points of representation which stand out on their own account from within the great compositional context.

Take, in this respect, so vast a composition as the *Iliad*. How do we know it? How do we think of the poem as a whole? We can hardly grasp it in its totality. What comes to mind, in such a case, is an idea of the plot or of the general contents, historical associations, vague notions of literary genre, or the thought of our own interests and studies—all things which, however valuable, have no bearing on the poem itself as an actuality in its own right. But take, on the other hand, even a single line like "along the shore of the wide-roaring sea in silence he walked" and the matter of the *Iliad* comes alive; for here is a way of representing nature and man, by realizing a given spot at a given moment. Within this compass we may fully recover the imaginative moment of expression.

It may be urged that my viewpoint is too narrow. But the line just quoted is but one instance. The narrowness of focus is made up for by implicitness. The poet's imagination lingers here in the same way it does elsewhere. The passage is resonant: there are other men, other shores; and yet they wonderfully coalesce in one perspective, in a haunting single perception of a solitary human figure placed on the margin of earth and sea. And we may apply the same approach to other kinds of instances. Clusters of images arise, flashes of resemblance strike throughout the poem. It is as though the narrative were but a foil to these identities of form.

This truth of independent focal points is typical of Homer. It is found not only in the noun-epithet phrases, in the recurring sentences, in the typical scenes which arrest in permanent form an act or a state of being, but also in the major dramatic passages. Look at Thersites, or Helen and Paris, or Hector and Andromache: these scenes cling to our memory in that they stand their own ground without any mechanical connection with the context, in that they are independent points of focus irradiating on their own account. Or how do we form our notion of Achilles as a character? It is on the strength of a few scenes which stand in connection with one another not so much through narration as through forcible contiguity; and each instance is complete in itself, the link of cause and effect as direct as that of a blow and counterblow. The parts do not so much make up the whole as the whole provides a framework wherein each part has a life of its own.

Our vague notion of an ancient epic thus sharpens into perspectives which are immediately relevant to the experience of life and reality. In the same way, we may be aware of the subject matter and general composition in a great painting; but the moment we get closer we gain a deeper knowledge of what makes the painting: incidences of light and shade, moments of depth and exposure, colors condensing into form and forms evaporating into color. Here, as in Homer, we find coincidences and sequences: points of focus which accumulate and are integrated into a movement of life. We cease to take the subject matter for granted; we recompose it in terms of existential values.

What Homer typifies is universally applicable. Our firsthand knowledge comes from a luminous instance which reverberates elsewhere. Such an instance is both typical and vivid in itself. You may call it a motif, a theme, a keynote; but, whatever it is, there is at its source a vivid point of realization which we transform into a mental image: such is, in *War and Peace,* the ball where Andrei meets Natasha: like other events in the novel, it is one in its constellation. We think of such essential recurrences, even when much of the plot is forgotten. An indefinite variety of incidents cannot be retained. It is both repellent to the poetic imagination and to our own interest in depth. A feeling for the underlying truth drives us to dwell upon some engrossing action or state of being which gathers around an image.

Our knowledge of literature in its most vivid aspects is thus necessarily made up of fragments. But these fragments are deeply significant. They abide in our mind in sequences sustained by some keenly realized value. Even a single solitary image summons analogies. It is indeed a sign of its significance to do so; it hardly could, if it were something merely peculiar, strange, curious. Hence the extraordinary resilience of many a fragment in Greek lyric poetry —in Sappho, for instance, that apple which gleams on the topmost branch like a blossom in a Chinese painting, or the mysterious figure of a man in φαίνεταί μοι κῆνος. These are like epithets amputated of their substantives. We see the light without knowing whence it comes; it is left to our own imagination to recompose and integrate the scattered parts on the strength of an inherent significance. But we do essentially the same thing even where the author's complete work is available—measuring, in this case, the author's expression against the vast domain of what is unwritten, potential, imaginable. In the case of Homer, we are fortunate enough to have the whole *Iliad* and *Odyssey;* but we must not take this fortune for granted. That is to say, we must elicit the value of each passage as from a fragment; and then, passing on to the whole, rediscover it on a major scale.

2. THE EPITHET AND HOMERIC POETRY

1

Bearing these ideas in mind, we may now turn to the epithets of Homer.
I shall at once define a Homeric epithet as a characterizing word or group
of words that is so intimately bound to a certain noun as to form with it one
sole image, and this without any pointed connection of meaning with the
context.

We recognize here the poetic value which I have dwelt upon. An object so
bound up with an epithet stands out in itself and by itself, in its own identity;
it is not simply a means to an end, it is not entirely subjected to circumstance
or to cause and effect. Take, for instance, such a familiar kind of sentence
as "He went to the hollow ship." What strikes us for a moment is the ship itself, its nature, its shape. If the poet had said merely, "He went to the ship,"
he would simply have given us a piece of information leading to something
else. If, on the other hand, he had used some pointed adjective and said, for
example, "He went to the ship made ready for him," he would have brought
out a purely practical or utilitarian connection. As it is, the effect is altogether different. What we find is a quality intrinsic to the idea of ship. The
hollow ship is what it is. It is moored wherever it may be, true to itself and,
as such, unsubjected to the particular requirement of the action at a certain point. Here is something perceived for what it is. The ship's hollowness
is poetic precisely because it is irrelevant to the narrative occasion. What
matters in the moment is a pure reality of shape.

2

We may now pass from a typical sentence to a passage and see this poetic
value of the epithet in some significant instance. Take such a line as *Il.* 1.219:

> So he spoke, and on the silver hilt he held the heavy hand.

It is the moment in which Achilles is about to attack Agamemnon and is stayed by Athena. That the sword's hilt is of silver or that Achilles' hand is heavy does not matter at all to what is happening. "Silver hilt" and "heavy hand" recur elsewhere. It is the property of a hand to have weight or pressure, it is the property of a sword's hilt to be of silver. Things are thus portrayed for what they basically are. We are so used to pointed description rather than pure representation that this is not immediately obvious: the English phrase "heavy hand" conveys a sense of oppressive burden, and the specification "silver" either gives us a piece of information or denotes costliness.

Now the poetic quality of this verse mainly consists in the fact that the epithets have no connection with the narrative context. They exclusively turn on the pertinent details, producing an image. We forget the wrath of Achilles. We are drawn to that hilt, to that hand as to a piece of sculpture. Our eyes rest on their stillness, and the pause is visualized. The sword's silver, the hand's heaviness give to the moment its glitter, its volume.

A storyteller would have ignored this natural suspense. In his eagerness for facts, he might have elaborated on the goddess or brought into the picture the surrounding crowd of Achaeans. A writer striving for effect, on the other hand, would have pressed his point, telling us perhaps how the hero's violent hand came to uneasy rest. Not so in Homer. The epithets keep us fixed to a certain object and, therefore, to the act, to the situation itself. No intrusive interest is allowed to interfere—no curiosity of description, no variety of episodes, no arbitrary effect. The situation is reduced to its core: Achilles' halt. But it is also expressed in its fullest materialization: the silver hilt, the heavy hand. A moment of experience is thus set off in visual focus. We are free to read into it whatever nuance we wish; but on condition of recognizing, first and foremost, the importance of so representing a thing in its own intrinsic evidence.

3

Let us now see this significance of the epithets as it appears within the range of a whole scene. Take the arrival of the embassy at Achilles' tent (*Il.* 9. 182-95):

> They went along the shore of the wide-roaring sea,
> intensely praying the earth-holding, earth-shaking god
> that they might smoothly overcome the pride of Achilles.
> To the Myrmidons came they, to their ships and their tents,
> and found him delighting his heart with a tuneful lyre
> lovely cunningly-wrought, and the bar upon it was silver,
> which he took from the spoils conquering Eetion's city.

> With it his soul he delighted and sang the glories of men.
> Patroclus sat before him in silence alone,
> waiting for Achilles to cease from his song.
> They came forward, divine Odysseus preceded,
> and over against him they stood; amazed Achilles sprang up,
> still holding the lyre, leaving the chair where he sat,
> and just so Patroclus rose beholding the men.

Consider now the epithets—and also the lack of epithets—from line to line.

The act of walking is immediately centralized, grounded where it belongs: hence the epithet of the sea on the coastline. Likewise the act of prayer must be given strong relief: hence the epithets of the god to whom the prayer is addressed. The whole effect is very similar to that achieved in the rendering of Chryses in 1.34-36:

> Silent he went by the shore of the wide-roaring sea.
> And then walking away intensely the old man prayed
> to lord Apollo whom lovely-haired Leto gave birth to.

Both the spot and the term of prayer are set off, thus giving to the moment its full value.

Then comes the object of the prayer "that they might smoothly overcome the pride of Achilles." This introduces a general sense of purpose which abstracts us from the actual presence of Achilles, who is, therefore, left without epithet. There is, instead, another point of interest: his proud mind; and this interest is a moral one, removing us even further from Achilles as an image.

Then the arrival at the Myrmidons' camp. There is no epithet for their tents and ships, as this is but a hendiadys signifying "camp" (cp. p. 193).

Achilles himself now comes into view. What draws the attention, however, is not the hero himself, but his striking occupation. Thus the lyre is set in sudden focus: whence its rich epithets, along with the stress on the silver bar and its place of origin. For what matters is the simple fact that Achilles is singing and playing, and the instrument is central to the act. The song and its theme, on the other hand, are but background music; hence simply "he sang the glories of men" without epithet. Nor is there any epithet for the city of Eetion. Why so? Because it occurs in a phrase which itself qualifies the lyre and it is therefore quite out of focus.

Patroclus is added to the picture, sitting in silence, alone. Notice the lack of epithet: it is not his sheer presence or coming that matters, but his silent mood, his loneliness, the fact that he is waiting for Achilles to finish his song.

The case is different with the visitors who presently approach. Odysseus steps in, leading the way; hence the epithet which brings him into full physical evidence.

At the sight Achilles is roused, amazed. Patroclus likewise. The stress falls on the emotion, on the new tension. Hence, again, no epithets for the heroes.

Nor is there any epithet for Achilles' chair, which is mentioned merely for the sake of explanation: "leaving the chair where he sat." It is thus a quite subordinate detail and, significantly, expressed with ἕδος, a colorless neuter noun.

Nowhere in this scene does Achilles have an epithet. He is too much in the mind of all the other characters. He is too much an object of general concern. He is too engrossed in himself. The epithets are found instead with what comes into play directly, clearly, tangibly. This is most notably the case of the lyre, which lights up the moment like a still life that conveys a sense of pure existence even in the midst of a crowded scene.

What is the charm of the whole passage? It lies in the points of focus, in the way they are distributed, and in the ensuing sense of balance, proportion, harmony. The epithets, and the absence of epithets, play here an important part. Zones of light and shade succeed one another accordingly. From the grand outline of the shore down to the chair of Achilles everything is given pertinent relief by pure emergence in the field of vision. We have perceptions that complete one another rather than narrative. As a result, the epithets do not occur at all where we most might expect them from a conventional point of view—as, for example, to characterize Achilles in his proud aloofness or Odysseus in his delicate mission. No, they unobtrusively contribute to the clear perspective.

Think now what a lesser composer might have done. He might have elaborated on the fears and hopes of the ambassadors, whereas Homer condenses all this in an act of prayer face to face with the sea. He might have had Achilles dwelling on some appropriate detailed theme, whereas Homer simply focuses on the lyre and tells us only that he was singing the glories of men. The form of representation hardly admits digressions or descriptions. The epithets, rather than describing, enhance the presence of what is there: the sea, the god, the lyre.

4

This nonnarrative, nondescriptive character of the epithets is further shown by the way they are used in the sentence. For the noun with its epithet (whether it is subject or object of a verb) cannot but be inextricably joined with the rendering of a certain act or state of being, firmly enclosed in the resulting sentence, centralizing it as one self-contained moment. This is to say that the epithet is no ordinary attribute whose meaning might be drawn out, commented upon, explained, made into a theme of narration or description. Take again Achilles' lyre in the passage quoted above: it is so bound up with its epithets and so integrated with the act of Achilles playing that its portrayal does not at all break the unity of the sentence. The point of focus thus produced is sufficient to keep all subsequent detail in place: the silver bar, the provenance from Eetion's city follow as if they were prolonged epithets. All digression is thus precluded: there can be no further description of the lyre, no narrative of Eetion. In the same way the "shore of the wide-roaring sea" is all one with the act of walking upon it; the "earth-holding, earth-shaking god" all one with the prayer addressed to him; "divine Odysseus" all one with his entering. As elsewhere throughout the poems, we have points of focus which oust all diffuse narration.

3. NARRATIVE AND REPRESENTATION

1

I mean by *narrative* all that body of expression which, in a story or in any
account of events, presents things insofar as they bear on a general plan or
on an ulterior motive. I include here such description as serves to convey the
atmosphere of a certain environment. What prevails is a sense of connection,
relation, purpose, cause and effect. There is, in any case, a superimposed interest which overshadows the facts of immediate experience. We are driven to
a general effect and conclusion.

I use the term *representation,* on the other hand, for all expression that
touches strongly and swiftly upon its immediate object. In a story or in any
account of events, it stands out as a highlight. It is not *about* a certain thing,
but identifies the thing. It is evocative rather than descriptive. Brief as it is,
it does not break the train of thought but adds to its vividness. It is self-
contained without being a digression. The narrative connections are not rejected, but naturally fade into the background.

I am no doubt using the terms *narrative* and *representation* arbitrarily,
for I am using them with a view to inner motives and not to any clear-cut category. It might thus be urged that such strains of expression continually
interpenetrate each other. They do, nevertheless, point to distinct values; and
this distinction may prove useful to our purpose.[1]

2

I have pointed out the nonnarrative, representational value of the epithet. It
now follows that epithets are most richly used in the passages of the poems
in which representation prevails over narrative.

Take *Il.* 15.696–705:

> Bitter again by the ships was the battle;
> unwearied unscathed, you would say,

> they faced one another at war, they fought with such fury.
> This was their mind as they struggled: the Achaeans
> thought they would not escape from ruin but verily perish,
> while the heart in each of the Trojans had hope
> to set the ships afire and slay the Achaean heroes.
> With such feelings against one another they stood;
> then did Hector lay hold, at the stern, of the sea-faring
> sea-swift beautiful ship. . . .

The general description of the battle seems a foil to Hector's gesture. It describes, it explains the situation. It therefore lacks epithets, even though the things mentioned might well have them (battle, war, Achaeans, Trojans, ships). Hector, on the other hand, stands apart. He is a point of focus and not just part of the narrative. The moment in which he touches the ship is thus given full representation. Hence the epithets of ship. They do not describe the ship but set it off. Hector's act is brightly materialized.

Compare *Od.* 22.8–21:

> So he said, and on Antinous the bitter arrow he pointed,
> He was about to lift a beautiful cup
> golden two-handled, his hands were around it
> that he might drink the wine. Death was not in his mind.
> Who in the midst of a banqueting throng would ever think
> that one man alone, were he even the strongest of men,
> would bring upon him cruel death and dark doom?
> Him Odysseus, aiming, struck at the throat with his shaft.
> Right through the delicate neck passed the point.
> He bent on the side, the cup fell down from his hand
> at the blow . . . at once he pushed the table away
> hitting it with his foot, and spilt the food on the ground;
> the bread and cooked meat were defiled.

Notice, again, how the epithets give relevance to the moment. Antinous's cup is enriched with epithets at the moment he is about to take it and is struck down; it has no epithet in the subsequent description of the fall. Why so? Because in the first instance the cup is a point of focus; it is caught in its intrinsic form in that it is a central object and reflects the imminent drama. The same might be said of the bitter arrow and Antinous's delicate neck. On the other hand, the epithets tend to vanish later on. The wine and the table have no epithets, though they often have them elsewhere. The poet does not linger upon them, drawn as he is to give the story its setting. The aftermath of the central act is treated narratively, descriptively.

3

Here are other instances which are perhaps less obvious but no less significant:

Il. 1.531–37 (Zeus and Thetis after their interview):

> So having counselled they parted. She
> sprang to the engulfing sea down from resplendent Olympus;
> Zeus to his dwelling; and the gods all arose
> up from the seats in meeting their father; none of them dared
> to await his coming, but all stood up before him.
> So he there sat on his throne; not did Hera
> ignore when she saw him. . . .

The clear, independent movement of Thetis is given in its self-contained fullness: hence the epithets of the sea and of Olympus. The following lines, on the other hand, dwell on Zeus's relation to the other gods and lead descriptively to the coming scene: hence no epithets for Zeus, Hera, the other gods, no epithets for Zeus's dwelling or his throne.

2.37–42 (Agamemnon after his dream):

> He thought he would conquer the city of Priam that day;
> fool! Nothing he knew of the works which Zeus was devising,
> of the woes and groans which he was going to bestow
> through their violent combats upon the Achaeans and the Trojans.
> He woke from sleep; the divine voice was shed all about him;
> he sat up, he put on the soft tunic
> beautiful newly-made, cast the wide cloak around him . . .

We find here, as often elsewhere, epithets of tunic, cloak, etc. because these things are brought out by punctual, momentary, self-contained acts. There are no epithets, on the other hand, for city, Priam, Zeus, Achaeans, Trojans: these names serve to trace the general course of action and are narratively connected with the plot.

4.105–08 (Pandarus preparing to shoot Menelaus):

> Forthwith he unsheathed the well-polished bow made of goat-horn—
> a strong wild goat which he smote once under the breast
> as it was descending a rock; he was waiting for it in ambush
> and hit its chest; there it fell back on the rock.

The bow's and goat's epithets are there to focalize Pandarus's momentary decisive act; but in the subordinate narrative of the hunt there is no epithet for "rock," which so often has it elsewhere.

5.794-97 (Athena finding Diomedes):

> She found the king by his chariot and horses
> cooling the wound which Pandarus struck on him with his arrow.
> Sweat chafed him under the broad strap of the well-rounded shield;
> . . . lifting the strap he was wiping away the dark blood.

It is the vexatious rub of the strap which is in focus here, a self-contained detail which might be removed without loss to the narrative sequence but at the cost of missing the vivid moment: hence the wealth of epithets with strap, shield, blood. On the other hand, the narrative explanation (Pandarus, arrow) has no epithets. Nor are there any for Diomedes cooling his wound, his chariots and horses: circumstances rather than central facts.

6.494-502 (Hector and Andromache):

> Thus bright Hector spoke and took the horse-tailed helmet;
> his wife was on her way home
> often turning around, shedding full-blown tears.
> Quickly she arrived at the well-founded house
> of man-slaying Hector, and joined there the many handmaids;
> in all she stirred lamentation.
> Upon Hector yet alive they mourned in his house;
> for they thought he would never return from the war,
> escaping the might and the hands of the Achaeans.

The epithets in the first part of the passage give body to each act, each movement; not least Andromache's arrival at the house ("of man-slaying Hector" as well as "well-founded" is epithet of "house"). On the other hand neither Hector yet alive nor his house has any epithet in the lines that follow: what stands uppermost is the women's foreboding, their sense of Hector's present condition and of what is to come.

8.53-74. In 53-67 there is a general account of the battle with very few epithets interspersed. But, in 67-74, the single acts of Zeus weighing the scales are each rendered with phrases which contain epithets, as if to mark the weight of the moment:

> Then did the father lay out the golden scales,
> put upon them two dooms of down-crushing death
> for the horse-taming Trojans and the bronze-clad Achaeans;
> he held them up at the midpoint, Achaea's fateful day swayed low.
> Down to the nourishing earth sank the dooms of the Achaeans,
> up to vast heaven those of the Trojans arose.

11.531-37 (Kebriones, Hector's charioteer):

> So he said and lashed at the horses-of-beautiful-mane
> with the clear-sounding whip; and hearing the blow
> quickly they drew the swift car among the Achaeans and the Trojans,
> crushing bodies and shields; with blood all the axle
> was bespattered beneath and the rims enclosing the chariot
> were struck with splashes from hooves of horses and wheels.

The central act of Kebriones fills and colors the moment: hence the epithets. The rest is descriptive, designed to produce a general effect: hence no epithets.

12.110-24. The onslaught of Asios against the Achaean wall is full of epithets (110-15): Asios son of Hyrtacos leader of men ... swift ships ... windy Ilium. But there follows (118-23) a passage which explains the direction, condition, circumstance of his attack: hence no epithets of such things as ships, Achaeans, horses, ships, gates.

13.1-6:

> Once he had made the Trojans and Hector come close to the ships,
> Zeus left them there to endure pain and toil
> relentlessly, and he himself turned his shining eyes far away—
> looking far over the land of the horse-herding Thracians,
> of the close-fighting Mysians and of the bright Hippemolgi
> that-feed-on-milk and of the Abioi the justest of men.

There are no epithets of Hector, Trojans, ships in the temporal sentence, which merely denotes a narrative connection. Contrast with this Zeus's shining eyes as they turn away. The epithets of people hold us to the visual focus. They give sustenance to Zeus's lingering expansive gaze.

16.218-22:

> In front of all two men were arming themselves,
> Patroclus and Automedon, united in spirit,
> to fight before the Myrmidons; and Achilles
> went to his tent, opened up the chest
> beautiful cunningly-made. . . .

It is significant that there are no epithets in the sentence which quite generally points out the arming of Patroclus, Automedon, the Myrmidons; but not so in the singling out of the opening of the chest. Likewise in the following lines each object is brought into strong focus by the central act of Achilles libating to Zeus: the well-shaped cup, the lovely flow of water, the gleaming wine.

18.490-508. There are epithets in the singling out of Hephaestus's creative act (490-91). Then follows the presentation of the city at peace. It is a description of human activities producing a general effect of social life: hence no epithets of things which have epithets elsewhere (women, chambers, lyres, porches, city). The only instance of epithets here is at 18.503-05:

> and the elders
> sat on the well-polished stones in the sacred circle
> holding in their hands the sceptres of the airy-voiced heralds.

The epithets of the place isolate the elders in their clear setting (so Nestor and Alcinous similarly sit in *Od.* 3.406, 8.6); and this in contrast to the descriptive situation of the litigants or of the public in the crowded scene.

Similar remarks could be made about 550-60 (cp. 541-43). Elsewhere the scenes depicted on the shield are made up of momentary acts which tend to take the color of actuality; and the epithets are frequent.

23.708-32. In the wrestling match between Odysseus and Ajax, the two heroes are represented each with his epithets when they appear in their full presence, engaged in a simple self-contained act (to stand, to speak, to lift): cp. 708, 709, 722, 729); but not so in explaining their maneuvers (cp. 719, 720, 725, 727).

Od. 1.102-12. Athena suddenly arriving and appearing at the threshold of Odysseus' palace is rich with epithets (102-06); but there are relatively few epithets in the lines which follow describing the general behavior of the suitors (none with gates, wine, crater, water, tables). Cp. 17.167-72.

Od. 5.291-96. General description of a storm: no epithets of earth, sea, sky, wind. But epithets of single winds suddenly breaking out:

> Eurus and Notus fell in and ill-breathing Zephyrus
> and Boreas born-of-the-sky.

6.85-100. Nausicaa's arrival at the washing-place is strongly focalized (85-87):

> When they arrived at the lovely streams of the river
> where were perpetual pools, and much beauteous water
> was flowing. . . .

The unyoking of the mules is similarly rendered (89-90):

> They turned them loose along the eddying river
> To graze on the honey-sweet grass.

Here the epithets are frequent; but not so in the following lines (90-100), which take a more narrative tone in describing the work and sport of the girls (no epithets of chariot, garments, sea, shore, river, headbands, etc.).

8.1-10. Alcinous and Odysseus arise, sit in the assembly of the Phaeacians. As often on such an occasion there are rich epithets of people and things: each act is strongly outlined and fixed where it belongs. But there are far fewer epithets or none at all for the picture of the general background, for the people that crowd about to watch and hear; cp. 15-17, 57-58, 109-10. Nor are there any epithets in the explanation of the design of Athena: 21-23.

9.216-23. The interior of Polyphemus's cave is described: there are cheeses, folds of kids and lambs, pails, bowls. In this general description there are very few or no epithets either for any of these things or for the cave itself. Compare, on the other hand, 240-49: here Polyphemus is presented as attending to each of his tasks, and there are epithets of the objects which serve to implement single acts (the doorstone, goats, milk, baskets).

9.415-35 (Description of the blind Cyclops sitting at the cave's entrance, groping, feeling his sheep): There is a general effect of his helplessness which blurs the incidence of single acts: no epithets (none for the Cyclops himself, the doorstone, the sheep) (cp. 415-19). There are rich epithets, on the other hand, for the rams that are suddenly involved in Odysseus' central stratagem (425-27); and likewise for the things which implement his single acts (well-twisted withes, shaggy belly, divine wool) (cp. 427-34).

10.81-132 (Odysseus in the country of the Laestrygons): The epithets are frequent according to whether the action is focused on a certain spot or moment (e.g., the harbor as it is entered, the hilltop as it is ascended, the spring as it is approached, Antiphates' daughter met there and then); but the epithets tend to disappear in any general account or question about the place (cp. 98-101, 108, 110, 118, 122-23). Most interesting in this respect is the use of epithets in Odysseus' escape; see 126-27 and 131:

> then quickly drawing the sharp sword from my thigh
> I cut off the cable of the dark-prowed ship . . .
> far into the sea my ship escaped
> the overhanging rocks, where all the others perished.

Through the epithets Odysseus' solitary act springs into evidence: so much so that the loss of the other ships is almost obscured, although this loss is most important in point of the narrative and plot.

10.203-43 (The approach to Circe): There are rich epithets at each step, as the action gathers round its point of focus. Note especially the house of Circe as it is approached (210-11), the standing on the doorway (220), the hearing of her voice (221), her plying the loom (222-23). On the other hand, the account of her magic craft is almost lacking in epithets (232-43); not even her wand has an epithet (238).

12.403-17 (The storm and wreck of Odysseus' ship): There is a heavy use of epithets at one point (405-06):

> then did Zeus bring up a dark cloud
> above the hollow ship.

Here is the focus. The rest of the narratively important scene has no epithets.

14.23-36 (Odysseus' arrival at Eumaeus's hut): There are epithets for the barking dogs, for the leather upon which Eumaeus is working at the moment (24, 29). But after this we find a realistic piece of narrative. In the haste of the occasion Eumaeus drops his leather, Odysseus his stick: neither these nor the dogs nor Eumaeus or Odysseus themselves have any epithets.

17.328-41. Eumaeus enters the palace, seen by Telemachus, who nods to him; he gets the message, peers around, takes an empty chair, and sits at Telemachus's table. . . . All this is plot, maneuver, and it is cursorily told: hence we have narrative without epithets. But the attention turns next to Odysseus; and it focuses upon the spot where he is sitting: the threshold and the doorpost are richly presented with epithets.

19.53-64. Penelope is richly presented as she appears in the hall after the suitors have left: thus, there are epithets of herself and of the chair on which she sits (53-59); then arrive "the white-armed handmaids." What follows is the tasks of the handmaids: clearing the tables, removing the cups, etc. This is descriptive narrative: hence no epithets.

21.1-21. The wealth of epithets which accrues to each act of Penelope as she goes to fetch Odysseus' bow (1-14) contrasts with the relative scantiness of epithets in the narrative, which tells us how the bow itself came to Odysseus.

These instances are but few among many. They simply highlight a principle of expression which is more or less manifest in any passage. While the details may at times appear controversial, the broad underlying principle is inevitably clear.

For this is a matter of the simplest logic: we have, on the one hand, zones of relief touched off by the epithets and, on the other, various forms of connection favored by their absence. Here is a basic distinction which, in many other different ways, we observe even in ordinary speech: how often any narrative is suddenly checked by a fleeting but rich notation of a shape, a color, a sound. But this instinctive trend becomes in poetry a form of art. Points of arrest are brightened into focus, transitions are quickened into movement. Hence we find in Homer a continuous ebb and flow within the narrative and a recurring climax bodied out in the noun-epithet phrases.

4. THE EPITHETS IN DIALOGUE

1

The pure representation of things also tends to be submerged in certain instances of direct speech. When we speak to another person we usually have some purpose in view: to ask a question or give news, to approve or reproach, to warn or encourage. In such cases we make an issue, we drive a point. Anything we mention subserves some other interest. There is no dwelling on things for their own sake. Imagination gives way to will or mere curiosity.

It follows that there is little room for epithets in speeches which mainly pursue an ulterior purpose. Some passages of Homer give us a cue. When the same object is mentioned in a speech and in the accompanying representation, it often happens that it has an epithet in the latter but not in the former. Thus, in *Od.* 21.176 Antinous orders Melanthius: "Come now, Melanthius, burn the fire in the hall. . . ." And in 21.181, we find: "So he said, and Melanthius kindled the weariless fire." This variation is quite natural. When Antinous thinks of fire, it is merely for the purpose of melting the fat and greasing the bow; but when Melanthius actually sets off the flame, it is fire itself which is at the center of the picture.

Other instances of this variation are: *Il.* 1.234 and 245-46, 5.359 and 363, 6.365 and 370, 11.528 and 531, 15.146 and 151, 16.518 and 529, 19.348 and 354, 23.141 and 146, 151, 23.239 and 252, *Od.* 7.179 and 182, 9.346 and 347, 10.340, 342, and 347, 12.19 and 23, 13.50 and 53, 14.29 and 37, 15.50 and 56, 16.4 and 9, 18.17 and 33, 18.173 and 192, 19.97 and 101, 19.594 and 600, 24.358 and 361-62.

2

We may move on to passages of greater import, where the purpose of the speaker does not hang on anything particular but has a wider range. As he drives his point home, broad issues occupy his mind and he surveys the whole situation. This is the case when the warriors of the *Iliad* give their urgent advice and impassioned view on the fortunes of the battle. Such is Polydamas urging on Hector a certain plan of action in 13.726-47 (cp. 12. 211-29); Glaucus in 17.141-68; Sarpedon in 5.472-92. In passages of this kind there are relatively few epithets. The Achaeans, the Trojans, the individual heroes, their arms, the city of Troy, the walls become part of a generalized mental picture. Concrete objects naturally pale in the perspective of a personal standpoint. Thus, when Glaucus, after Sarpedon's death, tells Hector (17.144-55),

> Think now how you will save the land and the city,
> you alone with the people who in Ilium are born.
> For none of the Lycians will now come to battle the Danaans
> for the city's sake: there was never any thanks
> for ever relentlessly fighting the foe.
> Fie on you! How will you save a lesser man in the throng,
> since now you abandoned Sarpedon, who was your guest and your friend,
> abandoned him to be spoil and prey for the Achaeans—
> he who was for the city and for you such a boon
> while living; but now you dared not chase from him the hounds . . .

it is the lack of epithets which is striking: the land, the city, Troy, Lycians, Danaans, Sarpedon himself are but reflections of Glaucus's mood and judgment.

The same might be said of any vehement speech that goes straight to the point. Such is that of Thersites in *Il.* 2.225-42, with each sentence coming like a blow; or the similar one of Achilles insulting Agamemnon in *Il.* 1.225-44. Compare Telemachus calling on the suitors to leave the house (*Od.* 2.130-45), or inciting the people against them (2.40-79). We find the same effect and the same lack or scarcity of epithets in the soliloquies of hard-pressed heroes: e.g., *Il.* 11.404-10, 21.553-570; and in appeals, implorations, boasts: e.g., *Il.* 7.96-102, 8.161-66, 12.269-76, 15.347-51, 399-404, 425-28, 661-66, 718-25.

3

A calmer mood may set in. Consideration, reflection, judgment are laid over the sensible world; and a moral strain conditions the view of things. Here again epithets tend to vanish, as people and their surroundings are placed in relative terms. We thus find hardly any epithets in Idomeneus's speech on courage, *Il.* 13.275-84: the external features of his ideal hero tend to become symbolic. There are no epithets where Odysseus opens the account of his wanderings by dwelling upon what is most beautiful in life (*Od.* 9.3-10): the people and things which he mentions (the minstrel, the cupbearer, wine, table, kraters, cups) are there, but to reflect an idealized happiness. Compare *Od.* 15.390–401, 18.130–50, *Il.* 15.490–99, 19.155–83.

Similarly, we should hardly expect epithets in maxims or moral sayings. Such is the case in Telemachus's excuse in removing the arms from the hall (*Od.* 16.294, 19.13): "Steel itself, ready, draws a man to blows" (Chapman's translation). Or Eumaeus's (17.246): "The evil shepherds do destroy the sheep." Compare the lack of epithets in the sententious passages of Hesiod's *Works and Days:* 21-26, 40–41, 276-80, 287-92, etc.

4

Nor, on the other hand, shall we find any wealth of epithets in the speeches of the great dialogues. Hector in conveying his feeling for Andromache surveys all at once her life and his own, Troy and the future of Troy. Priam speaking to Achilles in his grief summons up a whole warring world in which Trojans and Achaeans are subjected to the same destiny. In such cases the stress falls no longer upon any single act or object. There is an encompassing wholeness. What stands supreme is the speaker's feeling. It replaces action. In its broad sweep it passes over the outer show of things. We thus have sentences which simply portray modes of life and experience. Epithets, if they occur at all, merely serve to underpin occasional points of reference. Take, for instance, in *Il.* 24.486-501, Priam's words to Achilles:

> Think of your father, o Achilles, o kindred of gods,
> he is as old as I am, on the baneful verge of old age,
> hard-pressed perhaps by the neighbors that live all around him,
> with nobody there to ward off the doom and the ruin.
> But hearing of you still alive he is gladdened at heart,
> he hopes all his days to see his son back from Troy.
> But most wretched am I whose sons were the best ever born
> in the wide land of Troy; and none, none is left to me now.
> Fifty I had when the sons of the Achaeans first arrived;
> nineteen came from one womb, while the others
> by my women were bred in the house; and the most
> violent Ares has felled, unstringing their knees.
> He who alone was left me, who saved the city and its people,
> him you yesterday slew as he fought for his land,
> even Hector . . .

We find here no epithets for such things as Troy, Achaeans, women, city. Most remarkable is the absence of epithet with Hector. How could he have any epithet here? He is not seen in his bright presence engaged in any act; no, he is a feeling, a thought, the climax of a long grief.

This imponderability is true not only of tragic speech. Any speech of intense though delicate feeling naturally tends to the same impalpable kind of expression. See Odysseus' famous address to Nausicaa in *Od.* 6.149–85. He is passionate, tender, reverent, and cunning by turn. Each of his sentences has transparent depth, though it may seem a mere statement of fact. Any object he mentions is removed from its habitat, transplanted, recomposed to make up the train of his thoughts. If he mentions Nausicaa's family life (the parents, the brothers, her dance, the bridegroom who might take her to his house), he does so in fond surmise. If he mentions anything beautiful which he has seen in the past (the palm tree in Delos by Apollo's shrine), it is but in relation to her beauty. If he mentions the city and people of Phaeacia, it is only to know where he is and to find refuge. If he mentions clothing, it is only for his immediate need. Then, finally, if he conjures up the imagery of a happy life (man and woman living at peace in a house), this is a wish for Nausicaa. Now there is hardly any epithet for the things so mentioned, however suitable it might be. The undercurrents of emotion naturally soften the sharpness of contour.

5

Just as significant as their scarcity is the occasional wealth of epithets in the speeches of dialogue. We must see why and when they most often recur; this may throw yet more light on their poetic value.

When we speak, we are often carried away from the main drift of what we are saying. It mostly happens in expansive moments. A sympathetic train of thought develops on its own strength, and it touches on all manner of objects that present an imaginative relevance to the initial motive. Other events are summoned up in the widening range. As the volume increases, a principle of representation blends with the pure expression of feeling.

We find in Homer many examples of this kind. Thus, in *Il.* 3.46–49. Hector, after upbraiding Paris in the strongest terms, goes on to say:

Such as you are, indeed, on sea-faring ships
sailing over the sea with comrades dearly-beloved,
mixing with strangers, you carried away the woman-of-beautiful-form
from a distant land, the daughter of spear-wielding men.

Later on in the same book, Paris invites Helen to his bed, having just been saved from the hands of Menelaus. After minimizing his setback, he says (442–44):

Come . . .
for never did love, as now, so encompass my mind,

> not even when I first sailed from Lacedemon-the-lovely-one
> ravishing you away in sea-faring ships . . .

The eager invitation yields to poignant memory which gives body to things long past.

But let us take a passage of greater complexity—Andromache's speech to Hector in *Il.* 6.407-39. After her desperate concern for the future, she dwells on her bereavement (414 ff.):

> My father did Achilles-the-god-born slay
> when he conquered the well-placed city of Cilicia
> Thebes-of-the-lofty-gates; Eetion then he struck down,
> and stripped him not, in his heart he felt awe,
> but buried him together with his arms-wondrously-wrought
> and heaped a mound above; around it elms were grown
> by the mountain-nymphs, daughters-of-Zeus-aegis-bearing-god.
> And the seven brothers who were with me in the house
> all in one single day were sped down to Hades;
> them strong-footed god-born Achilles slew
> as they were tending the oxen-of-trailing-gait and the white-fleeced sheep.
> My mother who was queen under forest-rich Placos
> hither was brought with all her possessions,
> but he released her in exchange of measureless ransom,
> and in my father's hall Artemis struck her the goddess-of-arrows.
> Hector, you are now to me father and stately mother
> and brother, and you are my flourishing husband. . . .

Grief here stirs the imagination. Andromache is an unwitting artist. Her present feeling naturally overflows into past perspectives, touching experience into imagery and acquiring plastic power. This is not narrative but evocation. It is as if new blood were injected into the dead; and the envisaged scenes burst into full momentary evidence. The epithets are, therefore, at home. They fix the occasions where they belong. See how strongly implanted is the locality of what happened—the city of Thebes, Eetion's burial ground, the pasture lands, the queen's home. Especially the oxen-of-trailing-gait and the white-fleeced sheep have a startling effect through sheer representation: here is the tranquillity of daily life suddenly swept away. So strong is the realization of the events themselves in time and place that all biographical detail is left out. We are not even told the names of Andromache's mother and brothers, but the sharp identities of "brother" and "stately mother" arise, as it were, from the past to crown Hector's living image as its ultimate attributes.

It thus appears that the Homeric characters use epithets most richly when speaking about distant things and not when dealing with their own actions.

Compare Achilles dwelling on the distance that separates him from home, *Il.* 1.155-57; Odysseus recalling Aulis, 2.305-07; Pandarus thinking of the horses he left at home, 5.193-96; Dione remembering the gods injured by men, 382-402; Hector hoping for victory and projecting its effect in the future, 7.81-88; Phoenix conjuring up his escape to Phthia, 9.447-49 and 471-80; Briseis lamenting her past, 19.291-94; Poseidon reminding Apollo of a common experience, 21.446-49; Andromache mourning for Hector, remembering the past and anticipating the future, 22.499-514; Achilles dwelling on instances of Patroclus's life, 23.281-82; Priam on his sons, 24.751-54. Similarly, at times, the characters of the *Odyssey* use epithets when they think of the absent Odysseus: *Od.* 1.48-54, 196-98, 260-63, 4.814-18, 19.365-68; Nestor remembering his toils at Troy, 3.103-12; Odysseus talking about his old marriage bed, 23.190-204.

6

Frequent epithets in speech dealing with present action are hard to find. Hector's speech giving orders for the coming night in *Il.* 8.497-528 might seem exceptional in this respect. His orders however turn into a realization of what is going to happen. When, for instance, he says (517-19)

> Let the Zeus-beloved heralds proclaim through the city
> that the stripling boys and the hoary-templed old men
> be encamped on the god-built walls . . .

we are made to see the scenery itself. His speech is not so much the call for a particular action as a picture of people at bay. Compare the city at war on Achilles' shield, *Il.* 18.514-15.

Thus orders at times prefigure the action which is their object, and things with their epithets are mentioned therein rather than when the order is actually carried out: *Od.* 20.149-56, 22.437-45.

Or take, in *Il.* 14.3-7, Nestor inviting wounded Machaon to rest:

> Think you, divine Machaon, on what is now going to happen;
> greater is by the ships the cry of the flourishing yeomen.
> But, as for you, sitting down, drink now the sparkling wine,
> until well-tressed Hecamede make ready the warm-washing water
> and wipe off the bloody gore.

The very epithets seem to prolong the moment of rest. The invitation lingers. It is not so much a request as a picture.

In quite a different mood, but similarly visualizing what he says, Hector questions the handmaids in *Il.* 6.377-80: "Where did white-armed Andromache go . . . ?" His words linger on the image, preparing us for Andromache's central presence a few lines later.

Epithets depend here on the degree of exposure. They recur insofar as the speaker lets himself visualize and contemplate a certain action and its scene. It cannot be so, if the tone is too peremptory. The moment must be allowed to expand. See, in *Il.* 18.254-83, the speech of Polydamas warning Hector to withdraw within Troy. In 259-60 he recalls past occasions saying,

> To be encamped upon the swift ships was my joy,
> to take the curved ships was my hope.

Or, in 273-76, anticipating the future:

> In the town-square we shall keep our strength for the night.
> The high ramparts, the gates and door-boards fitted upon them
> tall, well-polished, well-joined—these will protect the city.

But in 255-56, 266, 277-78 all this is mentioned cursorily in a tone of command, urgency. And, of course, there are no epithets (cp. 21. 531-36).

It may thus be said, most generally, that the epithets reflect the speaker's standpoint, though not his mood. They are most at home when things are perceived, remembered, foreseen along with the moment or place of their occurrence. Pure representation is then absorbed into subjective speech. Quite the opposite is the case, on the other hand, when the speaker's overriding interest sets in, whatever that interest may be. Things are then passed over, reduced, wrenched away from their surroundings, disembodied on the strength of a more pressing motive. Here is a basic logic of expression. Poetry turns it into account.

5. FLAGRANT INSTANCES OF THE EPITHET

Instances displaying a certain phenomenon with unusual fullness are classified as "flagrant" (or "glaring," "coruscating") by Bacon. I accordingly call
"flagrant" certain typical instances in which the epithets appear to cluster.
Why the abundance of epithets in these cases? What occasion, what need summons them up so richly?

Any phenomenon is most likely to be understood in the places of its greater
frequency; by the same token, these flagrant instances cannot but be characteristic of epithets as a whole and give us an idea of why epithets are used at all.

A survey of such instances will show that they are mostly attributable to a
need of exposure at certain points in the action. What occasions them, in
other words, is some concrete reason. If this is so, we may touch upon a real
poetic value, and not merely on some kind of epic habit.

Note the following:

1. The sudden appearance of a character upon the scene. Such is the case of
Penelope (*Od.* 1.332-35, 18.208-11, cp. 16.414-16):

> When to the suitors she came the divine among women
> she stood by the pillar of the thickly-built roof
> holding before her cheeks the glistening veil
> and on either side a careful handmaid stood by her.

Compare Andromache, *Il.* 6.395-403; Briseis, 19.282-86; Nausicaa, *Od.* 8.457-
58; Helen, 4.121-25; Hector, *Il.* 6.318-20 (cp. 8.492-95). In such passages
epithets tend to cluster—not only joined to the characters, but to anything the
characters come into contact with.

2. Sudden encounter with a character. Here a character does not appear, but
rather is visited, reached, found. Thus Athena visiting Nausicaa in *Od.* 6.15-19:

> She went right to the rich-wrought room where the girl
> was sleeping like-to-the-gods-in-form-and-in-looks,
> Nausicaa daughter of great-hearted Alcinous,

> and, with her, two handmaids-who-had-from-the-Graces-their-beauty
> by the doorpost on either side; closed were the shining doors.

Compare the way characters are summoned up on being visited: epithets of their abode or of the things they are doing contribute to focus strongly and concisely on the moment of their presence: Helen, *Il.* 3.125-28; Achilles, 8.186-88; Nestor, 10.73-79; Hephaestus, 18.369-77; the Cyclops, *Od.* 9.182-92; Aeolus, 10.1-4; Circe, 10.210-11, 220-23. Let it not be said that this is due to the social or mythical importance of the characters. Eumaeus is similarly treated. Odysseus finds him sitting before his house (*Od.* 14.5-7)

> and there his court
> was standing high-built on a spot descried-from-all-sides
> beautiful, big, running-round.

This is hardly realistic description. No less than Nausicaa, Eumaeus must be identified, fixed where he is at a certain moment.

3. Welcoming of a guest—as in the typical lines (*Od.* 1.136-38, 4.52-54, etc.)

> A handmaid brought water in a jar
> beautiful golden, poured it in a silver basin,
> for washing, and laid there a polished table.

Or in Telemachus's welcome to Athena (*Od.* 1.126-28):

> When they were within the lofty hall,
> he laid her spear against the long-shaped column
> within the polished spear-stand . . .

Each act of welcome is strongly outlined, and the epithets give it its sensuous contour: *Od.* 4.39-43, 17.85-90, cp. 10.352-70. What favors the epithets is thus a sense of focus, a sense of the occasion itself, and not a ready-made phraseology. Compare Hecamede welcoming Nestor and Machaon in the tent (*Il.* 11.628-37) or Eumaeus welcoming Odysseus in his hut (14.49-51): these scenes show the same wealth of epithets, although the wording is quite different, as befits the difference of circumstances and of the objects mentioned.

4. Characters arising, dressing—as in the typical line (*Il.* 2.44, *Od.* 2.4, etc.) "under the glistening feet he fastened the beautiful sandals." Similarly, we often find any garment or piece of clothing enhanced by an epithet the moment it is taken, donned, worn: cp. *Il.* 2.42-47, 10.131-36, 14.175-86, *Od.* 15.60-62. Here belong the arming scenes of heroes: *Il.* 3.328-38, 11.17-46, 16.131-39, 19.369-83, cp. 14.9-15, 15.478-83; or those of Athena: 5.733-48, 8.382-91. The moment of dressing or arming obviously caught the poet's imagination. For it shines out in newly appropriated details of form and color. It implies

a fresh start, almost a new man or woman rising up to the occasion. Hence the abundance of epithets. Again we should not take this for conventional heroic treatment: herdsman's clothing is similarly treated in *Od.* 14.528-31, beggarly garb in 13.434-38. There is a similar principle of expression in a chariot or ship made ready: *Il.* 24.266-74, *Od.* 6.72-78, 2.424-32, 15.289-95.

5. Man-to-man fighting scenes rendered in the moment of the actual clash, as in the typical lines (*Il.* 3.355-59, 7.249-52)

> He swayed and hurled the far-shadowing spear,
> upon the all-even shield did it strike,
> through the bright shield the strong shaft flew,
> through the rich-wrought corslet it pressed.

Cp. 22. 289-91, 4.134-39, 11.434-36, etc. What stands out is the encounter, the blow. Homer brings matters to a head, to a point of focus where epithets tend to cluster. In *Il.* 12.175-84, for instance, there is a general description of the battle rather lacking in epithets, and then (182ff.) the instant thrust of Polypoetes:

> There Pirothous' son Polypoetes-the-strong-one
> struck Damasus with the spear through the bronze-cheeked helmet,
> nor could the bronze-helmet check it, right through
> did the brazen-point break. . . .

Cp. 13.143-62, 361-72, 16.101-07, 17.288-96.

More generally we may say that in the battle scenes the epithets make room for the point of contact, help isolate a central occasion. We are made to see what happens as it materializes there and then. Thus the clash of spear and shield is abstracted from the human drama. Both the gruesomeness and the glamor of war are neutralized. There is the percussion of metal rather than the cry of vanquished and victor. No bravery is especially extolled, no coward-ice or malice especially upbraided. It is the momentary event itself which, through the epithets, is caught in its sharp, clear outline.

6. Any action or event so summoned up as to be contemplated in the moment of its taking place, in one single impression.

The instances quoted above are of this kind, but they come under particular topics. What I wish to point out here is the instance of realization in itself and by itself. It will be seen that the epithets richly occur in such cases, quite apart from any special subject matter.

Take *Il.* 18.203-06 (Athena's effect on Achilles):

> Upon the mighty shoulders the tasseled aegis she threw,
> she surrounded his head with a golden cloud,
> up from his body she kindled a shining flame.

Or 5.314-15 (Aphrodite saving Aeneas):

> Around the dear son she spread her white arms,
> before him the shrouding folds of her shining robe.

Compare Zeus's embrace, 14.346-51; Achilles offering his locks, 23.140-43; sunset bringing the night, 8.495-96; Achilles crushed by Patroclus's death, 18.22-25; the play and dance of the Phaeacians, *Od.* 8.372-78; cp. *Il.* 18.593-96. Such passages are not at all descriptive. The compact imagery is scanned all at once; and the epithets give it both conciseness and quality.

Here may be mentioned the use of epithets in similes. See, for instance, *Il.* 13.62-64:

> As a swift-winged falcon arises to fly
> lifted up from a steep towering cliff . . .

Cp. 2.87-89, 459-63, 12.167-70, 13.703-07, 16.428-29, 487-89. Or 12.156-58:

> they fell down like snowflakes
> which a gusty wind, whirling the shadowy clouds,
> sheds thick upon the much-nourishing earth.

Cp. 12.278-86, 15.618-21, 16.297-300, 17.53-58. The epithets are here at home. By focalizing on pure values of form or function, they intensify rather than distract; and the action or event is drawn together, apprehended in one unique moment. Epithets are far less frequent, on the other hand, where the simile develops into the description of a certain action, as in *Il.* 4.275-79:

> As when a shepherd sees from a summit a cloud
> driven by the blast of Zephyrus over the sea;
> and to him far away darker than pitch it appears
> as it comes over the sea bringing with it much storm;
> he shudders then at the sight, and herds the sheep in a cave. . . .

Cp. 3.33-35, 13.470-75, 15.362-64, 586-88, 16.259-62, 17.657-64.

7. Cases of immediate and arresting visualization. The object is both seen and revealed, uncovered all at once—as the features of Ithaca appearing to Odysseus (*Od.* 13.195-96):

> the far-creeping paths and the ever-welcoming harbours,
> the steep-climbing cliffs and the flourishing trees.

Compare Scheria descried in the distance, 5.279-81; a hall suddenly lit up, 19.37-38; the forms of Aphrodite suddenly revealed, *Il.* 3.396-97. The outline is here sharp, clear, resilient. This is not the case where we have a panorama: cp. *Il.* 8.52, 13.13-14.

8. Points of arrival—as in *Il.* 6.242-50:

> But when he came to Priam's beautiful house
> made with polished verandahs; and in it . . .

Or *Il.* 22.147-56:

> They came to the fair-flowing springs; there two fountains
> gush up from deep-eddying Scamander. . . .

Cp. 6.313-15, *Od.* 4.1-2, 43-46, 6.85-87. Such passages are no more descriptive than those above. The appearance of a place is so presented as to be one and all with the act of arrival. It comes, again, all at once; and the epithets keep it in focus. This is quite understandable. The fact of arriving (no less than arming or dressing) is a fresh start, a new step, a moment that stands out; and nothing is more common in Homer than to find an epithet joined to the name of the place or thing which is reached, arrived at: *Il.* 1.12, 26, 432, *Od.* 1.104, 126, etc.

I may here mention the way in which epithets bring out the features of a place or landscape to the eyes of the newly arrived visitor, as most notably Calypso's island to Hermes, in *Od.* 5.63-76. It might be objected that this is nothing but description, as in any narrative when places are seen for the first time by any of the characters. But here it is not quite so. The passage does not develop into a digression. It does not give rise to a separate series of impressions, each object contained within the momentary gaze of Hermes (75-76). See how the epithets give weight to the mere presence of things so perceived, see how the verbs but convey the natural state of a thing: the blossoming trees *are in full growth,* the birds *roost,* the vine *stretches out,* the clear waters *flow.* The sense of *aspect* in the verbs does the same service as the epithets. Hence no incidental feature of the terrain, no remarks *about* the forest. There is a startling fullness in the visual suspense. Compare *Od.* 7.81-135.

This visual fullness is true even where there is no beholder. The cave of the Nymphs in *Od.* 13.96-112 is presented in sentences rich with epithets before the actual arrival of Odysseus, which follows immediately after (13.113). Again no description but visualization: each thing brought into focus at a point of contact, a moment of approach. Compare the little island close to the Cyclops (9.116-39). It is far more removed from the act of arrival, presented as part of the Cyclopean world. A point is made of its unexploited fertility— for example, "not bad it is, there are meadows watery, soft . . . , imperishable might be its vines." Accordingly we have attributes and predicates rather than epithets.

All these classes of instances may give us some idea of the epithet's poetic function in Homer. What is it that they all have in common? It is a momentary occasion which brings things into evidence. Penelope's glistening veil and the luxuriant vine of Calypso's cave both are objects instantly witnessed there and then, not details descriptively narrated.

The epithets here point to something permanent, to a quality rooted in the nature of the thing and not related to the circumstances. The momentary act or condition is thus given a burden which is not momentary. It ceases to be episodic, accidental. It is grounded in the nature of things.

Particularly significant in this respect are those typical instances in which the same epithets, the same phrases tend to occur (arming and dressing scenes, the clash of arms, etc.). The momentary and the typical, the individual and the general are here quite merged with each other. Such a verse as "under the glistening feet she [or he] fastened the beautiful sandals" could be applied to anyone at any time. The act is caught in the flash which is intrinsic to it. Thus the epithets of feet and sandals do not puzzle or distract us at all, but rather affirm the act itself for what it really is. The more a moment of experience is seen in its essential and nonepisodic nature, the more it tends to be general and universally true.

6. THE EPITHET IN NARRATIVE

Throughout the *Iliad* and the *Odyssey* the pure representational element continually tends to displace or absorb the narrative; and here, we have seen, the epithets play their full role. We may thus test this representational mode of expression insofar as it resists any narrative inclination, insofar as it maintains itself in passages which are most narrative in intent and in scope. This will be the case where a character looks back and recounts past experiences, for the moment of pure representation is most likely to be submerged in a flow of narrative which covers not days but months or years; and the way it maintains itself even in such cases will throw light upon its significance and resilience.

This happens especially in the *Odyssey*. I do not mean Odysseus' account to the Phaeacians, which is resolved in vivid, self-contained scenes, but pieces of spoken narrative which we find scattered in the poem. Among them are Nestor's account of the return from Troy, *Od.* 3.103-200, 254-312; Menelaus's story of Proteus and of his visit to Egypt, 4.356-586; Eumaeus's account of himself, 15.403-84; Odysseus' fictitious autobiography, 14.199-359, cp. 14.468-506, 13.256-86, 19.172-202, 24.302-14. We may add the story of young Odysseus and the boar hunt in 19.393-466.

2

Take Nestor, at the point he begins his narrative (*Od.* 3.130 ff.). There are in his story clear points of movement and action, but the sequences of cause and effect remain hardly intelligible. We are made to guess at rather than see the complexities of the situation. Instant acts are presented quite abruptly, and they seem to obscure all coherence.

Nestor first points to the woeful return of the Achaeans from Troy and to the wrongdoings which were the cause of their woe; but we are not told at all

what these wrongs were. We then have a quarrel between Menelaus and
Agamemnon (136); but it is weakly motivated, and what stands out most
prominently is the moment of confrontation (148-50):

> exchanging bitter words
> they stood; and they rose the well-grieved Achaeans
> with wondrous uproar.

Some stay with Agamemnon, others leave with Menelaus, including Nestor.
We are not told the right and wrong of the decision; but (153-55, 157-58):

> At dawn we drew the ships to the shining brine,
> we loaded our things and the deep-girt women . . .
> Swiftly the ships sailed out;
> a god smoothed out the hugely hollowed sea.

Another quarrel ensues (161); but its motive is again set aside and we are
drawn to the actuality of movement (162-63):

> they went, turned backward their curve-sided ships
> those round wise-minded crafty-souled Odysseus.

The next important stage is a stop in Lesbos, where a god signals them to
make for Euboea. We are not told anything about the god or the portent; but
the moment of setting off is stressed in full clarity (176-77):

> A sounding wind rose to blow; and very swiftly
> they crossed the fish-rich paths.

Later (254 ff.) Nestor tells Telemachus about Aegysthus, Clytaemnestra,
Orestes, and, at the same time, Menelaus's homecoming. All this is very cursory. What stands out is the moment of Menelaus's shipwreck and his landing in Egypt (286-300):

> When sailing over the wine-colored sea
> in hollow ships to Malea's lofty mountain
> speeding he came, then wide-eyed Zeus devised
> a hateful journey;
> the breath of sounding winds he poured upon him
> and swelling waves . . .
> . . . .
> There is a tall smooth cliff sheer on the water
> off Gortyn out in the mist-visaged sea;
> against the western headland the great waves
> are by the South-wind driven, toward Phaestus,
> and narrow stones keep out the huge sea-flood.

> There some arrived; the men hardly shunned death,
> while the waves shattered on the reefs the ships;
> but the five other blue-prowed ships to Egypt
> were brought by wind and water.

3

Compare Menelaus's narrative. It is longer, more varied, but it presents similar vantage points. Menelaus's long wanderings (cp. 3.301-02, 4.81-85) are dispatched in two lines (4.351-52). We come straight to the island Pharus where Proteus makes his revelations. The sense of place and locality is again brought out most richly (4.354-60):

> An island lies on the much-washing sea
> off against Egypt, and men call it Pharus,
> so far that in one day the hollow ships
> cover the distance, when the sounding wind
> blows from behind upon them; and therein
> a port fair-harboring whence they launch to sea
> the even ships and draw the deep-black water.
> For twenty days the gods detained me there. . . .

The narrative can hardly proceed without a clear term of reference. No less than the Cretan cliff in Nestor's story, Pharus stands out, breaking the narrative syntax but concurring with the narrated event. For it is neither described nor mentioned for the mere sake of geography. It is simply present as an indispensable ground for the action. It must thus be fully accounted for; and its characteristic existence is greatly enhanced by the epithets, which are neither decorative nor curiously descriptive.

A considerable part of Menelaus's narrative deals with the revelations of Proteus on the return of the Locrian Ajax and Agamemnon; here, as in Nestor's case, we find epithet phrases which again punctuate moments and places. Let us turn, rather, to the way Proteus is forced to yield and give his responses (4.363-459). The narrative is relatively short. The full details of the stratagem and of the attack (which might have engrossed a storyteller) appear neglected. Hence some inconsistencies: how do the men resist the terrific manifestations of the god? And where does the fight take place—in the god's cave (cp. 403) or out on the shore (cp. 449, 453)? In any case, the poet's interest lies elsewhere. He is concerned with things clearly and suddenly emerging on the scene rather than with the intricacies of the plot or marvellous exploits. Here is the appearance of Proteus and the seals on the shore (401-06):

> The infallible old sea-god comes ashore
> under the breeze of Zephyrus, concealed

> in the dark rippling of the water; thence
> he goes to rest inside a hollow cave;
> round him the seals, brood of the lovely sea-nymph,
> are gathered sleeping, having once emerged
> out of the foaming wave and breathing forth
> the pungent odor of the far-deep sea.

Notice that this presentation is given more space than any other single episode within this part of the narrative—more, most notably, than the actual forcing of Proteus. The moment is allowed to expand. And this is done mainly through the epithets. Rather than describing strangeness, they make strange things credible by fixing and exposing them in the reality of the element to which they belong: the sense of sea and brine stands out even more than the god.

The accounts of Odysseus (*Od.* 14.199-359) and of Eumaeus (15.403-84) are much better narrative. They come in the course of intimate conversation between the two men. The mood is one of reminiscence, communion, reflection on past and present. A reflecting narrative sets in, which extends the range at the cost of weakening the focus. Hence the epithets are less frequent, things are mentioned discursively, and events come up at a leisurely pace. Even here, however, the single scene, the single occasion—with the epithets which provide focus—inevitably emerges, conditioning or influencing the narrative.

Take Eumaeus's account (15.403-84), which is a story of how he was abducted as a child. Although it is excellent narrative, running smoothly with few epithets and exquisite touches of realism, yet it cannot begin without being strongly implanted in its setting through the use of noun-epithet phrases:

> There is an isle called Syrie, you may know,
> above Ortygia by the setting sun,
> a goodly land though not so populous,
> well-sheeped, well-meadowed, grain-rich, wine-abundant.
> . . . .
> Thither Phoenicians came men-famed-in-ships,
> grasping, with myriad gauds in the black ship.
> In the house lived a woman from Phoenicia
> beautiful, stately, versed-in-lovely-crafts.
> Her the Phoenicians subtle-witted duped;
> one first lay with her by the hollow ship
> when she came washing. . . .

An island, a ship arriving, people landing, an encounter: we find these throughout the *Odyssey,* with the epithets giving existential relevance to each thing and concurring to build up a strong point of focus, whence episodes follow. Homer does not begin a story with "once upon a time." He needs a concrete occasion grounded in the nature of things. Eumaeus's account would have been quite different in the hands of an ordinary storyteller. He would have started by giving us a picture of Eumaeus's happy childhood and introduced the Phoenicians later, whereas Homer conveys a sense of happiness in the image of the island itself by presenting it in its exuberant nature as the home of Eumaeus and the place to which the Phoenicians arrive. The qualitative presentation of the island is hardly separated from that of the ship's arrival.[1] (With Syrie and its epithets in *Od.* 15.406 compare a similar use of epithets in strongly establishing the image of a place as the scene of further action—for example, *Od.* 3.293-94, 4.844-45, 19.172-73. In 1.50-51, νήσῳ ἐν ἀμφιρύτῃ . . . νῆσος δενδρήεσσα, the need to focus on such an image leads to irregularity of construction. On the relative lack of epithets for the nameless island off the land of the Cyclops, compare p. 38 above.)

Compare the fictitious autobiography of Odysseus in *Od.* 14.199-359. It covers a whole lifetime. It is an admirable self-portrait. Birth, youth, and early proofs of a strong character are splendidly surveyed, up to his participation in the Trojan War and return from Troy. But this comprehensive narrative, which uses hardly any noun-epithet phrases, is abruptly broken at a certain point, when we are suddenly told (246): "My spirit stirred me to set sail for Egypt." There follows a characteristic Homeric scene strictly fixed in its day and place (252-57):

> Out of wide Crete we sailed the seventh day
> with Boreas strongly-blowing beauteous wind
> . . . .
> on the fifth day we reached the fair-flowing Nile,
> moored on the river the curve-sided ships.

The hero's people ravage the country, there is war. But this soon comes to a close (276-79):

> I doffed the well-wrought helmet off my head
> . . . .
> clasped the king's knees and kissed them.

He stays seven years with the king, until a Phoenician, baiting a trap, persuades him to leave with him. He soon finds himself sold into slavery; but a storm breaks out, the ship is wrecked—and here we have again the full relevance of the moment (302-04):

> then a black cloud above the hollow ship
> was placed by Zeus, so that it dimmed the sea.

He is the only one to be saved (311):

>Zeus brought into my hands
>the mast impregnable of the blue-prowed ship.

An ordinary narrator would have protracted the story of the hero's relations with the Phoenician trader—a good occasion for adventure and character drawing. Not so Homer. He refrains from mere variety. He passes over intrigues and complications. Where further narrative might be expected, nature comes again into its own: the noun-epithet phrases, at some crucial instance, merge the fleeting action with elementary reality.

7. ON THE REPETITION OF THE EPITHETS

1

The repetition of the Homeric epithets may be used as an argument against the idea that they present points of imaginative focus. "If this is so," it may be objected, "why is it that we do not find *any* kind of object so placed in focus? Why does it hardly ever happen that we find some unexpected thing to have an unexpected epithet? Why do these epithets fall into patterns? Does not this show that we have here traditional phrases, the poet's stock-in-trade?"

Such an objection ignores the relation between the noun-epithet phrases and the nature of the things they portray. It is as if a poetic phraseology just hung in the air to be appropriated by the poet and adapted to his subject matter. The question should rather be put in these terms: "Why is it that certain things are so singled out as to be rendered in self-consistent imagery? Why is the subject matter so perceived as to give rise to this kind of expression? Or, more particularly, what things are so highlighted while others are ignored? What kind of criterion prompts the choice? Does not this process of selection ultimately depend upon a sense of value?"

Tradition, stock-in-trade do not give us a real answer. They ignore the problem—transposing it from the poetic mind to an ill-defined collective entity.

2

What then is the reason for these repetitions? It lies in the recurrence of a certain kind of act or state of being. "Swift-footed (πόδας ὠκύς) Achilles," for instance, mostly occurs insofar as Achilles is speaking; and the recurrence of the epithet is all one with the importance which the act of speaking has in the poems. The noun-epithet phrase is part and parcel of the sentence in which it occurs. A certain action thus summons up a certain image, and the inverse is also true.

The repetition of epithets is thus proportionate to the importance of certain acts. What kind of importance? Such as is not due to any topical or narrative reason, but to what I might call existential incidence. Thus, again, Achilles often has the epithet when he is brought into immediate focus as the subject of simple verbs which trace existentially important moments (to stand, go, come, see, etc.).

The repetition of epithets thus reflects a repetition which makes up the very texture of existence. What prompts their recurrence is a sense of recurrence in life itself. Hence an existential value in the repetition of epithets. But how are we aware of such a value? Is it through the number of repetitions? If this were so, our argument would be circular. No, it is a quality in the expression which elicits the repetition and not the other way round. What makes a noun-epithet phrase is a property which is intrinsic to it—that of welding an image to a certain act or state, making it relevant only to that existential moment and removing it from the narrative context. Thus "swift-footed Achilles" vividly conjures up the image of the speaking hero, quite apart from what he is going to say. The epithet "swift-footed" is here particularly felicitous in that it focuses on the sheer vital presence of Achilles. The repetition would have a surfeiting effect with anything like "great," "valiant," "proud," "magnanimous."

"Swift-footed Achilles" recurs very often, and yet what produced it was a sense of this expressive value in one initial instance. An epithet may thus occur once only and yet be potentially recurrent, if the sentence itself also occurs once only although it be so incisive that we might imagine it recurring any number of times in other occasions not found in the poems. Take, in *Il.* 22.411, the unique Ἴλιος ὀφρυόεσσα: "as if brow-shaped Ilium were wasting in fire." We may wonder why the poet did not use the frequent and metrically equivalent ἠνεμόεσσα, "windy Troy." Because the instances of "windy" are all associated with Troy as a point of arrival, as a term of direction (*Il.* 3.305, 8.499, etc.), while "brow-shaped" occurs here in the image of a burning city. We may assume that if the burning of Troy had been similarly presented more than once, we should have found more than once the epithet ὀφρυόεσσα. The image is a haunting one. It would have been frequent if Homer had sung of the burning of Troy.

Why is it so? Why is the same city "windy" when approached, "brow-like" when seen burning? There is no facile answer. All we can do is to familiarize ourselves with a mode of expression which brings out concrete aspects of things in immediate connection with a passing event. It is this concreteness which strikes us here: the smoke-enveloped brow of a hill seen in the distance, a windswept height approached and climbed. The image of a place is all one with the occurrence which affects it. In the same way Troy is mostly called "well-built" as object of conquering. It is enough to note that such a connection with some incisive act keeps the noun-epithet phrase alive.

3

The repetition of the noun-epithet phrases is thus proportionate to that of certain acts and states of being; and this implies the vision of a world in which occurrences become recurrences, in which events as well as things are seen in a persistent relevance of form. Our problem thus expands and we may ask: what events are those which lend themselves to such repetition of expression? What sort of poetic mind responds to them so persistently?

We must look at the repetition of these noun-epithet phrases in the light of those larger recurrences which come from representing events or action in themselves and by themselves—from representing them, that is to say, in their large, comprehensive outline, in a way which is neither casual nor deliberately descriptive. Such a style cannot be isolated in a mental vacuum. It is all one with a vision of things.

What is, more precisely, the import of such a vision? We find, for instance, storm and calm, toil and rest, youth and old age, but hardly those wavering intermediate states which most lend themselves to descriptive virtuosity. This is true down to the smallest occasions: any work or task is seen in its outright performance, and not with any view to whether it is carried out more or less well. What stands out is thus a necessary cadence rather than any tentative, wayward stage.

The outcome is a self-coherent world-representation. Just as the nouns with their epithets present the recurring images of things, so the sentences draw out persisting trends of action and being. The principle of expression is the same. In both cases the multiplicity of phenomena is reduced, essentialized, refined into form. An imagined clarity of outline seems to absorb the entanglements of experience. A correspondence is thus discovered between the way things exist or happen and the way they are perceived by the subjective mind. A significant shape, a significant incidence stands out. It strikes a common chord. Hence the felicity of a refrain.

4

This sense of form in the refrain is the sense of an existential cadence. Proof of this lies in the fact that these repetitions and recurrences dwell on basic events and not on desultory details. We do not have mannerisms, peculiar preferences, gratifications of a punctilious taste. No, the very repetition is justified by the nature of things.

See, in this respect, those verses which reproduce in its unremitting cadence the break of day (*Il.* 1.477, *Od.* 2.1, etc.), the fall of night (*Od.* 2.388, 3.487, etc., cp. *Il.* 1.475, *Od.* 9.168, 558, etc.), the increasing daylight (*Il.* 8.66, *Od.* 9.56), high noon (*Il.* 8.68, 16.777, *Od.* 4.400). A sudden storm is rendered the same way in *Od.* 9.67-69, 12.313-15, cp. 5.292-94; so the serenity of a calm sea (5.391-92, 12.168-69, cp. 10.94).

Compare with these those instances which are like human counterparts to the succession of day and night: the rising from bed which rhythmically accompanies the break of day (*Od.* 2.2, 3.405, etc.); the taking of meals, when (*Il.* 1.468, 602, etc.) "the spirit lacks not its even portion" or (*Il.* 1.469, 2.432, etc.) "the yearning for food and for drink is expended"; the act of lying down for the night and "seizing the boon of sleep" (*Il.* 7.482, 9.713, etc.).

Less regular, but no less indicative of a necessary incidence, are those sentences which mark with the same words the inevitable moments of any congregation or struggle. Such is the assembling of people (*Il.* 1.57, *Od.* 2.9, etc.), the clashing of masses (*Il.* 4.446-49, 8.60-63), the closing in of two opponents (*Il.* 3.15, 5.630, etc.), the impact of body upon body in men pressing forward (*Il.* 13.131-33, 16.215-17), pursuit (8.341-42, 11.177-78), withdrawal (15.727, 16.102), resistance (5.527, 15.622).

To address, to speak, to answer, to question: we hardly need illustrate how regularly self-coherent is in Homer the formulation of these essential acts of human intercourse. Add to this such moments as those of meeting (*Il.* 6.253, 406, etc.), parting or leaving (1.428, 2.35, etc.): "clung fast to his hand, spoke word and said" or "so having spoken he went and there left him." Such sentences—which would hardly strike us if they occurred once only—have a cumulative effect: they bring out a taste of all possible human contact by simply touching upon an inevitable moment.

Rarer and more solemn experiences are similarly treated in that they are pervasive. For instance (*Il.* 8.147, 15.208, etc.): "Here is dread grief that comes to my heart and mind. . . ." Or (*Il.* 17.695-96, *Od.* 4.704-05): "Speechlessness seized him for long, and the eyes/filled with tears, checked was the flourishing voice." Cp. *Od.* 19.472, *Il.* 23.397.

The effect of any strong feeling or passion is similarly portrayed: a force that seizes, possesses the individual. Cp. *Il.* 14.475, 16.599, 1.387, etc. There are variations in the wording, but the expressive form remains the same. Compare, for instance, the black cloud of grief which encompasses Achilles in *Il.* 18.22 and the dark night that falls on Andromache in 22.466. What matters is the existential shock, the feeling of a power that overwhelms a man or woman. Here is a proof, if any were needed, that we are dealing with a persistent imaginative form and not with a convenient formula.

Even individual characters tend to assume a stance or position which is typical of their nature, and the same words portray them more than once. This is done by focusing on an act which is both universally significant and individually pertinent. We have, as it were, one great, typical moment. So Penelope (*Od.* 1.362-64, 19.602-04, 21.356-58, cp. 16.449-51):

> up to the chamber she went with the women attendants
> and cried for Odysseus her husband till sleep
> sweet on her eyelids was shed by bright-eyed Athena.

Or Hector (*Il.* 5.494-97, 6.103-06, 11.211-13):

> at once from the chariot in arms he sprang to the ground,
> waving two sharp spears he went to and fro through the host
> spurring to fight, and roused the dread battle-din;
> they rallied and stood face to face with the Achaeans.

Cp. 3.77-78 = 7.55-56.
Or (7.219, 11.485, 17.128):

> Ajax came carrying his shield like a tower—

a massive, bulwarklike figure which suits the hero's character.

5

The same appeal of a self-repeating outline is found in the presentation of general human tasks and behavior. Such is the arming of a warrior; a sacrifice; the welcoming of a guest; laying a bed for the night; the yoking or unyoking of horses; a ship drawn to sea, sailing off, landing, mooring. Or the question about a stranger's identity (*Od.* 3.71-74, 9.252-55); or the wonder at his presence on an island (*Od.* 1.173, 14.190, etc.).

Consider, again, the existential importance of the instances. There is always a recurring moment which is necessarily critical in that it portends some new step, phase, or initiative—imminent contest in arming oneself, destination in departing or arriving, a solemn token in a sacrifice. Here then are junctures grounded in human life. They have their own self-contained nature, they have their own inevitable way of taking place irrespectively of any specific occasion or purpose. The poetic touch consists in bringing out this great pervasiveness of form and contents—in giving us, for instance, a cumulative sense of meeting and parting moments rather than stressing the mood of a certain welcome or farewell.

Hence no description of peculiar habits. The sources of character lie elsewhere. Insofar as he arms himself, Achilles is no different from Paris. Nor does the poet describe strange customs of distant people. If anything extraordinary happens, we are immediately transposed to the world of myth or tale: the Cyclops, Circe; and, apart from the fantastic element, even these lead lives which are rooted in the coherence of daily familiar acts: the Cyclops is a herdsman, and Circe weaves, sings, behaves like a genial hostess.

This sense of a pervasive form in any act is intrinsic to the poetry. It is, again, a value which is not determined by the number of instances. Even actions mentioned once only seem to fall into an inevitable pattern. Such are the contests in *Il.* 23, the displays of the Phaeacians in *Od.* 8. Or take such a rare occurrence as Eyryclea recognizing Odysseus (*Od.* 19.468-69). What happens? There is a foot let go, a drop, a fall, a clang. The fact really *takes place,* expanding in its physical dimensions, breaking up into its essential moments of motion and sound—much as in the rendering of a battle scene. There might have been countless other ways of describing the suspense and excitement of the incident: this simplicity was hard to achieve; and yet we read the lines as if no other rendering would have been possible.

6

Actual word-for-word repetitions are only the most obvious aspect of a far wider mode of expression which encompasses the whole poems.

The minor battle scenes of the *Iliad* are a good instance. They take up a large portion of the whole poem, and yet nowhere do they develop into a lengthy narrative of a general battle. Rather, we have self-contained encounters following one upon another. Although we find of course unlimited variations, yet there is throughout the same prevailing pattern. Consider the first encounter in *Il.* 4.457-62:

> First Antilochus slew, of the Trojans, a helmeted man
> brave in the foremost Echepolus son of Thalysius;
> him he first struck on the ridge of the horse-haired helmet,
> transfixed the brow; it pierced within through the bone
> the brazen point; darkness covered his eyes;
> he fell, as falls a tower, in the strong combat.

Everything centers on the clash, the blow, the fall. Epithet or simile, where present, has no complicating effect; it simply enhances the outline. Cp. 5.533-40, 612-17, 6.5-11, 8.256-60, 312-15, 11.95-98, 12.182-86, 13.541-44, 545-49, 576-80, 14.449-52, 516-19, 15.575-78, 16.307-11, 313-16, 321-25, 411-14, 17.312-15, 516-24, 20.395-400, 413-18, 472-89.

The briefest mention of the victim's background sometimes prolongs the visual presentation—as in the case of Simoeisius (4.474-79):

> whom once his mother
> on her way from Ida begot on the banks of Simois
> since she followed her parents in tending the sheep;

> therefore the name Simoeisius; nor to his parents
> he gave return for his rearing, brief was his life
> under the blow. . . .

Cp. 5.69-75, 152-58, 541-53, 6.20-28, 8.302-08, 14.442-48, 489-96, 20.382-88.

Or life's activity is mentioned—as in the case of Phereclus (5.60-61):

> who knew how to make with his hands
> all cunning work, for Pallas Athena supremely loved him.

Cp. 5.49-58, 6.12-19, 16.603-07.

Or an irony of fate is recalled—as in the case of Euchenor, who sailed to Troy (13.665-68):

> of his doom well aware;
> for often his father had told him, old Polyidus,
> that either of cruel disease in the house he should die
> or be subdued by the Trojans. . . .

Cp. 5.148-51, 11.328-35.

Or a Trojan's special relation to Priam: 13.173-76, 365-69.

The *Iliad* never dwells on the causes of the war, much less on its history; but these scenes, with their steady focus on the fact itself, tell us what war is all about. This is achieved through the uniformity of treatment. The underlying form is more important than any variation, or, we might say, the variations are a foil to the clash, the blow, the fall. What we see is a process which spells out its deadly round. Hence there is no room for exaggeration, glorification, vilification. It is, again, a basic form of expression which sets the measure; and the ultimate reason for its effectiveness lies in its voicing, again and again, the truth of experience. No other eloquence, here, shows friend and foe subjected to the same fate.

7

Let us turn further afield. Beyond this basic recurrence of single encounters there are other recurrences which are less constant, less regular, but wider in range.

Take *Il.* 11.248-50. Coon sees his brother Iphidamas slain by Agamemnon: "and a mighty grief enveloped his eyes at his brother's fall." He proceeds forthwith to avenge him and fights Agamemnon. This is the most frequent kind of complication we find in the battle scenes. Time and again we find brother or friend similarly intervening in the action: cp. 5.9-21, 541-64, 11.231-50, 426-33, 13.383-88, 402-20, 576-82, 14.442-60, 15.430-41,

518-22, 16.319-25, 482-533, 570-81, 17.344-53, 575-91, 20.419-54.
Achilles grieving for Patroclus and avenging him is no different. The poem's
great theme is reflected in countless other instances; and what justifies the
recurrence is a central human significance.

Compare the struggles over the bodies of Sarpedon in *Il.* 16.548-665 and
Cebriones in 16.737-83. These rehearse the greater struggle over Patroclus in
the following book. Many single man-to-man combats flare up around the
bodies of these three heroes, continually producing their recurring beat; but
these are in their turn encompassed by that larger recurrence which has the
three heroes as its theme.

Or consider the fatal advance of Asius through the Achaean wall, *Il.* 12.110-
74. It is like a prelude to that of Hector: 12.195-200, 437-71. Compare
Hector, again, in 8.492-542, 13.802-37, 15.688-95, 717-25. There is no war
plan that might lend itself to narrative. There is only the basic instinct to
advance, to drive the Achaeans into the sea; and this cannot but be presented
as a repeated endeavor.

Agenor's desperate stand before Achilles in *Il.* 21.550-70 is, similarly, a prelude to Hector's in 22.91-130. The same self-questioning, fear, resolution,
although the words are quite different. Compare the soliloquy of Odysseus in
11.401-10 and that of Menelaus in 17.91-105. Here are plights which are
typically human and thus tend to similarity of form. The strongest heroes are
no exception, not even Achilles (21.273-83).

And, beyond all such instances, look at the battle itself: it remains obscure
in point of strategy or topography, presented as a continuous ebb and flow.
All we have is a space between hill and sea, the two sides like scales in a balance.
Actions thus appear punctually reciprocal. Note how similar is the impersonal public voice of Trojans and Achaeans: *Il.* 3.298-301, 320-23, 17.414-19,
420-22; or how simultaneously they crave for a truce to bury their dead:
7.333-35 and 375-78. The general narrative could not be more reduced to its
essential outlines; and the recurrence of these outlines is in proportion to
the volume of the material.

8

The creation of characters relies, to some extent, on the same principle of
recurrence. Just as they have standing epithets, so do recurring positions
and attitudes cling to them. The human individual significance is here far
greater, but repetition or recurrence is no less a source of its effectiveness.

We see Achilles aloof on the seashore in *Il.* 1.348-50, 18.1-137, 23.59-107,
crying over a destiny which is as apparent at the beginning of the poem as it
is at the end. We hear him pleading his cause against Agamemnon in *Il.* 1.149-
244, 9.308-429, 16.49-100. In each set of instances we find words which

echo one another. The same strain endures and expands. There is again and
again an image which is so affirmed and insisted upon as to become a powerful character.

Or take Hector. Apart from the great scene of *Il.* 6.390-502, what is, as it
were, the raw material which builds him up as a hero? The extremities of
advance and retreat in their all too human succession. They follow one another
in *Il.* 8, 11, 12, 13, 14, 15, 17, 18, 20, hardly introducing any new characteristic element but affirming over and over the sharp outline of the hero. His
final flight before Achilles and his final resolve are like an ultimate consum-
mation of what has happened many times before.

The burden of Andromache's speeches remains essentially the same on the
three occasions in which she appears. The widow's and orphan's woe is
expressed no less in her speech of *Il.* 6.407-39 than in her mourning of 22.477-
514, 24.725-45. Compare self-recriminating Helen in *Il.* 3.172-80, 6.344-
58, 24.762-75.

These characterizing recurrences are no less obvious in the *Odyssey*. The
character of Odysseus is largely conveyed in the same way: see how constantly
his adventures rehearse the state of a man finding himself on a solitary unknown shore, discovering his bearings, ascending a height to view the land,
wondering what people are there. When he is finally back in Ithaca, he does
not know at first where he is (*Od.* 13.187-235). We see once more (as in
books 9-12) a wanderer seeking human contact. Later, in disguise, he gives
accounts of himself which, though fictitious and varied in detail, repeat the
same essential truth. These are, of course, stratagems required by the plot,
but they give us pictures of an experience which could be endlessly illustrated.
The poet himself, unobtrusively, lets us draw the message: 19.363-81, 20.
199-207.

Or Penelope: how is she conveyed as a character? Again, through recurrences
of mood and action. There is the thrice-told tale of the web, there is the oft-
repeated withdrawal to the upper chambers, with sleep coming upon her tears,
and dreams, omens. Here is a life of hope, hanging between calamity and
vision. We are made to feel its persistence through the rendering of recurring
moments.

We might make similar remarks about all the major Homeric characters.
What stands out is a speech, an act, a pose which is neither casual nor deliberately descriptive of a certain trait but permanently significant. Achilles
is all one with his wrath, Odysseus all one with his wanderings. Here is a way
of being. Quality, character is a state, an action. A hero can hardly be conceived outside an intrinsic stance. We thus have a perfect coincidence of image,
moment, place; and, to be effective, this needs focus, concentration, repetition.

9

Quite apart from individual characterization, we may further trace this self-repeating beat in the way it serves to bring out the general human contents of the poems. Experiences are proved to be both unique and universal. The suffering of one person implies the suffering of all.

Is it not particularly significant, for instance, that the poet should apply to the death of the two great opposing heroes, Hector and Patroclus, the same kind of phraseology which he applies to others, but in a form at once fuller and more intimately personal? See *Il.* 16.856-57 and 22.361-62:

> From his being, in flight, the soul to Hades was gone
> bewailing its fate, leaving manhood and youth.

Manhood, youth, the disfeatured countenance:[1] we are made to feel strong sympathy for both sides by the pregnant and uniform presentation.

Or take the fall of Troy intimated in *Il.* 4.164-65, 6.448-49. It is important in the *Iliad* as a premonition, a feeling. But at the same time the fall of all other cities is borne in mind: 2.117-18, 9.24-25. Even Argos and Mycenae are no exception: 4.52-54.

Troy is reflected throughout the world; the slaying or enslavement of people is not presented as a narrative of particular events but as the measure of a common doom. Compare the speeches of Priam (*Il.* 22.38-76, 24.493-501) with those of Andromache (6.414-28), of Briseis (19.290-300). The poet himself seems to insist on this point in saying that Briseis' companions mourned ostensibly for Patroclus, but in reality each mourned for her own woe: 19.301-02, cp. 338-39.

A key point of the *Iliad* is the scene between Priam and Achilles in the last book. What is it that makes possible their moment of communion? It is the thought of old Peleus in the same plight as Priam himself; and, with it, the common fate of Patroclus and Hector (*Il.* 24.486-89, 509-12).

In *Od.* 1.336-59 Telemachus rebukes his mother for bidding Phemius to cease singing the return of the Achaeans from Troy. That woeful return, he says, is no fault of the poet but of Zeus; it is the poet's task to sing what affects most the minds of men:

> for not Odysseus alone missed the homecoming day
> out in Troy; many more men also perished.

What this implies is the bearing of poetry on one and all, quite apart from any particular story that might be found more or less interesting.

In all such cases there is juxtaposition. Just as recurrences in a hero's activity build up his character, so do these juxtapositions give us a picture of humanity. The sense of universality is thus brought out by the simplest means: through

the concrete perception of parallel instances. A single event is seen in itself
and by itself; but so strong is the sense of its incidence that it inevitably summons up its likeness. This is not so much narrative as an account of the human
condition.

10

The repetition of the noun-epithet phrases, the most obvious case of repetition, can thus be appreciated only in the light of the larger recurrences which
we find throughout the poems.

There are literal repetitions. There are recurrences in which the wording is
varied but the essential mold remains the same. There are passages that echo
one another in meaning, quite apart from any exact correspondence of form.
This principle of recurrence is naturally loosened where the meanings are
wider and more complex; but there is everywhere a focus, a core which tends
to preclude digression and self-seeking variety. Swift-footed Achilles, for
instance, appears over and over again in simple, concrete acts; but with similar,
though less regular, persistence we see him in the recurrences of his solitary
stance by the seashore or of his fighting scenes. Right from the beginning the
hero must have loomed in the poet's mind—a vitally recurring image once
and for all associated with the occasions of its presence in place and time. A
narrator whose characters develop through a lifetime of incidents and experiences works in a different way. This is why the use of recurring epithets
in a novel would be quite intolerable, but appears natural in Homer.

How account for these repetitions and recurrences which are so characteristic of Homer, which are right at the source of his poetry? W. Arend relates
them to the characteristics of primitive poetry and also points out the Greek
perception of the typical, the essential.[2] But what is "primitive," what is
"Greek" in this respect? And what is essential? Arend hardly elaborates on
these concepts. The Parryists, on the other hand, ascribe this style to traditional phraseology, to traditional themes, and to the need of oral composition,
thus leaving us in the dark as to any fundamentally poetic reason.[3]

If we wish to find such a reason, we must look for it in a principle which is
as abstracted as possible from the culture of a certain age. I appeal to that
representational principle which I have been expounding. It is universally poetic. It is essentially nonnarrative, nondescriptive; and it thus tends to render the object of representation in itself and by itself—as imagery, as form. In
doing so it naturally sacrifices variety of accident to persistence of outline,
complication of events to points of focus. What narrative there is naturally
flows from juxtaposed actions and situations. We have expansion rather
than survey. Hence fighting scenes and not the account of a battle, hence individual acts and not a hero's biography. This is especially remarkable in the

Odyssey, where the complications of the plot might lead us to expect otherwise. There are separate zones of action, each contained within its own separate days, as in a picture: Ithaca, Phaeacia, Pylus and Sparta, Olympus. We repeatedly see the suitors at their wanton task, Penelope in her continual withdrawals, Telemachus taking the initiative, Odysseus as a wanderer, the gods taking counsel, until the various threads concur and merge through the intrinsic pressure of each action or situation.

That nonnarrative principle which led Homer to sing the wrath of Achilles rather than the whole Trojan War, the return of Odysseus rather than the life of Odysseus—that nonnarrative principle led him to the last details of his composition. It was not so much a brilliant intuition as a form of art. In the same way we find the single stroke rather than the long exploit, single acts rather than activities, strong recurring emotions rather than moody states of mind.

Now this extreme concentration on pertinent moments is all one with an intense feeling for form. For it is the way of all art to catch a point of utmost significance and give it pregnant consistency, ignoring the rest. We thus have in Homer the triumph of form over matter. The sense of form continually contends with the multiplicity of the material and overcomes it to an extraordinary extent. Hence a pervasive style, provided we understand style in its broadest and truest sense—not as a manner of saying things but as at once a way of perceiving, conceiving, expressing. For, ultimately, it is a vital sense of truth that keeps this style alive and saves it from falling into mere stylization.

But, we may object, if these Homeric repetitions and recurrences are explained on the basis of a representational, nonnarrative principle which is universally poetic, why is it that we do not find the same thing everywhere in literature?

The answer lies, I think, in the unique process of gathering into form so vast a material while focusing upon immediate concrete acts and states of being. Here art, perhaps for the first time, came into its own exclusive domain, conditioning to itself history, myth, religion. Phenomena appeared in their bare multiplicity and brightness, outside the blurring effect of homage, worship, glorification. How would the war of Troy appear in this light? Not, certainly, as the glory of any city or warlord; not as an exploit of heroes, demigods, gods; not as a chronicle; no, it had to be seen in the way of its concrete realization—as the pressure of body upon body, of arms against arms, as the blow and the fall, as life saved or lost, as anguish, mourning, in short, as incidence after incidence. Or Odysseus' return? Not as a myth or tale, but in all those actualities of rest and movement which are the existential pattern of any journey.

The keen, concrete perception of events in themselves and by themselves could hardly admit any generalized narrative; the greatness and extent of the theme, on the other hand, could hardly admit any perfunctory treatment. The action was thus envisaged in its voluminous realization. But how? How cover a multitude of facts without losing the strong, concrete focus? This was possible only by presenting instance after instance in such a way that the insistent form, common to all, gave through its recurrences the sense of an encompassing rhythm. We might find any number of parallels in nature and art: the repeated beat of waves on the shore gives a sense of the whole sea, the juxtaposed groups of the Parthenon frieze give the sense of a whole charmed city at peace. Such are, in Odysseus' wanderings, the regular succession of night and day, of landing and sailing, of plashing oars and driving winds.

If, say, we had only one instance of "when early-born rose-fingered Dawn appeared" we should simply regard it as a happy image; being repeated many times, it also acquires, in any single instance, that sense of bright continuity which it has in nature. Repetition or recurrence is here not repetitious. Phenomena and events are presented in their voluminous essence and not in their mere multiplicity. The quantity of instances is thus prompted by a qualitative stress. There is concretion and not accretion. The mass is relieved, as it were, of its dead weight. It becomes outline, rhythm, cadence, form. In such succession things tend to lose their episodic connotations and are made symbolic while remaining true to themselves.

The representational, nonnarrative principle is most obvious in these repetitions and recurrences: an event presented once and for all as form. This is most conspicuous in Homer; but the tendency is poetic in the broadest sense. For it is a character of poetry to dwell most insistently on certain themes of experience, isolating them from the accidental or arbitrary course of things. The richest imagery revolves around a few points of focus. We shall thus find in all poetry some kind of keynote, a persistence of touch, a continual return to its centers, a deepening stress. We shall thus everywhere discover repetitions and recurrences, though quite different from Homer's. They will be, especially in modern poetry, more elusive, more subtle, more intimate. But they will lack Homer's persistent coherence with actuality. Why so? Because of a treatment which is at once so concrete and so voluminous: in Homer the points of focus are such as to condition the vast material and not be submerged by it. The act in itself, the state of being in itself was discovered as something to be celebrated in its own right, liberated from the chaos of myth, history, or everyday living. It comes up again and again, imparting the constant beat of life to the vast composition.

PART II: THE CONCRETE VALUE OF THE EPITHET

8. THE EPITHET IN THE SENTENCE

1

We have dealt so far with the epithets in relation to Homer and poetry as a whole, using some significant poetic passages by way of illustration. This, however, will hardly suffice to show the value of the epithet in any single instance; for there are epithets more or less everywhere in the poems. We must therefore pass from poetry to language itself and seek consistent trends, abstracting as much as possible from the quality of any particular passage.

Since meaning (in a poetic, not a literal sense) is my first concern, I shall avoid taking the noun-epithet phrases as abstractions, as compositional elements divorced from their immediate context. I shall rather look at them always in relation to the sentence in which they occur, in relation to the ways in which a thought is enunciated. I shall therefore concentrate on the sentence and posit the matter of inquiry in these terms: is there within a sentence any expressive reason for the occurrence or nonoccurrence of an epithet? What difference does it make whether a certain name or noun has an epithet or not, and what value does thence accrue to the sentence?

2

The nature of the question involves, again, that representational principle which I have been expounding. Though most manifest in the imagery of a whole passage, this principle may be implicit in the single sentence. Though eminently poetic, it naturally grows out of the ordinary usage of language.

Take, for instance, any sentence in which Achilles appears. He will mostly be mentioned by name and epithet or by name without epithet or by a pronoun or simply understood as subject or object of a verb. Ordinary speech of course requires the name to make it known who the person in question happens to be, but not so where the syntax is sufficient to make this clear: the name serves the need of establishing a person's identity. This also applies to

61

Homer (and to poetic speech), but in quite a different way. What in ordinary speech is practical identification often becomes in poetry a concrete realization of a person's identity; and the name or name-epithet may occur even where it is not required by the context, as, for example, in *Il.* 9.193: "They stood before him; amazed Achilles rose up." We may make similar remarks about the pronoun. Poetic expressive need often infringes upon expediency. We thus find in Homer ὁ δέ, "and he," where, for the sake of practical clarity, we would rather use the proper name: cp. *Il.* 17.608, 610, 11.94, 13.698, 7.186-89, 18.33-35; in 15.557-58 neither name nor pronoun marks a change of subject and object. Actions quickly succeeding in close relation with one another leave no room for the concrete presentation of heroes.

It follows that the name, and even more so the name with its epithet, underlines a person's actual presence in any act or situation. Such an occurrence of the name (or name and epithet) has thus nothing to do with the importance of what is being done either in praise or blame. It rather draws our attention to whatever passes before us, acquiring distinctive outline. In other terms, it confers independent standing to a sentence within its context.

Consider in this respect *Il.* 21.1-63. From the end of the preceding book it is quite clear that Achilles is pursuing the Trojans. He reaches the river Scamander. The river, coming into sudden evidence, is named with epithets, but Achilles himself, who charges with full might, is hardly mentioned by name; pronouns and bare verbs without pronoun suffice: cp. 3, 17-20, 26-33. Only at 1.39, in a self-standing sentence, do we first find the full name and epithet. Why here? Because an isolated, particular scene is suddenly summoned up from the past: the attack on Lycaon. Achilles is thus removed from the preceding close sequence of warlike acts. He is fully embodied in a different occasion which singularly stands out. Then again a strong presentation—a double epithet at 1.49. Why? Because Achilles is now instantly visualized in a concrete and self-contained stance as he perceives Lycaon. This contrasts with the lack of epithet at 11.15, 47 ("under the impact of Achilles," "in the hands of Achilles")—instances in which Achilles is indeed presented in his full might, but for the mere sake of specification or explanation. A nonpoetic punctiliousness would have required the epithet in the latter rather than in the former case (in which Achilles simply perceives).

3

It might be worthwhile to examine in the same way all the cases in which Achilles is mentioned. Quite generally we may say that the epithet will imply various degrees of focus, visualization, realization, while the lack of epithet (or the mere pronoun) will in turn imply various degrees of transition, connection, cause and effect, subordination, explanation.

These remarks about Achilles could be qualified and extended to include anything which in Homer is given an epithet. Constantly to be borne in mind is the absence as well as the presence of the epithet. Absence may be here just as important as presence. They are complementary to each other through the succeeding sentences. Their interplay constitutes a modulation in the flow of the action. As events pass before us, they must necessarily involve some tangible or identifiable thing whose outline sharpens or blurs according to the moment; and the way this particular thing is named (with or without epithet) will take into account these changes. Just as the signs of punctuation tell us where to modulate our voice according to relations of meaning, so the noun-epithet phrases by their presence or absence tune us to modes of articulation. But they work on quite a different level. Whereas the punctuation signs are merely conventional, the nouns and epithets are most concrete. It is as if the lingering moments of pause or focus came to the fore and acquired a body; as if certain basic relations which are implicit in all discourse were given self-standing evidence. Through its sheer presence a noun-epithet phrase portends a thickening of the representational material; while, through its mere absence, room is left open to the full scope of those relations and conditions whereby things reflect upon one another.

4

How give an account of such complexities? A running commentary of the poems along these lines would achieve some results; but its bulk and repetitiveness would be intolerable. We may, rather, consider instances of certain nouns in their respective sentences, trying to evaluate the reasons for the epithet's presence or absence. Any noun that has an epithet would serve our purpose; or, from the viewpoint of meaning, any tangible or ideal object so bodied forth in its identity as to be susceptible of being expressed with a noun and epithet.

We may thus further qualify our inquiry: if there is a principle of concrete focus which produces the noun-epithet phrases, how does this principle work within a sentence? In what syntactic conditions is it most effective? How does it affect a certain noun in accordance with the noun's meaning? Or in other words: since the most disparate things have an epithet (as, for example, Achilles and a ship), how do the syntactic occasions of the epithet differ from one to the other? And, on the other hand, what common value accrues to one and all from this principle of concrete focus embodied in the epithet?

As we inquire into the various sets of instances, we shall refine the notions both of *focus* and *concreteness*. These cannot be rigidly understood. They are a matter of degree and nuance. While retaining their poetic value, they necessarily differ from case to case. Hence, on their strength, we can give no general rule on the use of epithets; but what we can do is to establish unmistakable poetic tendencies.

9. SHIP

The noun "ship" (νηῦς) recurs some thousand times in the poems, about as frequently with an epithet as without.[1]

1. Ship as place

Most frequent is "ship" indicating place in sentences which express rest or action "by the ships," movement "to [from, over] . . . the ships." The epithet tends to be used when such rest, action, or movement is simply rendered in itself and by itself without any intrusive connection with other ideas. The measure of such intrusion is, of course, a matter of feeling or judgment; but it is generally clear that the noun-epithet phrase imparts self-standing body to the sentence.

Notice the following sentences:

Il. 1.12: ὁ γὰρ ἦλθε θοὰς ἐπὶ νῆας Ἀχαιῶν
    1.26-27: μή σε, γέρον, κοίλῃσιν ἐγὼ παρὰ νηυσὶ κιχείω
        ἢ νῦν δηθύνοντ' ἢ ὕστερον αὖτις ἰόντα
    1.439: ἐκ δὲ Χρυσηὶς νηὸς βῆ ποντοπόροιο
    8.22: στῆ δ' ἐπ' Ὀδυσσῆος μεγακήτεϊ νηὶ μελαίνῃ

In these sentences there is a natural stress on "ship" as the scene of what is actually happening. No other interest comes in the way. The bare rendering of an act thus acquires fullness of contour. The epithet is necessary to the full expression. Indeed such simple meanings as "go to [or from] the ships," "stand [stay, be held] by the ships," when fully or independently expressed, seem to require the epithet. Compare *Il.* 1.89, 300, 421, 488, 2.17, 168, 392, 3.119, 5.700, 7.229, 372, 381, 419, 432, 8.98, 9.332, 609, 10.74, 308, 510, 514, 525, 11.193, 274, 281, 520, 569, 600, 12.38, 471, 13.57-8, 267, 14.367, 15.423, 693, 743, 16.247, 295-96, 304, 17.383, 416, 454, 625, 18.3, 19.344, 356, 22.392, 465, 23.248, 892, 24.1, 115, 780, *Od.* 1.303, 3.344, 360, 365, 431, 4.731, 779, 10.156, 244, 272, 402, 408, 11.331, 12.368, 13.116, 15.205,

464, 24.50. Significantly we always find the epithet with "to fall [irrupt ($\pi i \pi \tau \epsilon \iota \nu$)] into the ships": *Il.* 2.175, 9.235, 11.824, 12.126, 13.742, 15.63, 624, 17.639. An exception is *Il.* 11.311, a conditional sentence.

Similarly we normally find the epithet in the independent or full expression of such meanings as:

a. "Send [bring, spur] to [or from] the ships": *Il.* 5.26, 327, 6.52, 7.78, 8.334, 10.389, 442, 11.3, 828, 13.423, 15.259, 603, 16.664-65, 17.397, 453, 708, 736, 21.32, 23.162, 883, 24.336, 564, *Od.* 9.226. So "to throw in front of . . . ," *Od.* 9.482, cp. 539, 11.6; "to drive over . . . ," *Od.* 12.406, 14.304; "to send away from . . . ," *Od.* 15.280.

b. "Fight [slay, die] by the ships": *Il.* 5.791, 7.72, 8.531, 12.90, 13.107, 14.57, 15.488, 673, 16.1, 547, 18.304, 21.135, 22.508, 24.254, *Od.* 4.499. So "fight from the ships . . . ," *Il.* 15.387. Exceptions in *Il.* 13.69, 778.

c. Other actions concretely rendered: "to arm," *Il.* 20.1; "to eat," *Il.* 19.160, *Od.* 9.86, 10.57, 272, 12.292; "to float," *Od.* 12.418. Compare also *Od.* 15.420, 258.

Consider, on the other hand, other instances of the same motion, rest, action, but with "ship" lacking the epithet:

Il. 1.167-68: ἐγὼ δ᾽ ὀλίγον τε φίλον τε / ἔρχομ᾽ ἔχων ἐπὶ νῆας.

Il. 15.44: τειρομένους ἐπὶ νηυσὶν ἰδὼν ἐλέησεν Ἀχαιούς.

Od. 17.516: πρῶτον γάρ ἔμ᾽ ἵκετο νηὸς ἀποδράς.

Il. 18.104: ἀλλ᾽ ἦμαι παρὰ νηυσὶν ἐτώσιον ἄχθος ἀρούρης.

In these sentences we find the same relation to ship ("by the ship," "to the ship"); but the sense of motion, rest, action is overlaid with other meanings and inevitably weakened. "With what little prize is my own I go to the ships," says Achilles (*Il.* 1.167-68). "A vain burden to the earth I sit by the ships," he laments (*Il.* 18.104). It is clear that a supervening experience makes the gist of the sentence. Likewise in *Il.* 15.44 (of the god Poseidon): "seeing them hard-pressed by the ships he pitied the Achaeans." In *Od.* 17.516 Eumaeus says about Odysseus: "to me did he first come a fugitive from the ship." The simple meaning "came from the ship" is here filled with a sense of escape and rescue. It is easy, therefore, to account in such instances for the lack of epithets: we are drawn to a mood or to a state of things which removes us from the actual point of contact. Compare *Il.* 1.415, 2.149-50, 6.69, 8.149, 183, 512, 10.82, 141, 281, 336-37, 385, 549, 11.659, 826, 12.114, 123, 225, 411, 418, 13.123-24, 738-39, 744, 746-47, 14.28, 15.407, 494, 655-56, 746, 16.66-67, 204, 305 (contrast 304), 17.340-41, 692-93, 18.7, 22.386, 24.681, *Od.* 1.311, 9.98, 144, 10.117, 146.

Other instances in which the lack of the epithet is due to lack of visualization:

a. What takes place by the ship is a general activity or achievement, and the local connection with "ship" is quite abstract—as in *Il.* 18.294, "to win renown by the ships"; 9.631; "we honored him by the ships." Cp. *Il.* 2.725, 4.513, 7.294, 15.512-13, 16.281, 22.217, *Od.* 11.545. Exceptions: *Il.* 13.84, 16.201, 2.297. In *Il.* 9.609 we must understand Achilles as saying: "the destiny which will keep me [that is, make me stay] by the beaked ships." It is the same case with the meaning "the best of the Achaeans by the ships"; *Il.* 16.272, 17.165, cp. 10.214, 13.276. Exception in *Od.* 4.409, cp. *Il.* 10.306. Similarly "to be a steward by the ships," in *Il.* 19.44. Compare p. 71 below.

b. The connection with ship is casual: *Il.* 11.603, "calling me from the ship." Or it is indefinite: 8.515, "anyone jumping from the ship." Or we have a vague view: *Od.* 9.144, "there was deep fog round the ships."

Elsewhere the lack of epithet is due to facts of construction and relation between sentences. There is a subordinating impact or encroachment which blurs the visual sense of what is happening by the ship:

a. The act involving ship is so markedly presented as a counterpart to other acts that it loses its edge.

In *Il.* 15.367-71, "So by the ships they were halted calling upon one another . . . and Gerenian Nestor . . . most of all was praying," the focus shifts swiftly from the Achaeans by the ships to the hero's image. So *Il.* 8.345-49, 10.1-4, 15.414-15, cp. 13.1, 15.295, 23.2.

b. With successive acts in view of their outcome: *Od.* 14.499-501, "Then Thoas . . . swiftly arose, put down his red cloak, ran out to the ships." Cp. *Il.* 16.293, *Od.* 10.172.

c. With coordinated imperatives: *Il.* 10.53-54, 11.512-13, 16.87.

d. With simultaneous acts which make up one general task, as in *Od.* 9.193, "to stand by the ship and to guard it." So 10.444, 17.429, 19.289.

e. In a closely knit temporal construction: *Il.* 8.473-74, 10.365-68, 13.778-80, 15.232-33, *Od.* 9.465-66. Or the stress falls on the timing of the act: *Il.* 24.401, "Now I have come from the plain to the ships; for tomorrow. . . ." Consider in this connection the difference between the lack of epithet in "after coming to the ships and the sea" (*Od.* 11.1, cp. 4.428, 573, 11.636, 12.144, 13.70) and, on the other hand, the epithet in "they went to the swift ship and the shore" (*Od.* 4.779, cp. 10.154, 407, 569, 12.367). Stress on temporal sequence works against the epithet.

f. With a participle or infinitive in wholly subordinate position: *Il.* 13.69, 15.420, 18.13-14, 278-79, cp. 2.701-02, 19.70-71, *Od.* 14.498.

g. In a parenthesis: *Il.* 10.256.

h. After a simile. In *Il.* 16.259-67 the Myrmidons are compared to wasps sallying out: "with such a heart did they pour out of the ships." What fills our mind is the simile, and the ships are necessarily dimmed out. Cp. *Il.* 2.91, 15.593, 19.360.

2. Ship as a means of transport

Ship, again, has the epithet when the act stands out and the ship is viewed in its bodily presence. In *Il.* 19.328-32 (cp. *Od.* 11.508-09) Achilles thus addresses Patroclus in his fancy: "My heart had hoped that I alone should die, so that from Skyrus you might take my child in the dark swift ship and show everything. . . ." The journey itself is lingeringly realized in the "dark swift ship"; no exacting purpose obscures it.

On the other hand, ship has no epithet if it is no more than a means of conveyance, as when a few lines earlier (19.297-99) Briseis mourns for Patroclus, saying, "'You said you would make me Achilles' wedded wife, and take me in the ships to Phthia, and give the marriage-feast.'"

In this light let us survey other instances. With *Il.* 19.328-32 compare the epithet of ship in rendering the carrying away of Helen: *Il.* 3.46, 444, 22.115, 7.389. Penelope remembers Odysseus as he left "in the hollow ship": *Od.* 18.181, 19.259, 23.176; cp. 1.211, 260, 2.18, 27, 3.288, 10.332, 19.182, 193, 339, 21.39, *Il.* 2.351, 3.240, 5.550, 11.228. In such instances the occasion is haunting, lingers on its own account. Hence the epithet whenever the act of sailing, going, carrying is sufficiently self-contained: *Il.* 7.88, 8.239, 528, *Od.* 3.61, 4.173, 10.502, 12.186, 14.357, 15.416, 16.368; sailing in a ship as distinguished from walking in *Od.* 11.58, *Il.* 24.438.

Consider, on the other hand, opposing instances without epithet:

a. As in the Briseis passage quoted above, there is the impact of another meaning: *Il.* 16.832, "you thought you would take as slaves in the ships the women of Troy." What stands out is the idea of slavery. Cp. *Il.* 4.239, 8.166, 21.41.

b. There is uppermost a sense of purpose; or the simple act of sailing, carrying, is replaced by a more complex one: *Od.* 2.263, "to seek my father in the ships"; 3.105-06, "wandering in the ships for booty"; 3.301-02. So *Od.* 12.99, *Il.* 18.213, "to escape, to rescue with the ships"; *Il.* 9.328, "to conquer with the ships"; *Od.* 15.387, "to take captive with the ships"; 9.129, "to cross." Exceptions: *Od.* 4.512, 13.425.

3. Ship as object

a. "To steer [direct, drive, moor] a ship." Ship has here the epithet because it is the concrete object of a simple concrete act: *Od.* 3.162, 180, 7.109, 8.161, 9.279, 10.91, 95, 11.70, 106, 159, 12.82, 305, 14.258, 15.33, 503, 17.427, *Il.* 23.317. Exceptions are few: *Od.* 4.582, 12.185. In *Od.* 11.456 there is stress on the manner of landing, in 12.109, 219-20 on the complicated steering.

Compare by way of contrast the meaning "to lead the ships, to be a captain of ships." We find here no epithet because no concrete action is brought to bear on the ship itself: *Il.* 1.71, *Od.* 3.283, 8.247, cp. 15.37. So often in the *Catalogue of Ships: Il.* 2.557, 576, etc. Exceptions are few: *Il.* 2.671, *Od.* 14.230.

b. "To draw a ship to the sea." Here is immediate action and a point of focus. Ship has therefore the epithet: *Il.* 1.141, 308, 2.165, 9.683, 11.8-9, 14.97, 106, *Od.* 2.389, 4.358-59, 8.34, 51, 16.348. Similarly "to draw the ships to land": *Il.* 1.485, *Od.* 9.148, 16.325.

The examples without epithet are few, mainly due to additional detail and temporal construction. So in *Od.* 3.153, "at dawn we drew, some of us, the ship to the sea. . . ." Cp. 4.666, 780 (contrast 8.51), 9.546, 10.403, 423, 511, 11.2, 12.5, *Il.* 14.79, 100.

In *Od.* 9.495 no epithet is used for the ship which the splash of Polyphemus's rock throws back toward the shore. What matters is the extraordinary event. In *Od.* 10.26 the ships, without epithet, are borne along or smitten by the winds, cp. 9.67-70, 283-85. But in *Od.* 3.299-300 there is an epithet for wind-driven ships actually arriving at Egypt.

c. Ship as object of attack or defence. We do not normally find the epithet. Consider the following:

"To take [conquer] the ships": *Il.* 11.315, 13.813-14, 14.365, 15.504, 720, 16.128. Exception: 15.477. For 18.260, cp. above, p. 33.

"To defend [fight for] the ships": *Il.* 9.347, 602, 674, 12.142, 179, 216, 227, 13.687, 700, 15.503, 566, 688, 731, 16.246, 251, 301. Exceptions in *Il.* 9.435, 11.277, 12.7, 156, 13.110.

"To save the ships": *Il.* 8.501, 9.424, 681, 10.45, 13.96, cp. 12.5, 16.95.

"To fear for the ships": *Il.* 9.433, 11.557.

"To burn the ships": *Il.* 8.182, 235, 9.653, 12.198, 14.47, 15.702, 16.82, 22.374. Exception: 8.217.

Why do we lack the epithets in these instances? Because the predominant idea lies in the effect and not in the act itself. The ships become a symbol of safety, victory, defeat.

Contrast now the meaning of "throw fire into . . ." with that of "burning." Here we do have the epithet: *Il.* 16.122-23, "into the swift ship they threw the weariless fire," cp. 13.320 (contrast with 13.319), 628-29, 15.597-98. Why the epithet? Because the immediate act is visualized as taking place in the ship. An exception is in *Il.* 12.441 with coordinated imperatives.

Similarly we do not find the epithet in such a general account of destruction as *Od.* 3.298, "the waves shattered the ships on the reefs," cp. 12.67, 290, 9.283-84. Nor in the general statement: "a god might destroy our ship": *Od.* 12.349, 23.319. But we do find the epithet when Zeus is represented in the act of breaking the ship with his thunderbolt (*Od.* 5.131-32, 7.249-50, 12.387-88, 13.148-51, 23.234-35, 330-31, cp. 8. 567-68, 13.148-51). No epithet, however, in *Od.* 14.305, where there are both lightning and thunder.

d. "To touch [to hold] the ship." This concrete act requires the epithet: *Il.* 15.704-05, 2.170-71, 358. Not, however, 2.151-52, "they called on one another to lay hold of the ships and draw them to the sea," where the act is both subordinate and coordinate to others.

4. Ship as subject

Ship has the epithet in the simple statement that it is actually present in a certain place: *Od.* 15.473, "where there was . . . the sea-swift ship." So 6. 264, 9.544, 13.100-01, *Il.* 16.168, cp. 10.309=396, 11.666, 11.229, "in Percote he left the well-balanced ships."

Ship has similarly the epithet when it is represented as actually sailing, coming, arriving: *Od.* 12.69, "the sea-faring ship sailed by," cp. 4.356, 5.175-76, 9.64, 12.166, 13.95, 161, 14.339, 16.322, *Il.* 13.174, 15.549, cp. 24.396. So, generally, in the *Catalogue of Ships: Il.* 2.516, 524, etc.

There is no epithet, on the other hand, where the presence of the ship is immediately set in relation with some other overbalancing meaning. Note the following cases:

a. The ship's location is expanded upon, as in *Il.* 14.30, "far away from the battle the ships are drawn up," 9.43-44, 10.113, 13.681, 15.653-54, 18.69, cp. 14.75.

b. "The ships resounded": *Il.* 2.333-34, 16.276-77, 20.60. Sound has an encompassing effect, and the ships but refract the echo. Cp. *Od.* 10.122, *Il.* 14.4, 16.63.

c. The ship is involved in swift successive events: *Od.* 12.204-05, "the oars crashed down in the flood, the ship was arrested. . . ." Cp. 10.131-32, 12.1-2.

d. What stands uppermost is the purpose, the destination. *Il.* 2.303-04, "the ships assembled in Aulis bringing woe to Priam . . . ," cp. 7.467, 9.71-72, 306, 13.453-54. So *Od.* 8.150-51, "already the ship is hauled down and your friends are ready," cp. 14.332, 19.289, *Il.* 9.43. The ship is similarly weakened in *Od.* 16.330, "Telemachus ordered the ship to sail."

5. Supplementary remarks

Other factors tend to undermine the ship image and deprive it of its epithet.

When "ship" has a pointed attribute or a predicate, the sentence is naturally explicative. Thus we have no epithet with the "half-burnt ship" of Protesilaus (*Il.* 16.294), or with Agamemnon's "empty ships" (*Il.* 4.181); nor in such a sentence as *Od.* 2.292-93, "there are many ships . . . old and new." Cp. *Il.* 20. 247, *Od.* 8.556, 558. Similarly when the emphasis is on the ship's owner: *Il.* 2.54, 10.326, 13.101, 15.707, *Od.* 9.535, etc. So "each to his ship" in *Il.*

19.277. (In *Od.* 3.423, however, an unwonted stress both on ship and owner; cp. *Il.* 15.63-64).

We have seen that the concrete value of a noun-epithet phrase mainly lies in its intimate connection with the representation of a concrete act. For the epithet with ship, it is therefore essential that the act therewith connected be expressed with a verb. Thus we do not normally find the epithet when this act is expressed with an agent or action noun. We have "they fight by the hollow ships" (*Il.* 5.791) but "there was battle by the ships" (*Il.* 15.696). So 15.601, "retreat from the ships"; 16.366, "flight from the ships"; *Od.* 9.126, "craftsmen of ships"; *Il.* 10.342, "a spy on the ships." Cp. *Il.* 13.333, 14.4, 15.69, 601, 653, 16.63, 127, 18.171-72, *Od.* 2.319, 4.361-62, 5.404, 11.112-13, 12.286. "Bulwark of the ships" (εἶλαρ νηῶν), *Il.* 7.338, 437, 14.56, 68.[2]

This distinction is quite natural. In the name of an agent or of an action the act is crystallized. It is taken for granted. It is descriptively related to its scene. We are thus told that there was a battle and that it took place by the ships: a statement of fact. The verb, on the other hand, gives us the act which naturally spreads out in its characteristic scene. The language itself thus evinces a representational principle; and this confirms the concrete, nonornamental nature of the epithet. For the noun-epithet phrase subtends an act; and if it were purely ornamental we should find it more or less anywhere, with action and agent nouns as well as with verbs.[3]

10. HORSE

The noun "horse" (ἵππος) recurs some four hundred and fifty times. The instances with epithet are a little less than one third of the total. I give here some of the main trends.

1. Horse with epithet[1]

1. Horse is the subject of a verb of motion, as *Il.* 8.122-23, 314-15, "the swift-footed horses swerved." Cp. *Il.* 5.257, 295-96, 772, 8.88, 10.491, 11.708, 13.31, 16.367-68, 375, 380, 866, 18.223, 20.498, 22.162, 464, 23. 303-04, 373, 376, 475, *Od.* 3.496. Cp. *Il.* 23.503-04. In such instances the horse appears in the full evidence of immediate, simple, appropriate action. Exceptions occur where the movement is described, explained: *Il.* 12.58, 23.392-93; or amplified: *Il.* 11.615, 23.500-01.

2. Horse is the object of driving, directing, curbing, etc., as *Il.* 5.329, "towards the son of Tydeus he drove the strong-hooved horses." Cp. *Il.* 2.764, 5.236, 240, 261, 275, 321, 323, 581, 752, 829, 841, 8.139, 157, 254, 348, 432, 10.527, 537, 564, 11.127, 289, 513, 760, 12.62, 15.259, 354, 16.712, 732, 17.465, 496, 18.280, 19.424, 23.13, 347, 423, 536. So *Il.* 11.280-81, "the charioteer lashed the fair-maned horses to the hollow ships"; cp. 11-531, 17.624-25, *Od.* 5.380, 15.215. Other concrete acts: *Il.* 21.132, 8.402. In such cases the epithet is at home: the action is immediate, full, bringing the horses into sudden evidence.

The few exceptions occur when the stress shifts away from the bare act. Note the following:

a. The act is weakened by descriptive detail, as *Il.* 23.426, "hold back the horses" (in a passage concerning the maneuvering of the chariot). Cp. *Il.* 3.113, 4.302, 11.48, 15.352, 17.501, 23.533.

b. The attention turns to the mood of the charioteer, as *Il.* 12.124, "there with straight purpose he drove the horses," cp. 13.395-96, 15.456-57, 23.514-15, 24.696-97.

c. The act is regarded as a professional activity: *Il.* 23.357, "the best in driving horses," cp. 2.553-54, 15.679, *Od.* 9.49-50.

d. The horse is pointedly qualified: *Il.* 16.506, "hold the snorting horses."

e. The weakening of the act is due to the construction of the sentence. There is a strongly subordinate clause in *Il.* 8.168, 20.488; both subordinate and containing additional detail in *Il.* 11.48=12.85; a parenthesis: 8.257-58; a μέν . . . δέ construction: 12.76-77, cp. 15.385, 24.324-26.

2. Horse without epithet

1. There is no epithet when horse is object to an act which is not concrete, not visualized in any single instance. Thus *Il.* 5.263, "thinking of the horses"; 5.202, "sparing the horses"; 8.113, "to take care of the horses" (cp. 10.481); 10.401-02, "to desire the horses"; 11.702; "grieving for the horses"; 11.718, "to hide the horses"; 17.76, "to pursue the horses"; 23.571, "to harm the horses"; 8.184 (cp. 19.399, 23.372, 402), "to address the horses." Of gods infusing might into the horses: 17.456, 23.390, 400, 24.442. (But in 2.383, "give food to the swift-footed horses." Affectation?)

2. Horse as subject of the sentence. There is no epithet when horses are portrayed in striking postures which distract us from the simple, concrete act. Thus *Il.* 8.136, "the horses in fear crouched down." So usually in all plight, strain, exertion: *Il.* 2.390 (cp. 12.58), 4.27, 5.588, 6.38, 8.81, 15.452-53, 20.394, 489, 23.321.

Il. 17.426, "the horses of Achilles were . . . weeping"; 8.127, "the horses were missing their charioteer."

There are a few remarkable exceptions which are self-explaining. Thus the epithet is an element of high relief in *Il.* 12.50-51, the splendid lines:

> they dared not,
> the swift-footed horses, but neighed on the uttermost brink,
> standing. . . .

Cp. 16.370-71. In 19.404 the unique προσέφη πόδας αἰόλος ἵππος introduces —as though it were a human speaker—the horse Xanthos speaking to Achilles.

3. Supplementary remarks

As in the case of "ship," the horse has no epithet when it has a predicate of a particular attribute: *Il.* 8.104, "slow are your horses"; 10.437, "the most beautiful horses I saw"; 12.96, "him the horses bore from Arisba, tawny ones, huge ones"; *Il.* 2.770, 5.222, 6.506, 8.106, 9.124, 10.473, etc. So with emphatic point: *Il.* 10.477, "These are the horses . . ."; cp. 558.

Like "ship," "horse" has no epithet when the accompanying act is expressed not by a verb but by an agent or action noun. So "driver of horses" in *Il.* 6.18-19, cp. 5.102. Contrast *Il.* 23.375, ἵπποισι τάθη δρόμος with 16.375, τανύοντο δὲ μώνυχες ἵπποι. In *Od.* 18.263 the exceptional ἵππων τ᾽ ὠκυπόδων ἐπιβήτορας perhaps pointedly means "riders of horses"; cp. *Il.* 18.531-32, ἐφ᾽ ἵππων βάντες ἀερσιπόδων. Another rare expression is in *Il.* 10.535, "the sound of swift-footed horses," suggested perhaps by 11.152, "of horses the high-sounding feet."[2]

11. SEA, EARTH, SKY, AND ZEUS

"Sea" (ἅλς, θάλασσα, πόντος, πέλαγος) recurs in the poems some four hundred times, about as frequently with an epithet as without.

1. Sea with epithet[1]

Sea has an epithet when it gives concrete setting to simple human acts or events distinctly taking place:

a. *Od.* 1.183, "sailing through the wine-colored sea"; *Il.* 15.27, "sped over the unvintaged sea"; *Il.* 2.159, "flee over the sea's broad shoulders."

With the sense of "traveling in [through, over] . . . ," we find the most extensive and varied use of the epithet: cp. *Il.* 1.312, 2.613, 20.228, 23.744, 24.752, *Od.* 2.263, 370, 421, 3.177, 4.362, 510, 5.52, 174, etc.

Similarly "to look over . . . ": *Il.* 1.350, 5.771, *Od.* 5.158.

Without epithet, actuality fades into circumstance, cause and effect, point, question: *Il.* 2.665, "assembling many people he escaped over the sea; for they threatened him . . . "; *Od.* 3.15, "Therefore you traveled over the sea: to know . . ."; 5.330, after a simile, "so did the winds bear the raft hither and thither on the sea"; cp. 7.239, 9.491.

b. *Il.* 1.34, "silent he walked along the shore of the wide-roaring sea." In any such picturing of the extended shore, the epithet is seldom lacking: *Il.* 1.327, 9.182, *Od.* 4.432; cp. *Il.* 1.316, *Od.* 10.179.[2] Equally so for exposure *on* a certain spot: *Il.* 1.350 (cp. 23.59), "going far aloof from his friends he sat on the white-sea's shore." Cp. *Od.* 11.75, *Il.* 14.31.

By way of analogy, *Od.* 9.132, "there were fields along the white-sea's shores. . . ." Cp. *Il.* 15.619.

The lack of epithet implies some kind of complication. There is singular tension and behavior in *Il.* 24.12, "he kept circling in frenzy along the seashore"; cp. 19.40-41. There is an unwonted act in 11.621-22, "they cooled the sweat off their tunics, standing to the breeze on the seashore." Compare the description of sundry occupations in *Il.* 2.773-75; a quick meal in

Od. 14.347. Or pure exposure is weakened by curious interest: the bedding of seals in *Od.* 4.449, the transformation of Odysseus in 6.236.

c. *Od.* 5.281, "[Scheria] appeared like a shield out in the mist-colored sea." So we find the epithet when anything is distinctly witnessed, carried out, situated on the high seas: *Od.* 1.197 (=4.498, 552), 3.294, 6.204, 19.172, 5.132, 221, 7.250, etc.

2. Sea without epithet

Sea, on the other hand, has no epithet when it is a loose term of reference— a mere specification of place or an explaining detail or an addition which is not intrinsically integrated into the vivid realization of acts and events:

a. *Od.* 4.428 (cp. 573, 8.50, 10.569, 11.1, 12.367, 13.70), "when I came to the ships and the sea." Similarly in all routine accounts of "disembarking [resting] on the seashore": *Il.* 1.437, *Od.* 4.430, etc. Such instances are far removed from those quoted above in section 1b. To appreciate the difference, consider *Od.* 4.428-33: Menelaus mentions the sea without epithet in saying, "we rested on the seashore," but adds on a different level of realization:

> then along the shore of the wide-passaged sea
> I walked with keen prayer to the gods.

b. "Near the sea," "up to the sea," "beyond the sea": *Il.* 14.75, 13.143, 15.362, 17.265, *Od.* 3.293, 9.182, 13.257. These have no epithet because they are but definitions of place. So with emphasis on relative positions: *Il.* 15. 740, "with our backs against the sea"; cp. 1.409, 16.67, 18.294, *Od.* 4.608, 9.25, 13.235. For *Il.* 15.619, "a rock by the white-foaming sea," see 1b above. An exception exists in *Il.* 23.374, a controversial passage.

c. *Od.* 1.4, "many woes did he suffer at sea. . . ." Cp. *Od.* 3.91, 4.821, 5.301, 335, 377, 12.27, 14.135. There is a reason for the lack of epithet: the sea refers to a general condition; it does not give focus to a particular act. An exception is in *Od.* 10.458. In 16.367, "at sea . . . sailing," the meaning "to sail" passes into that of waiting, expecting, toiling.

d. More generally "sea" without epithet merely completes the required sense from a practical point of view: *Il.* 10.572, "they washed with the sea," that is, "with seawater" (contrast the different value of *Od.* 2.261, where the actual contact with the sea stands out), *Od.* 14.350, "I set my chest to the sea" [that is, "to the water"] in order to swim" (cp. 5.374), 5.455, "the sea [that is, seawater] bubbled out from his mouth and nostrils." The phrase "to ply the sea with oars" has no epithet, perhaps for the same reasons, in *Il.* 7.6, *Od.* 13.78. Cp. 12.172 (but see p. 122 for the oar *touching, beating* the sea).

e. "To throw into the sea," "to fall into the sea." Here again seawater; and there is no epithet: *Il.* 1.314, *Od.* 4.508, 5.318, 431. cp. *Il.* 14.258, 15.219, *Od.* 5.50, 374. "To come out of the sea": *Il.* 13.15, 16.408, *Od.* 4.401, 5.422, 446, 9.285, 11.134, etc. The corresponding examples with epithet bring out the plunge, the splash, the emergence: *Od.* 4.425, 570, 5.352–53, *Il.* 1.532, 6.347, 1.359, *Od.* 4.405, 5.56). Stale instances are few: *Od.* 5.349.

What generally stands out is the epithet's function of evincing the sea-element insofar as it comes into contact with a certain human (or animal) act, when this act is roundly or fully expressed. This is no less true of, say, *Il.* 1.34, "he walked along the shore of the wide-roaring sea" than of *Od.* 6.226 (cp. 4.406), "he wiped from his head the scurf of the unvintaged sea."

Hence, with few exceptions (as the mythical *Il.* 14.204, 272), the sea has no epithets when it is presented as one of the elements or without any human act impinging upon it. So *Od.* 12.404, 14.302, "nothing appeared but the sea and the sky"; *Il.* 21.196, "[Oceanus] whence spring the rivers and the sea." So *Il.* 18.483, 8.24. In *Od.* 11.122, 23.269, the sea as an idea: "those who know not the sea" (cp. 1.52).[3] In *Il.* 1.157, "there are in between / many shadowy mountains and the echoing sea," the sea is not the element itself but a familiar presence that fills the intervening distance, a space to be seen, experienced, crossed over. The spondaic line (θάλασσά τε ἠχήεσσα) helps the effect.

Thus, curiously but significantly, we find no epithet where we might most have expected it from a conventional or ornamental point of view—in the Homeric passage that gives us most forcibly a religious sense of the sea, *Il.* 13.29:

> Poseidon drove over the waves; up sprang the sea-beasts beneath him
> everywhere out of the depth; they ignored not their lord;
> *and in joy the sea clove apart.*

Cp. 14.392, 18.66, 24.96.

Nor for the same reason is there any epithet when the sea is regarded as an active power, hostile or beneficial: *Od.* 5.454, "by the sea his heart was subdued"; 19.113, "the sheep give birth, the sea provides fish"; cp. 1.12, 3.192, *Il.* 2.294. None where the sea is pictured acting by itself: *Od.* 6.95, "the sea washed the pebbles clean"; cp. 9.484, 541. In *Il.* 16.34, "the gray sea gave you birth," we have no epithet but an attribute that fits the feeling of the passage.[4]

It follows that the sea has no epithet when it is disturbed by Poseidon or Zeus: *Od.* 5.291, 304, 7.273,[5] 12.315; nor when it darkens under the clouds: *Od.* 12.406, 14.304. Nor, with few exceptions (*Il.* 9.4, 11.298), in the similes depicting a storm: *Il.* 2.144–45, 4.276, 424, 14.16, 13.797, 17.265, cp. 7.64, 23.214.

Epithets do occur, however, when waves are singled out of the general mass, as *Il.* 13.798:

> blustering waves of the wide-roaring sea
> curving white-crested one before the other.

Cp. *Il.* 2.209, 15.381, *Od.* 12.2, 13.85. The sea, with its epithet, is the necessary field of action to the waves, which are given separate form. There is some analogy to the image of a man walking along the shore.

Earth (γαῖα, αἶα, γῆ, χθών, ἄρουρα) occurs in the poems some two hundred and fifty times, three times less frequently with the epithet than without.[6]

3. Earth as a particular spot

Earth is most frequently the ground upon which anything falls or lies. As such it is naturally taken for granted. It need not be mentioned at all; and, if mentioned, it usually has no epithet: *Il.* 1.245, "he threw the scepter on the earth"; cp. 3.114, 13.565, 654, 14.438, 20.483, 23.731, etc.

There are exceptions. So in *Il.* 12.194=8.277, 16.418, "all of them one on the other he brought down upon the much-nourishing earth." There is here the massive fall of many heroes, no detail of the fight; what stands out is the receiving earth with its epithet, while the slain men hardly have any epithets at all.

Consider now, in this connection, other instances with the epithet, from *Iliad* 3:

3.89 (Hector proclaims Paris's challenge): "he bids all lay down the fine arms upon the much-nourishing earth, alone in the midst . . . he will fight."

3.195 (Priam pointing to Odysseus): "the arms are laid by him upon the much-nourishing earth, and he . . ."

3.265 (Priam and Antenor): "from the chariot descended upon the much-nourishing earth, they stepped out . . . "

Why the epithets here? Because *Iliad* 3 presents the action in self-contained tranquillity. There is momentary peace. The interval is contemplative. Removed from the battle, things are shown for what they are. Arms resting on the ground, an old man descending from the chariot thus become points of focus that fill the passing moment. It is the earth, not the battle scene, which makes the setting.

Compare *Il.* 6.213, "he planted the spear upon the much-nourishing earth." Again, a moment of peace in the genial encounter of Diomedes and Glaucus. Likewise *Il.* 11.619, "they stepped down upon the much-nourishing earth" of Nestor and Machaon, at last away from the battlefield.[7]

The lack of epithet reflects quite a different feeling:

Il. 8.492: in the height of victory the Trojans "descend on earth" from their chariots to hear Hector's speech.

Il. 20.345: "Ah, here his spear lies on the earth, and I see not the man," exclaims Achilles when Aeneas is wafted away, saved from his attack.

Il. 10.472. A description of the Thracian camp: "their fine arms were laid by their side on the earth in good order, in three rows." The interest in detail naturally robs the earth of its effect.

Hence earth has its epithet whenever it is not mentioned as a matter of fact, neither encumbered by the tense human action nor lost in description. This happens when movement is contemplated for its own sake. The very spot is then part of the picture. Feet touch the ground as much as ground touches feet. See the mares of Erichthonius in *Il.* 20.226-27:

> when they leaped on the grain-giving earth
> they would run on the asphodel-tops and not break them.

Or the horse race in *Il.* 23.368-69:

> the chariots now closed down upon the much-nourishing earth,
> now rose up in the air.

So the Phaeacian dancers in *Od.* 8.378. The earth is here the surface touched, ground giving resilience to the act.

4. Earth as extended place or space

More generally, earth has an epithet when its relation to a certain event is both vitally pertinent and fully realized in the breadth of its range.

Il. 12.158 (stones): "they fell to the ground like snowflakes which the strong-blowing wind, whirling the shadowy clouds, thickly sheds down upon the much-nourishing earth. . . ." The picture expands full scale, with earth in its inevitable place to receive the falling snow. Note the cursory "stones fall to the ground (ἔραζε)" in contrast with the snowflakes alighting upon the much-nourishing earth.

Il. 16.635: "As the sound of foresters rises in a mountain valley and it is heard from afar, so did their din rise up from the wide-pathed earth." The sense of distance suggested by the simile confers reality to "wide-pathed earth." The same sense of space occurs in *Od.* 10.149, "I stood on a rocky hill . . . and smoke appeared from the wide-pathed earth." With this compare earth without epithet in 10.99, "there appeared no fields of men, no oxen, smoke only we saw arising from the earth," where the smoke is merely something noticed along with other things. (In *Od.* 3.453, on the other hand, the epithet appears trite).

Il. 8.73: "the fates of the Achaeans sank down to the much-nourishing earth, those of the Trojans rose up to wide heaven." The epithets focalize points exposed and brought into sudden range by Zeus tipping the scales first one way, then the other.

Strong self-evidence of place may also be felt when events or human conditions are presented in terms of their extension the world over. The earth and what takes place in it are complementary, both grasped at once as elements of one phenomenon.

Earth naturally has the epithet in such cases: *Od.* 19.593, "upon each mortal have the gods bestowed his portion over the grain-giving earth"; cp. 7.332, 17.386, 19.107, 408, *Il.* 7.446.

The same applies to the visual rendering of daybreak or nightfall: *Il.* 8.486, "into Oceanus sank the bright light of the sun, drawing black night over the grain-giving earth"; cp. 21.232, *Od.* 3.3, 12.386. Of Hermes's and Athena's worldwide task: *Il.* 24.342, *Od.* 1.98.

The corresponding examples without epithet show earth as a mere point of reference:

Od. 6.153: "if you are a mortal, of those that live upon earth . . ."; cp. 8.222, 9.89, 10.101, 7.67, 1.196, *Il.* 17.447, *Od.* 4.417. *Il.* 1.88, "whilst I live and see upon earth . . ."; cp. *Od.* 16.417. Similarly *Il.* 2.850 (Axios): "whose water is the loveliest shed upon earth"; cp. 5.545, *Od.* 11.239.

Od. 23.371: "they went out. . . . Already there was light on earth"; cp. *Il.* 23.226, 7.421. Daylight here but marks the timing, and earth is out of focus.

5. Earth as object of touch

Od. 5.463 (Odysseus washed ashore): "he kissed the grain-giving earth." So 13.354. Compare *Il.* 9.568 (Althaea): "beat the much-feeding earth with her hand, calling Hades." These are pregnant acts, and the earth is in full focus. Cp. *Il.* 24.54. Contrast *Od.* 21.122 (Telemachus fixing the axes for the contest): "he pressed the earth all around them"—a matter-of-fact explanation.

Il. 14.271–72 (the goddess Hera taking her oath): "with one hand she seized the much-nourishing earth, with the other the sparkling sea." This is also a pregnant act; but on the level of gods, with earth and sea mythically simplified. See also p. 77 above.

6. Earth in the function of what it does

Il. 3.243: "the life-begetting earth enclosed them." So *Il.* 2.699, *Od.* 11.301; cp. *Il.* 21.63. The earth holds the dead, both an agency and a place of rest. It keeps what is laid within it. Here is an act, a condition which is intrinsic to earth's nature and fully expressed, realized. Hence the epithet to bring out a full basic identity.

Consider, on the other hand, corresponding examples without epithet:

Il. 16.629: "sooner will the earth hold them," that is, "before that happens
they will die." Cp. *Il.* 18.332, *Od.* 11.549, 13.427, 15.31. The phrase becomes a trope fitting the speaker's viewpoint. Or consider the epithet in the
simple cry, "may the wide earth hide me" (*Il.* 8.150, 4.182, 17.416-17), and
the same idea without epithet in *Il.* 6.282, "may the earth swallow him; a
great woe he is . . . ," where the more complex train of thought puts earth out
of focus (cp. 6.411, 464).

Parallel are instances of the generating earth:

Il. 14.347: "under them the divine earth put forth new-blossoming grass"
(cp. *Od.* 4.229, 9.357, 19.111); *Il.* 2.547 (of Erechtheus): "Athena reared him
. . . and the grain-giving earth begot him" (cp. *Od.* 11.309, 365). The epithet
is here quite regular. What stands out is, again, the earth's identity. She is no
goddess, no detached power. The generative act is one and all with her nature.

7. Earth endowed with acts, states not intrinsic to it

These reasons for the use of the epithet may be better appreciated if we observe how earth lacks the epithet when acts or modes of being are ascribed
to it which are not intrinsically pertinent to its nature. It is remarkable that
the epithet should be missing in such cases, for it would be most appropriate from a rhetorical point of view. Note the following:

Il. 2.780-81: "they trod as if the land were afire, and the earth groaned as
if under the wrath of Zeus." Cp. 2.95, 465-66, 784, 20.157. See also p. 77
above.

Il. 19.362: "the flash reached the sky and the earth laughed at the glitter of
bronze."

Il. 4.451: "the earth flowed with blood." Cp. 8.65, 10.484, 13.655, 17.360,
18.329. The epithet is rare: *Il.* 15.715.[8]

All these effects are but incidental to the earth. Anything else might as well
refract, reflect, moisten. We have an added detail rather than an event native
to the earth, and therefore no epithet.

For the same reason we find no epithet when earth is a theme of human
emotion. The stress falls on man, not on anything which is inevitably pertinent
to the earth:

Od. 23.233: "as the earth appears welcome to swimmers whose ship Poseidon shattered at sea . . . "; 4.523, "gladly he saw the land." Cp. 5.392, 398,
439. The sentence quoted above, "he kissed the grain-giving earth," is otherwise incisive. It does not explain the joy of touching earth, but makes it
implicit in a concrete act.

8. Earth as one of the elements

Od. 1.54: "the pillars of Atlas hold apart the earth and sky." Cp. 5.294 (=9.69, 12.315), *Il.* 18.483.

Zeus pounding the earth: *Il.* 2.781, cp. 8.24, 20.63.

Od. 10.191: "we know not where the shining sun goes under the earth," that is, "which is the West." Cp. 11.18, 12.381, *Il.* 23.226.

Earth as the domain of all the gods: *Il.* 15.193.

There is normally no epithet in such cases. This is easily explained: earth as a cosmic element is mentioned in its own abstraction, removed from any clearly realized action or event impinging upon it. (There are few exceptions: cp. *Il.* 20.58. For *Il.* 14.271-72, cp. p. 80.)

It follows that earth has no epithet when presented as a goddess, in prayer or oath or sacrifice: *Il.* 3.104, 278, 15.36, 19.259, *Od.* 5.184. This is striking in that conventional usage would require the epithet. Cp. p. 77 above.

Sky (οὐρανός; compare αἰθήρ) occurs about two hundred times in the poems, about as frequently with the epithet as without. Instances and epithets are less varied than in the case of earth and sea.[9]

9. Sky as place, space

Take *Il.* 19.257, "in prayer he spoke looking to the vast sky"; cp. 3.364, 21.272; similarly *Il.* 15.371, *Od.* 9.527, "stretching his hands to the starry sky." In these sentences the epithet is fully justified. It furthers the sense of height, extension, space which is intrinsic to the act. For in all these passages there is a turning to heaven in prayer or anguish, and this needs an opening perspective.

Exceptions occur in *Il.* 16.232, 24.307. The wording is different: οὐρανὸν εἰσανιδών for ἰδὼν εἰς οὐρανὸν εὐρύν. The shorter phrase suits in both passages the detailed rendering of a libation; we are drawn to implements and ritual acts rather than to one broad gesture.

Similarly, the epithet makes us aware of any rising movement losing itself in the sky:

Il. 21.522: "as when smoke arising reaches up to the vast sky." Cp. 5.867.

Il. 5.504: dust "which the feet of the horses struck up to the bronze-wrought sky"; 17.424-25, "the iron din arose to the brazen sky through the unvintaged air."

Od. 3.2: "the sun arose . . . to the bronze-wrought sky." Cp. 11.17, 12.380.

Od. 12.73: the rock of Scylla "towering up to the vast sky."

When the epithet is lacking, our interest lies somewhere other than in the upward motion, which is therefore taken for granted:

Il. 1.317: "the flavor enwrapped in smoke rose to the sky." Cp. 8.549.
What captures our attention is the fragrant mass.

Il. 2.458: "from the wondrous bronze the all-shining flash . . . reached the
sky." What matters is the light, the glitter. Cp. 8.509, 11.44, 18.214, 19.362.

Of the war cry: *Il.* 2.153 (=12.338, 14.60). This is merely taken for granted.
The phrase underlines the loudness of the cry.

Or we have a circumstance rather than a phenomenon in its own right:
Il. 7.423, "the sun now was just hitting the fields . . . rising up to the sky, and
they met one another." Cp. *Od.* 4.400.

Or there is no more than a fact narratively told: *Il.* 23.868, "then the dove
flew to the sky." Cp. 24.97.

The phrase "whose glory [or infamy] reaches the sky" recurs both with
the epithet (*Od.* 8.74, 15.329, 19.108) and without (*Il.* 8.192, *Od.* 9.20). The
transferred sense tends to blur the value of the epithet.

10. Other instances with and without epithet

Il. 6.128: "if a god you are come down from the sky . . . ," that is, "if you
are a god and not a man." Compare 6.108 (the Achaeans seeing Hector),
"they thought that a god had come down from the starry sky." In the latter
instance the sentence expands to give the full sense of a descent from the
sky.

Similarly, compare the colorless οὐρανόθεν, "from the sky" (*Il.* 1.195,
17.545, etc.), with *Od.* 20.113 (addressed to Zeus), "you thundered from the
starry sky." Cp. 20.102-03.

Od. 5.303: "with what clouds Zeus enwreathes the starry sky." The act
of Zeus is so rendered as to give body to the sky. Contrast instances in which
the same effect is presented as an interplay of the elements: *Od.* 5.294 (=9.69,
12.315), "night [or storm] fell from the sky"; *Od.* 13.269, "murky night
held the sky."

Il. 20.299: "the gods who inhabit the vast sky." This is frequent: *Il.* 21.
267, *Od.* 1.67, 4.378, 479, etc. Cp. *Il.* 15.192, "Zeus, who had as his lot the
vast sky." The sky is at once a place and a distinctive habitation which sets off
the gods in relation to men (men, however, are said merely to "inhabit the
earth"; see p. 80 above).

A concrete sense of space is also evident in *Il.* 4.44, "all the cities of men
. . . laid out under the starry sky." Contrast *Il.* 22.318, "Hesperus, the loveliest star in the sky" (cp. p. 80 above).

The epithet is also lacking when we are distracted by emphasis on position:
Il. 15.20, "you hung suspended in the sky"; cp. 4.443.

11. Sky as one of the elements

As in the case of sea and earth (see pp. 77, 82 above), there is no epithet when sky is the element itself separated from the affecting impact of men and gods:

Od. 12.404, 14.302: "nothing appeared but sea and sky."

Il. 8.16: "as far below Hades as the sky is from the earth."

Il. 18.483-85 (Hephaestus on Achilles' shield): "he forged therein the • sky . . . and all the stars wherewith the sky is crowned."

An exception occurs in *Il.* 15.36=*Od.* 5.184, "let the earth know and the vast sky above," where the epithet is favored perhaps because "above" imparts a sense of space. "Great sky" appears in the mock-heroic *Il.* 21.388, "the great sky gave a trumpet-blast," and in the mythical *Il.* 5.750=8.394, "the Hours, to whom the great sky . . . is entrusted."

Zeus

Zeus frequently lacks the epithet when he is presented as an impersonal power:

Generally ruling over human life, as in *Il.* 20.242-44: "Zeus impairs and increases in men their worth; for he is the strongest of all." Cp. *Od.* 1.348-49, 4.237. In 6.188 the rather weak Ὀλύμπιος.

Inflicting ruin: *Il.* 22.403-04, "then did Zeus give him up to his foes, to be defiled in his land." Cp. 6.357, 159, 14.85-87, *Od.* 3.152, 14.300, 18.273, 19.363.

Bestowing wealth: *Il.* 2.670, 23.299.

Granting victory: *Il.* 17.331, 627, 19.204.

Credited with any final decision: *Il.* 18.116, "my doom I shall then receive, when Zeus . . . wills to bring it about." So 22.366. Cp. 18.328, 20.92, *Od.* 2.144, 3.160, 5.409, 9.38, 262.

Taken for granted as the source of natural phenomena: *Od.* 14.457, "Zeus was raining all night." Cp. *Il.* 16.365, 17.548.

In prayers, wishes, exclamations, as *Od.* 3.346, "may Zeus never bring this to pass." Cp. 2.34, 3.346, 4.34, 668, 14.53, 158, 17.597, 18.112, 22.252.[10]

In such instances Zeus almost becomes a symbol of generalized power. He is equivalent to an indefinite god or gods, and the lack of epithet reflects the lack of a definite form, a definite act. For the same reason we hardly find in Homer any characteristic epithets for the dark, fathomless idea of fate (*moros, moira, aisa*).

Now these instances without epithet stand in sharp contrast to those frequent cases in which Zeus is presented with his familiar epithets in the concrete image of a real person, speaking or spoken to, acting, involved in all manner of situations: *Il.* 1.397, 498, 511, 544, 609, etc.

It might be interesting, in this respect, to note Zeus's epithets νεφεληγερέτα, στεροπηγερέτα, μητίετα (cp. κυανοχαῖτα of Poseidon, ἀκάκητα of Hermes). If, as it was supposed, the -τα ending harks back to an original vocative form, this has a bearing on my argument. For this means that these impressive epithets were earlier used in invocations, and that they were adapted in Homer to serve simply as nominatives—that is to say, to compose the image of a god presented in a certain act. Such composition was not accidental. What was originally an evocation of divine power becomes here pure representation; and the epithets preserve this divine significance, but express it in the ordinary self-evidence of the god's passing acts rather than in any unusual manifestation.

This use of epithets to bring out even the presence of the supreme god within the compass of an experienced moment stands out against the relative lack of epithets where the same god is treated as an almighty agent. Here is another proof of the concrete value of the Homeric epithets. Again the epithet is often lacking where we might most expect it from a conventional, or rhetorical, point of view.

12. PERSONS

The epithets of persons (namely, proper names with their epithets) present
a far greater complexity than those I have surveyed so far. Their presence
or absence is again affected by the act or state expressed in the sentence; but
a person's acts and states are immeasurably diversified and related to one
another in most complex, delicate ways. Hence no easy classification is possible, and full treatment would require a separate study.

I shall therefore limit myself to only a few significant trends and illustrate
them insofar as they may shed some light upon the concrete function of
a person's epithet.

1. Instances with epithet

Il. 1.84: "to him in reply so spoke swift-footed Achilles." The epithet so
coherently used in this type of sentence needs no further illustration. It is
highly significant; for it gives body to the speaker whenever he (or she) stands
out simply to speak in self-contained outline, and no immediate detail is
added.

Hence we find the epithet with characters coming into full evidence in the
performance of any act which is visualized or perceived in itself and by itself. Consider *Il.* 1.6-7, "from the moment they first stood apart in strife /
Atreides-lord-of-men and divine Achilles." Two names with their epithets
within the same line are quite singular; but they naturally bring into focus
the moment which is here portrayed. Compare *Il.* 13.422, 14.380, 390, 16.760,
17.754, 19.48, 20.160.

Acts suddenly and strongly exposed naturally lend themselves most to
this kind of representation. Consider the following sets of instances:

a. *Il.* 1.102: "among them stood up the hero-son-of Atreus Agamemnon-
wide-ruling." Epithets thus serve to assert the presence of a man rising,
taking position. Cp. 1.68-69, 247-48, 2.100, 278, 3.216, etc.

b. Heroes responding to a challenge, as in *Il.* 7.162-68, "first arose the lord-of-men-Agamemnon, after him rose Diomedes-the-strong-one son-of-Tydeus. . . ." In such a series the epithets do not so much distinguish the heroes from one another as solidify the impact of each movement. Cp. *Il.* 8.261-67, 10.228-32, 23.288-303, 3.267-68.

    c. *Il.* 6.394-95: "There the bountiful wife ran out to meet him Andromache daughter of great-hearted Eetion." Epithets thus assert the presence of anyone newly arriving, meeting, coming: cp. 6.251-52, 11.809-10, 13.210, 246, 14.27-29, etc.

    What matters, however, is not the meaning of the verb or the idea expressed. It is, rather, a question of impact, of incidence filling the moment. We thus have, for instance:

    Il. 4.148: "he then shuddered the lord-of-men-Agamemnon." Cp. 4.150, 11.254, 15.34, etc.

    Il. 4.255: "at their sight he rejoiced the lord-of-men-Agamemnon." Cp. 4.311, 336, 8.350, 5.561, 610, etc.

    Il. 17.483: "bright Hector perceived," Hector's perception presented in itself and by itself, as a self-contained moment. Cp. 5.669, 9.223, *Od.* 22.162, *Il.* 14.293.

    Il. 3.21: "when Menelaus-dear-to-Ares perceived him . . ."; 3.30, "when as-fair-as-a-god-Alexander perceived him. . . ." Cp. 5.95, 596, 711, 7.17, 11.575, 581, etc. Although there is a temporal clause, the act of perceiving stands out, expanding the whole line. On the other hand, the person's name has no epithet in passages which have the same meaning but are quite subordinate to the narrative context, as *Il.* 11.284, "and when Hector perceived Agamemnon withdrawing"; cp. 14.440, 15.279, 16.818.

    The epithet is no less frequent when a person is presented as direct object of a verb meaning "to find," as in *Il.* 4.89-90, "she [Athena] found the blameless strong son of Lycaon/standing; around him strong ranks of warriors. . . ." Cp. *Il.* 1.498, 4.293, 327, 365, 5.169, 6.371, 515, 7.482, 11.197, etc.

    Thus, very often in the battle scenes we find an epithet with the stricken warrior in the accusative rather than the striker in the nominative (for example, *Il.* 11.92, 93, 123): what stands out is the transitive act insofar as it reaches its object, and the agent naturally falls into the background.

    Hence, also, the normal use of name and epithet with the preposition ἀμφί, "around," centering around. This preposition—unlike περί—brings out a character as a rallying point, as a focus to others.[1]

2. Instances without epithet

    a. *Il.* 1.199: "amazed was Achilles, turned, immediately knew/Pallas Athene. . . ." The swift sequence hardly allows the hero to solidify into his image. We are impressed with his state rather than with any single act. The lack of epithet frees the emotions, and Achilles is carried away by them. Compare *Il.* 11.777-79, 22.312-14, 16.119-22, 530-37, 22.291-95. Thus, generally, the epithet is less at home when the same individual is the subject of several acts: *Il.* 4.494-97, 11.15-16, 354-56, 566-71, *Od.* 2.296-300, 8.438-42, etc. A good example is that of Hector descending from the chariot, brandishing the spears, surveying, stirring the battle: *Il.* 5.494-96 (=6.103-05, 11.211-13).

b. *Il.* 17.620-21: "Meriones bending down seized the reigns"; 21.120, "him Achilles seized by the foot and slung into the river to be swept away." Cp. 10.391, 23.224-25, *Od.* 19.506, 20.300, 21.245. There is, in such cases, complication. The interest lies in the way something is brought about rather than in a simple instant realization. Hence a relevance of detail. We are drawn away from the simple image of the agent caught in the act.

c. *Il.* 3.38: "Him Hector ... upbraided with shaming words." The lack of epithet is here all one with the qualification of the utterance. Contrast the instances in which a character is presented as simply speaking, simply uttering his statement—for example, *Il.* 6.263, "and to her then replied great-Hector-of-the-shining-helm" (cp. p. 86 above). We thus find the character's name without epithet when the act of speaking is qualified in various ways: "spoke with honeyed words," "spoke with crafty words," "spoke loudly crying," etc: cp. *Il.* 3.275, 364, 6.110, 343, 16.616, etc. We have here a question of poetic logic and not of "hexametric economy." The dwelling upon a detail necessarily detracts from the person's full-fledged image, while the dwelling upon the person's image necessarily tends to oust details.

d. *Il.* 8.124 (=316, 17.83): "great grief did Hector encompass." Cp. 1.188, 9.553, 10.25, 13.470, etc. The epithet is normally absent in such sentences. The focus is entirely upon a powerful feeling which annihilates, as it were, the person's image.

e. *Il.* 6.403: "Hector alone saved Ilium"; 20.347, "Aeneas also is dear to the gods"; 11.556, "thus Ajax withdrew grieved at heart, unwilling"; 22.138, "Pelides sprang trusting in his swift feet"; *Od.* 19.286, "most of all Odysseus knows guiles"; *Il.* 13.361-62, "though middle-aged .../Idomeneus stirred rout"; *Od.* 2.59 (cp. 1.265, 4.689 etc.), "such as Odysseus was." Cp. *Il.* 24. 58-59, 5.801, 13.53-54, *Od.* 19.358-59, 5.436, 11.184-85, etc. In such instances—which are many and varied—the epithet is missing because of the predicates, which give us qualifying statements rather than pure representation. They condition the person's appearance, blurring the field of vision.

f. A person's name likewise lacks the epithet when it is emotionally emphasized, when the person's mention is loaded in tone, and again we are drawn away from pure, objective representation. Consider the following sets of instances:

Od. 1.60: "did not Odysseus offer you sacrifice in the wide land of Troy?"

Thus elsewhere in impassioned questioning of a similar kind: cp. *Il.* 9.339, 341, 11.656, 24.34.

Il. 15.288: "oh, how Hector stood up again, escaping his doom!" Cp. 15.288, 22.374. In *Od.* 23.7, Euryclea's tidings: "Odysseus has arrived!" So with the deictic ὅδε, as in *Il.* 20.117, "here comes Aeneas"; cp. 21.532-33.

Il. 24.501: "he who alone was left ..., him you yesterday slew ... even Hector." Cp. 18.115, 17.244, 22.170. The epithet would be inconsistent with the emotion of the statement.

Od. 17.412: "indeed was Odysseus about to make test of the Achaeans. ..." There is irony, threat; no pure act. Compare the assurance of 19.306 (=14.161).

g. *Il.* 13.370: "Idomeneus aimed with the shining spear"; cp. 16.466, 17.525, 11.61, etc.

Il. 7.206: "Ajax armed himself in shining bronze"; cp. 11.16, 13.240-41, 16.130 (contrast 19.364).

Il. 17.624-25: "Idomeneus lashed the horses-of-beautiful-mane to the hollow ships"; cp. 8.348, 5.731-32, 16.148.

Od. 2.12 (=17.63): "divine grace did Athena shed upon him"; cp. 8.18-19, 16.172, *Il.* 21.342.

Od. 1.260: "even there did Odysseus go in the swift ship." Compare the way in which Penelope refers to Odysseus as κεῖνος in a similar sentence: 18.181; cp. 4.731. *Il.* 23.59, "Pelides lay on the shore of the wide-roaring sea." Cp. *Od.* 1.425-27, 4.499, 10.244, *Il.* 3.312.

In such cases the characters have no epithet because they are overshadowed by an object or element of nature which their immediate action brings in to view; and it is the latter which has the epithet. This is especially frequent in the battle scenes: a brandished spear, for instance, or an uplifted shield suddenly becomes a point of focus. The same is true of anything striking which a person may carry, touch, approach. The spot of a person's rest or motion may have a similar effect—whether it be a feature of the landscape or a chariot or ship. We thus see an act materializing in the implements that make it possible or the spot which gives it its proper ground; and what stands out is not so much the agent as the act, which acquires, as it were, its own dimension, its own qualitative substance.

3. Connection, relation

The presence or absence of epithets also depends on the connection of sentence with sentence. Here relations arise which affect the visualization of a character.

Notice the following:

1. A character usually has no epithet when opposed to another character in a μέν ... δέ relation, "on the one hand ... on the other," as in *Il.* 1.306-08,

THE CONCRETE VALUE OF THE EPITHET

"thus having fought with words . . . they disbanded the assembly: Pelides went to his tent . . . "Atreides drew to sea a swift ship." Cp. 3.439-40, 7.258-60, 11.233-34, 13.347-51, 605-06, 16.702-03, 477-80, 731-34, etc. What stands out in such cases is the *relation* between acts rather than acts in their own right.

This tendency is especially frequent in the battle scenes, even quite apart from the μέν . . . δέ construction. In *Il.* 16.335-47, for instance: what matters is not so much the individuals themselves as the tension which opposes them to each other; and epithets would destroy the effect. Cp. 17.125-36, 13.159-63, 182-91, 5.655-62, 297-310, 21.173-83, etc. If epithets do occur, they are the epithets of weapons or armor, and these draw us to the massive clash.

The absence of a person's epithets in a μέν . . . δέ construction is typical. Here are instances with other disjunctive particles:

μέν . . . ἀλλά: *Od.* 4.282-84; cp. 16.428-30, 21.128-30.
ἐτέρωθεν: *Il.* 11.647, 13.489, 15.501, 18.32, etc.
μέν . . . αὐτάρ: *Il.* 8.364-65; cp. 9.216-17.
ὄφρα . . . τόφρα: *Il.* 11.357-59; ὄφρ᾽ ἔτι: 14.358; ὅτε δή . . . αὐτίκα: 23.768.
Compare ὅσσα . . . τόσσα: *Od.* 4.106-07.

2. There is no epithet in the line ending - αὐτὰρ Ἀχιλλεύς, "then Achilles . . . ," which marks a narrative or discursive transition, as, for example, in *Il.* 23.257, "then Achilles / stayed the people . . . brought the prizes out of the ships." This is very frequent. Compare especially the change of subject matter in *Il.* 20.75, 21.520, 23.128. The same applies to αὐτὰρ Ὀδυσσεύς, "then Odysseus": *Od.* 1.57, 2.182, 5.370, 7.81, 8.83, 521; cp. 367, 13.28, 367, etc. Thus with a similar value at the end of the line, ἐν δ᾽ Ἀγαμέμνων, *Il.* 11. 91, 216; ἂν δ᾽ Ἀγαμέμνων, 9.13; ἀλλ᾽ Ἀγαμέμνων, 6.53.

Even more the lack of epithet is justified in the causative connection οὕνεκ᾽ Ἀχιλλεύς, also at the end of a line: *Il.* 18.247, 19.45, 20.42; so οὐ γὰρ Ἀχιλλεύς, *Il.* 24.394. Cp. *Il.* 1.12.

3. We find, on the other hand, the epithet where juxtaposition prevails over narrative connection or relation of cause and effect. This happens when a person's act is perceived on the same level of vision as its counterpart, without any contrast or particular relation being underlined. Consider the following:

Od. 6.117: "they shouted; he awoke divine Odysseus."

16.164: "with her brow did she beckon; divine Odysseus perceived." Cp. *Il.* 14.293.

Od. 7.133: (before Alcinous's garden): "standing there did he wonder, much-suffering, divine Odysseus." Cp. 7.1 and 344.

13.353 (Ithaca appearing before him): "he rejoiced, much-suffering, divine Odysseus." Cp. 21.414.

The epithet is particularly effective where the acts portrayed are quite ordinary but implicitly grave, as in *Il.* 3.423-26:

> to the high-roofed chamber went the divine-among-women,
> for her reached a chair Aphrodite-lover-of-smiles
> . . . .
> there sat Helen-daughter-of-aegis-bearing-Zeus.

A character similarly has the epithet when presented after hearing someone speak and, without replying, lingering a moment, as in *Il.* 6.342, "so did he [Paris] speak, and helm-gleaming Hector replied not." This is very frequent: *Il.* 3.324, 418, 8.97, 198, 381, 484, etc. The hearer's reaction is not elaborated, but rather comes to a full stop; he (or she) simply stands out, juxtaposed to the speaker, in the same field of vision or conception.

There are some passages which show both interdependent connection (such as we find in a μέν . . . δέ relation) and pure juxtaposition. These may be taken to clarify my meaning. We thus have in *Il.* 9.663-67:

> Achilles slept in the depth of the well-built tent;
> by him lay the woman whom from Lesbos he took,
> the daughter of Phorbas Diomede-of-the-beautiful-cheeks.
> Opposite Patroclus lay; and there at his side
> fair-waisted Iphis, whom divine Achilles once gave him.

The two main characters, Achilles and Patroclus, have no epithet. It is as we should expect. They are presented in their solitary relation to each other after the departure of Agamemnon's emissaries. But it is not so with Diomede and Iphis, the girls sleeping at their side. These have epithets. We simply see them, contemplate them where they are, suddenly conjured up insofar as they lie at a particular spot. See how the lines expand to enclose them fully, their presence as perspicuous as that of the "well-built tent." Achilles, on the other hand, has an epithet later on ("whom divine Achilles once gave him"), summoned up as he is in a self-contained act far removed from the present situation, an act which thus acquires its own self-consistency: cp. p. 62 above on *Il.* 21.39.

A similar mode of perception and expression may be found where a character is presented twice performing the same act—first, without epithet, in narrative connection with the situation; and then, with epithet, in self-contained relief. Consider *Il.* 6.312-13 and 318. In 312-13:

> They prayed on their part to the daughter of mighty Zeus,
> while Hector went to Alexander's home. . . .

Then in 318:

There did Zeus-beloved Hector arrive.

Compare *Od.* 6.2 and 13, 15.104 and 106, *Il.* 18.203 and 205, 19.3 and 6, 5.43 and 45, 69 and 72, 134 and 143, 533 and 537, 7.219 and 224, 17.356 and 360.

Such passages are short instances of "ring-composition" with the enclosing final verse bringing out a character's figure; and the epithet, as is so often the case, marks this evidence in the passing act—a moment of actuality against the narrative background.[2]

4. Concluding remarks

What stands out is a purely existential stress—both removed from pointed emphasis and subordination to something else.

A most typical example is such a line as "so spoke swift-footed Achilles." The epithet has nothing to do with the hero's eminence. Anyone so presented would tend to have an epithet. Note the following:

Od. 18.25: τὸν δὲ χολωσάμενος προσεφώνεεν Ἶρος ἀλήτης
21.199: τὸν δ' αὖτε προσέειπε βοῶν ἐπιβουκόλος ἀνήρ
Il. 19.404: τὸν δ' ἄρ' ὑπὸ ζυγόφι προσέφη πόδας αἰόλος ἵππος
21.212: εἰ μὴ χωσάμενος προσέφη ποταμὸς βαθυδίνης

On the other hand, persons whose characteristics are described or pointed out in detail tend to have no epithet. What prevails is a narrative rather than a representational interest. Thus Thersites's lack of epithets (*Il.* 2.212-20) should not be attributed to his status as a commoner, but to the fact that he is no sooner mentioned than qualified both in character and appearance. He naturally has predicates instead of epithets. Compare Nireus in *Il.* 2.671-75, Eurybates in *Od.* 19.246-48, Elpenor in *Od.* 10.552-53. Similarly the dog Argos, *Od.* 17.291.

We see, again, how inconsistent is the epithet with predication and pointedness. In connection with the epithets of persons, note again this felicitous unobtrusiveness. It is all one with the epithet's image-making function. It delicately governs the choice of one epithet rather than another. We never find, for instance, the line-ending ἀμύμων δῖος' Ἀχιλλεύς; only once do we find μεγάθυμος 'Ἀχιλλεύς. Why is this so? Because such epithets would introduce a tedious laudatory strain. The phrase ποδάρκης δῖος 'Ἀχιλλεύς is much more effective in its plastic simplicity. Similarly we never find anything like μένος ἄσχετος Ἕκτωρ, which would be intolerable if often repeated; but we are never wearied by κορυθαίολος Ἕκτωρ, which presents us the hero in the flashing instant of his appearance. For the same reason such a phrase as ἀνδροφόνος θρασὺς Ἕκτωρ would be cloying; it is interesting that Hector's epithet ἀνδροφόνος is relegated to the genitive case; mostly in phrases which have the meaning "under the impact of . . . ," "at the hands of. . . ."

Poets less sensitive to the spell of form would here give vent to a facile, transparent characterization. In Homer only Odysseus has recurring epithets which obviously highlight his character; but these are made forcible by the whole action of the *Odyssey*.

13. PRESENCE AND ABSENCE OF EPITHETS

1. Concreteness

I have maintained that the Homeric epithets stress the concrete value of
whatever they refer to.

What do I mean by "concrete"? A thing will be concrete to the extent that
it is quite simply experienced, that we come into actual contact with it.
The grammatical definition of "concrete" is therefore not relevant here. We
shall not oppose concrete to abstract as something materially existent to
something ideal. When, for instance, Homer says, "he reached the measure of
glorious youth" (*Il.* 11.225), he identifies youth as something keenly experienced or realized, he gives concrete value to a word which commonly passes as
abstract.

It follows that I shall not distinguish between concrete and abstract nouns.
There are, rather, various degrees of concreteness or abstraction within the
same noun, according to the way it is used. Take, for instance, the two sentences "he sailed the ship" and "he was skillful in sailing ships" (*Od.* 3.283).
Obviously "ship" is more concrete in the first (as object of a certain act)
than in the second (as object of a general activity).

Moreover this concreteness does not depend only on the meaning of the
sentence, but on modes of apprehension. Consider the following:

The seafaring ship sailed by (cp. *Od.* 12.69).
A ship happened to pass by . . . (*Od.* 19.291).
Gladly my ship escaped . . . away from the cliffs (*Od.* 10.132).
The ships from Lemnos came bearing wine . . . (*Il.* 7.467).

All of these four instances are concerned with actual motion, but in the first
the ship is most concrete, appearing as it does in full focus. In the second
the casualness of "a ship happened to pass" weakens the effect. In the third
and fourth, circumstances come up which are integrated into the sentence
and outweigh the ship image.

We might thus say that the phrase with epithet naturally arrests the occurrence, and no less naturally the phrase without epithet passes on without stop to the general drift of the passage. Consider the following:

he sailed (for example, *Od.* 5.278)
he sailed in the ship (cp. *Od.* 2.226)
he sailed in the hollow ship (cp. *Od.* 1.211)
he sailed with the hollow ship over the wine-colored sea (cp. *Il.* 7.88)

In this series the act of sailing is enriched more and more. In the first example the interest lies not so much in the sailing as in the journey; but in the following examples, it is the sailing itself which stands out; we are drawn more and more to the fleeting moment. The concreteness of the ship image depends on the realization of the act.

By using or not using names with their epithets the poet thus follows basic trends of expression which implicitly affect the contents of his poetry.

An example in point is the idea of Patroclus's corpse lying by the ships. In expressing this idea Achilles cries out (*Il.* 22.386), "by the ships lies the corpse unburied, unmourned." The sense of Patroclus's state is such as to oust any epithet of ship. Elsewhere (*Il.* 19.319), Achilles expresses the same idea more passionately, and all reference to the ship is left out:

> Now you lie slain; and my heart
> is fasting of food and of drink.

But on another occasion, in a cooler mood, Achilles plans his revenge, and, visualizing the scene by the ships, he adds (*Il.* 18.338):

> Until then by the curve-sided ships you will lie even so,
> and they shall mourn. . . .

Or consider the idea of Odysseus' sailing to Ilium. When expressed by Penelope, it is a haunting, lingering thought, and we find the word "ship" with its epithet, as in *Od.* 18.181, "ever since in the hollow ships he departed." Cp. 19.259-60, 23.175-76, and see chapter 9, section 2 above. But there is no epithet when the same idea is expressed in anger by Antinous's father, Epeithes (*Od.* 24.427):

> ah, a great deed truly this man devised on the Achaeans!
> Taking them off in the ships. . . .

Similarly Penelope misses Telemachus, saying (*Od.* 4.731, cp. 817): "he went in the dark hollow ship"; but there is no epithet in Antinous's angry mention of the same event in 4.666. The concreteness of the epithet is quite suited to a sense of sympathetic, heartfelt, even anguished objectivity.

2. Aspects of concreteness

What I have said about *ship* and its epithets could in a very general way be said about any other thing. The general principle would be the same, but its application different in each case. For not all things appear concrete in the same way.

Take the two phrases "in front of the ship" and "in front of the horse." The epithet occurs with "ship" but not with "horse"; and we may understand why this is so (cp. p. 198). What appears as an intentional position in relation to horse (and therefore in a sentence denoting purpose) is most often a pure indication of space in relation to ship. For, in the *Iliad,* the ships are quite essential to the locality of the action.

This notion of concreteness is one of natural pertinence: the act or state expressed in a sentence must be in its own way fundamentally appropriate or intrinsic to the thing which is mentioned with name and epithet. Thus in such sentences as "he steered the ship," "he drove the horse," "he crossed the sea," the acts of steering, driving, crossing have a necessary, inevitable bearing upon their objects; and we thus naturally find the epithet with ship, horse, sea. The epithet, in other words, gives substance to the act. Any pointed reference or meaning would destroy its value. Hence the basic concreteness.

Conversely, such sentences as "he saved the ship," "he spared the horse," "he was subdued by the sea," we find no epithet. Why? Because the acts here envisaged are not so intrinsic to the nature of their objects. Neither ship nor horse is necessarily to be saved or spared, nor does the sea necessarily subdue. Such acts are connected with them by the narrative context. If an adjective were to be used here, it would probably be a pointed adjective: "endangered ship," "weary horse," "stormy sea." But such expressions would be quite un-Homeric.

People are presented in the same way. It is a person's most pertinent function to be direct subject or object of such acts as I have listed above: pp. 86–87; and it is in the full expression of such acts that we mostly find the epithet. On the other hand, the epithet is absent rather than present when persons are mentioned as terms of direction or approach or any interest affecting them in any way: see pp. 202–03. This is obviously quite a different case from that of ship, house, place.

The same applies to man-made objects; they are tools, possessions; they are most pertinent as things which someone holds or uses; and it is in such a function that they normally have the epithet. Even the most prestigious implements are never made into a theme of high-flown attributes. On the contrary, such things tend to lose their epithet when they become subject or theme of discourse: Achilles' scepter in *Il.* 1.234–39; the boar's-tusk helmet in *Il.* 10.261–71; Odysseus' bed in *Od.* 23.184–204. Odysseus' fateful bow has no epithet in *Od.* 21.153, where it is the subject of the sentence.

It might thus be said that the epithets hold the world in balance. This is well shown by the epithets of earth, sea, and sky. We have seen the great wealth of the sea's epithets with the meaning "sail over," "cross over." Earth is much poorer in this respect. Why is this so? Because the earth is not visualized as one single whole; we rather have mountains, valleys, plains. But the sea is an experience in itself. As we sail it, nothing else impairs its presence. As for the sky, it is much poorer in this respect than both sea and earth; and this is because it lies outside the pale of human action. The most significant instances are "to look at the vast sky" and "to stretch the hands toward the vast sky," both of which give a physical extension to individual acts. Note in this respect the epithets "brazen," "of iron" (χάλκεος, πολύχαλκος, σιδήρε-ος), which are always used with the sky in the accusative as an imagined term of arrival. Whatever their original conception, they point to something tangible, solid, reachable: as in the phrase "to reach the brazen threshold." Instead of any sublime attribute, we have epithets which present the sky as something to be reached.

3. Concrete opposed to ornamental

The Homeric epithet is not ornamental. The instances I have given show that its concrete function is as alien to decorative effect as it is to any pointed reference.

This is so, at least, if the term *ornament* is given its usual meaning. For to adorn means to embellish, add agreeable accessories. Thus, we are told, there is in poetry an essential meaning overlaid with beautiful trappings. But this can hardly be the case where meaning and form make up one inextricable whole.

The way in which Homer's epithets integrate an image with its occasion excludes any narrow idea of ornamentation. In this respect Homer would appear to be far less ornamental than other poets. Consider, for instance, Bacchylides, 17.1-7:

> The blue-prowed ship
> carrying Theseus-steadfast-in-battle
> and fourteen splendid sons of the Ionians
> was cleaving the Cretan main;
> and into the far-gleaming sail
> the gusts of Boreas were falling
> by the will of glorious Athena,
> holder-of-the-warlike-aegis.

Compare now the way in which Homer would express similar meanings by considering the following:

a. We do not normally find an epithet with "ship" in Homer when the ship is the subject of the sentence and is presented in the act of sailing to a certain destination or accomplishing a certain task. See chapter 9, section 4.

b. Homer would probably not have, in the accusative, the name and epithet of a man whom the ship carries: *Il.* 15.705, *Od.* 16.323, 13.87-92. In any case we should find in Homer men sailing in a ship rather than a ship carrying men: cp. *Il.* 2.509-10, 618-19.

c. As for "Cretan main," Homer would not so give the sea a local epithet, but an existential epithet like "wine-colored," "foaming," etc.

d. Bacchylides's epithet of the sail is used in a way which is not Homeric. Homer would not say, "the wind blew into the white sail," but he does say "to spread [or hoist] the white sail." In Homer there is a concrete connection between the act of "spreading out" and the sail's whiteness. Cp. *Il.* 1.480-82.

e. Bacchylides's rich epithets of Athena are un-Homeric in this position. Homer tends rather to use the god's name without epithet when the god's intervention is in the background, an act merely accessory to the human. Cp. p. 199.

It is quite possible, of course, that even in Bacchylides the epithets are not merely ornamental, but serve a higher poetic purpose.[1] They are, however, extrinsic. No necessary connection binds them to the act in itself. Their weight lies outside the passing existential moment. They serve to present a picture which might be indefinitely enriched. Or, we might say, the epithets do not grow out of the perception of each act, but are grafted upon the narrative material: the ship carrying Theseus . . . the Cretan main . . . the will of Athena —all are elements which are fused by mythical association rather than by a sense of inevitable connections between act and agent, between motion and its space.

As far as the ship's image is concerned, Shakespeare's lines (*Henry V, 3,* Prologue, 10ff.):

> behold the threaden sails,
> borne by the invisible and creeping wind,
> draw the huge bottoms through the furrowed sea,
> breasting the lofty surge

are in their way much closer to Homer. There is as keen a sense of the concrete. Actions and their impact, things and their qualities are drawn together by natural affinities and not by incidental ornamentation; and, as a result, the epithets but keep the ship in focus.

4. Logic of the epithets

A further conclusion to be gathered from our examples is that the epithets are not used loosely. There is a poetic reason for their presence and absence;

98

there is a poetic logic at work. This consists in the reasons why things are presented at one with their qualities at certain points of poetic speech. We may call it appropriateness, naturalness; but these terms hardly do justice to the underlying sense of truth.

Can we come any closer to this logic? However we may define it, it underlies all artistic expression. It strikes a delicate balance between the complexity of a thought and the outrightness of an impression, between the outline of a whole situation and the picture of single object emerging in the field of vision. Here are points of relative material weight; and, if such relations are put into words, the ensuing sentences will either linger or drive their point, stand out or give way, fix an object in its emergence or drift off into further regions of awareness.

Here is a logic embedded in the nature of things and in the truth of perception. It is no matter of deliberate construction or of cause and effect. It resides at a deeper level. Underneath the contents of any narrative or speech, over and beyond any deliberate effect, there are inevitable areas of stress or extension which are the existential basis of any theme or subject matter. A language will be truly poetic insomuch as it is responsive to this secret logic of things and free from superfluous accretion.

Although this logic cannot be pressed and defies analysis, it is by no means something abstruse. It is all one with a native sense of discrimination. While too baffling to be predetermined, it is open to anyone. Look at a landscape or a multitude of people, mark any striking feature the moment it comes to view, then follow up the vision and see it in its more distant relations. Insofar as you can put this into words, your sentences will move from the center to the outer reaches, thinning out, developing and complicating their thread, gaining in range what they lose in sensuous evidence. You will enhance some central image, giving it names, without burdening the distant margins. William James expresses well what I wish to say. About the "stream of consciousness," he writes,

As we take, in fact, a general view of the wonderful stream of consciousness, what strikes us first is this different pace of its parts. Like a bird's life, it seems to be made of an alternation of flights and perchings. The rhythm of language expresses this, where every thought is expressed in a sentence, and every sentence closed by a period. The resting-places are usually occupied by sensorial imaginations of some sort, whose peculiarity is that they can be held before the mind for some time, and contemplated without changing; the places of flight are filled with thoughts of relations, static or dynamic, that for the most part obtain between the matters contemplated in the periods of comparative rest.

Let us call the resting-places the "substantive parts", and the places of

flight the "transitive parts", of the stream of thought. It then appears that the main end of our thinking is at all times the attainment of some other substantive part than the one from which we have just been dislodged. And we may say that the main use of the transitive parts is to lead us from one substantive conclusion to another.[2]

This activity which we dimly carry out is realized in Homer on a vast scale. His epithets arrest the evidence of things; or, by their very absence, let it vanish in the drift of events. Self-contained images stand out, but only insofar as they do not obstruct the flow which binds sentence to sentence and passage to passage. As an action takes shape, it is joined to the imagery of those things which make it possible; but then it develops, it prolongs, it takes its own direction, and, as it does so, the epithets are thinned out. But then, again, the rarefying process cannot last for long. The sensuous elements must soon reappear to provide sustenance and points of vantage.

The logic of the epithets is thus founded on the ways of perception and thought. The very clarity of the representation is a proof. If the epithets were purely ornamental or mere devices of versification, we should find them scattered anywhere they might fit the meter. And this would produce confusion, not clarity.

14. EPITHET AND PREDICATE

There is striking confirmation of the principle of the epithet's concrete function in an important characteristic of language which has not been sufficiently noticed:[1] the use of different adjectives in the expression of quality according to whether they are epithets or predicates. This is especially notable in Homer. We must look further into the facts in relation to our argument.

1. Different values of epithet and predicate

The grammatical difference between attribute and predicate is, of course, a familiar one. What I wish to point out is a difference of values or meaning. There is thus a variation of nuance in the two sentences "he is a good man" and "he is good." The variation is even more pronounced in "he is a gentleman" and "he is gentle." We also use different words or expressions attributively or predicatively. Composite adjectives, for instance, appear to be attributive. We say, "a good-hearted man," but "he is good-hearted" does not come so naturally; we would rather say, "he has a good heart."

Here is a distinction which is deeply rooted in language. But in Homer the distinction is far more radical: the same adjective is not normally used both as attribute and predicate. Furthermore, in the case of human attributes, Homer does not usually use the same adjective both as an appellative (that is, as attribute of a common noun like "man," "woman," "servant") and as personal attribute with a proper name. These limitations greatly contribute to the particular character of the Homeric epithet.

Take, for instance, the epithet μεγάθυμος. It recurs with a hero's proper name, as in *Il*. 23.168, ἐκάλυψε νέκυν μεγάθυμος Ἀχιλλεύς, where "great-spirited Achilles" is subject of a simple concrete act; we instantly catch a glimpse of Achilles as an image, covering Patroclus's corpse. But it would be un-Homeric to say anything like μεγάθυμος γίγνετ' Ἀχιλλεύς, "high-spirited was Achilles," or ἦλθε δ' ἀνὴρ μεγάθυμος, "he came that high-spirited man" —sentences in which the attribute of quality would outbalance any concrete meaning and, by making a point, nullify the epithet's property to arrest a presence, an image in the passing moment. In order to convey quality Homer would use different words and sentences. Compare, for example, *Od.* 4.242–43:

> ἀλλ᾽ οἷον τόδ᾽ ἔρεξε καὶ ἔτλη καρτερὸς ἀνήρ
> δήμῳ ἔνι Τρώων, ὅθι πάσχετε πήματ᾽ Ἀχαιοί.

2. Epithet versus predication in Homer

This differentiation between predicative and attributive expression of the same quality seems to be nowhere so extensive and coherent as it is in Homer. It is the nature of the Homeric epithet which makes it so remarkable.

Thus the epithets of "ship," "horse," "sea," "sky," many as they are, hardly ever occur as predicates. In many cases this is just as we should expect. We should not normally say, for example, "Hollow is the ship," "long-necked are the horses," "wine-colored is the sea," "bronze-vaulted is the sky." Such attributes are too much part and parcel of the image to be separated from it and bear the general meaning of a predicate. But why should it not be possible to say, for example, "the horses are swift"? In this case Homer constantly uses a different turn of expression whose general sense is, "the horses run fast." So in *Il.* 8.106–07=5.222–23:

> οἷοι Τρώϊοι ἵπποι, ἐπιστάμενοι πεδίοιο
> κραιπνὰ μάλ᾽ ἔνθα καὶ ἔνθα διωκέμεν ἠδὲ φέβεσθαι

Cp. 11.533, 22.22–23, 162–163, 23.372.

Similarly we often have "swift ship," "sea-swift ship," "swift-faring ship," but not "swift is the ship." For the latter case, we find again the rendering of swiftness in the movement itself, as in *Od.* 13.86–88:

> ἡ δὲ μάλ᾽ ἀσφαλέως θέεν ἔμπεδον· οὐδέ κεν ἴρηξ
> κίρκος ὁμαρτήσειεν ἐλαφρότατος πετεηνῶν.
> ὡς ἡ ῥίμφα θέουσα θαλάσσης κύματ᾽ ἔταμνεν

Cp. 13.162, *Il.* 1.483, *Od.* 15.294; cp. 11.10–11. Only once do I find the adjective "swift" as a predicate of ship. In *Od.* 7.36 Athena tells Odysseus of the sea-faring Phaeacians: τῶν νέες ὠκεῖαι ὡς εἰ πτερὸν ἠὲ νόημα. This exception, however, is a further illustration of the same tendency. The verse's literal translation is: swift their ships like a wing or a thought. Notice the nominal phrase without verb. The adjective "swift" is as yet scarcely separated from "ship," only marked by a stress to which the comparison with "wing" and "thought" gives support—as if we said, "wing-swift ship" or "thought-swift ship." The sense of motion is still contained within the imagery. On this particular passage, see further, p. 105.

I have pointed out elsewhere the same tendency in the qualification of characters.[2] There are, for instance, many epithets for "strong," "brave" (ἄλκιμος, ἐρισθενής, εὐρυσθενής, ἴφθιμος, κρατερός or καρτερός, ὄβριμος), which are hardly ever used as predicates; for the meaning "he is strong" and "he is brave" other words, other forms of expression are commonly used: a verb (μέμαα, μενεαίνω), such a phrase as "reliant on strength and on hands" (cp. *Il.* 8.226=11.9, 12.135, 17.329, *Od.* 21.315, etc.), a whole sentence of the general meaning "strength is present within him" (cp. *Il.* 17.210, 499, 22. 312, *Od.* 21.281, 2.271, etc.). See, in *Od.* 8.167-81, Odysseus dwelling on human characteristics. Qualities are there expressed as actions, occurrences, presences; no epithets are used. The strength of Homer's personal epithets lies elsewhere: to denote a person's actuality in an instant occasion.

3. Distinct synonymous adjectives used as epithets and predicates

A stronger proof of the epithet's nature may be found in those cases in which there are alternative adjectives of the same general meaning used as epithets and predicates respectively. I shall list them below according to meaning.

Wise, prudent. There are the following epithets with personal names: περίφρων, ἐχέφρων, πολύφρων, πολύμητις, πολύβουλος, μητίετα. These hardly ever occur as predicates: πολύφρων only concessive "though wise," *Il.* 18. 108, *Od.* 14.464; ἐχέφρων only in coordination with other adjectives: *Il.* 9. 341, *Od.* 13.332.

Consider now, by way of contrast, the following adjectives, which are never used as personal epithets but as predicates or as pointed, emphatic attributes: ἐπίφρων (*Od.* 16.242, 23.12), σαόφρων (*Il.* 21.462, *Od.* 4.158), ἀρτίφρων (*Od.* 24.261), ἀγχίνοος (*Od.* 13.332), ἐπιστήμων (*Od.* 16.374), νοήμων (*Od.* 2.282, 3.133), πινυτός (*Od.* 11.445, 1.229, etc.); cp. ἐχέθυμος (*Od.* 8.320). Note also the affirmative predicative sense coming from negation of a negative: οὐδ᾽ ἀνοήμων (*Od.* 2.270, 278, 17.273), οὐκ ἄφρων (*Od.* 17.586), οὐδ᾽ ἀεσίφρων (*Il.* 20.183).

Warlike, brave. Epithets of heroes and people: ἀρήιος, βοὴν ἀγαθός, μενεπτόλεμος, φιλοπτόλεμος. Contrast with these the predicate μενεδήιος (*Il.* 12.247, 13.228), μαχήμων (*Il.* 12.247), οὐδὲ φυγοπτόλεμος (*Od.* 14.213).

We may also oppose the form μενέχαρμος, with predicative force in *Il.* 14.376, to the epithet μενεχάρμης (*Il.* 13.396, etc.).

Similarly, on the one hand, the epithet θρασύς (of Hector and others) and, on the other hand, the predicates θρασυκάρδιος (*Il.* 13.343, 10.41), θάρσυνος (*Il.* 16.70, 13.83), θαρσαλέος (*Il.* 19.169, 21.430),[3] ἀτάρβητος (*Il.* 3.63).

Glorious. There are many epithets referring to gods, people, things (κλυτός, κλειτός, ἀγακλυτός, ἀγακλειτός, ἀγακλεής, etc.). On the other hand, εὐκλεής occurs only as predicate (*Il.* 10.281, 17.415, *Od.* 21.331). Compare ἀριδείκετος in *Od.* 11.540; τμήεις (*Od.* 18.161, *Il.* 9.605, etc.). Here again note the predicative sense coming from negation of a negative: οὐ μὰν ἀκληεῖς in *Il.* 12.318.

Πολύτλας, the epithet of patient, suffering, daring Odysseus. When Odysseus applies the same quality to himself as a predicate, he uses a different form: *Od.* 18.319, πολυτλήμων δὲ μάλ᾽ εἰμί; 17.284, τολμήεις μοι θυμός, ἐπεὶ κακὰ πολλὰ πέπονθα. Compare 5.222. Note the pointed qualification in *Il.* 10.231-32:

> ῞Ηθελε δ᾽ ὁ τλήμων Ὀδυσεὺς καταδῦναι ὅμιλον
> Τρώων· αἰεὶ γάρ οἱ ἐνὶ φρεσὶ θυμὸς ἐτόλμα.

Bitter, hard to bear, disagreeable. There are such epithets as: πικρός, of pain, of arrows, of things naturally pungent; πευκεδανός, κρυερός, κρυόεις, ὀκρυόεις, of war, panic, mourning; cp. δυσκέλαδος, of rout; δυσηχής, of war; δυσηλεγής, of death; δύσπονος, of fatigue; δυσθαλπής, of winter. In such instances, clearly, quality and actuality merge into one, epithet and noun make up one single idea.

Oppose now to these epithets such adjectives as χαλεπός, ἀργαλέος, ἀλεγεινός, which are often used as predicates—for example, *Il.* 13.569:

> ἔνθα μάλιστα
> γίγνετ᾽ Ἄρης ἀλεγεινός

or 5.658, αἰχμή ... ἦλθ᾽ ἀλεγεινή. These adjectives are never pure epithets. Note their loose frame of reference and their frequently emphatic pointed meaning (*Il.* 17.544, 21.386, *Od.* 11.291, etc.). In *Od.* 14.226 the solitary predicate καταριγηλός.

θυμοδακής, "heart-biting," strongly predicative in *Od.* 8.185, θυμοδακὴς γὰρ μῦθος. Oppose to this the epithets θυμοβόρος, θυμοφθόρος, θυμαλγής.

Sweet, agreeable. There are the epithets γλυκύς, γλυκερός, ἡδύς, νήδυμος (ἥδυμος), ἡδύποτος, μελίφρων, μελιηδής, all joined to things which are naturally sweet, on a wider range than "sweet" is applicable in English: wine, milk, wheaten meal, barley, grazing grass as well as honey and figs; and equally so of sleep, desire, life when jeopardized or lost and therefore missed (cp. *Od.* 5.152, 11.203), Odysseus' long-desired return (*Od.* 11.100). On the other hand, the epithet does not lend itself to such metaphors as when we apply "sweet" to a person. For "sweet man" we have γλυκερὸν φάος addressed to Telemachus (*Od.* 16.23, 17.41): "sweet light," for light is naturally sweet. The epithet can thus extend its range only with delicate circumspection. Predicative use is barred. If the occasion presents itself, the whole sentence is altered. Thus Homer will not say, "sweet was his voice," but "sweeter than honey flowed his voice," where the natural sweetness of honey favors the expression: *Il.* 1.249. Cp. 2.453 (=11.13-14), *Od.* 9.28, 34-35.

Consider now the predicates, adjectives of similar meaning but never used as epithets:

μείλιχος. *Il.* 17.671, πᾶσιν γὰρ ἐπίστατο μείλιχος εἶναι Cp. 19.300, 24.739. ἤπιος. *Il.* 8.40, ἐθέλω δέ τοι ἤπιος εἶναι. Cp. 22.184, *Od.* 10.337, 13.314, etc.

θυμηδής. Only in *Od.* 16.389: μή οἱ χρήματ᾽ ἔπειτα ἅλις θυμηδέ᾽ ἔδωμεν, where it may be predicative: "then let us not eat up all his substance to please ourselves." In any case, it was never generalized as an epithet in spite of its fitness both in meaning and in form.

Similarly θυμαρής in *Od.* 23.232, ἔχων ἄλοχον θυμαρέα. Cp. 10.362, θυμῆρες κεράσασα. 17.199, σκῆπτρον θυμαρὲς ἔδωκεν. ἐπιήρανος in *Od.* 19.343, οὐδέ τί μοι ποδάνιπτρα . . . ἐπιήρανα θυμῷ. λαρός, a predicate in *Il.* 17.572, λαρόν τέ οἱ αἷμ᾽ ἀνθρώπου·, a superlative in *Od.* 2.350, proleptic in *Il.* 19.316, *Od.* 14.408. ἀσπάσιος, ἀσπαστός, frequent and always predicative: *Il.* 8.488, *Od.* 5.394, etc.

Cp. μενοεικής: *Od.* 5.166, 16.429, *Il.* 23.29, etc.

Swift as applied to ship. There are the regular epithets θοή, ὠκύαλος, ὠκύπορος. On the other hand, ὠκύς with predicative force in *Od.* 7.36: see p. 102 above. It is elsewhere applied to ships in *Il.* 8.197, *Od.* 9.101, 7.34; all instances in which the notion of swiftness plays a role. It is possible that, in this case, we might oppose ὠκύς to its synonyms. If so, the poet's choice of words reflects a general tendency of the language. It would not have been Homeric to say, for example, τῶν νέες εἰσὶ θοαί᾽ or τῶν νέες ὠκυπόροι.

ποτιφωνήεις, "capable of addressing," that is, "capable of speech," used by Cyclops speaking to his ram in *Od.* 9.456: "if . . . you were speech-endowed." We might oppose this predicate to αὐδήεις, an epithet of men.

4. The same adjective as epithet and predicate but with change of meaning

The same adjective may be used as epithet and predicate, but at the cost of strikingly changing its meaning. Such an alteration again points to the special nature of the Homeric epithet. For the epithet's concrete value is so bound up with an image and its occasion, that any loss of this bond undermines the very meaning of the epithet.

Consider the following instances:

θοός᾽ (cp. θέω, "I run") basically means "swift," and so it does as an epithet of "chariot" and "ship." But as predicate, referred to heroes, it means "courageous": εἰ θοός ἐσσι (*Il.* 16.494; cp. 5.536). This is especially striking in *Il.* 16.422, νῦν θοοὶ ἔστε, which is addressed to men in flight: the meaning "swift" would be quite contradictory.[4]

ἀγήνωρ. It has the positive sense "valiant" as epithet of θυμός and of heroes.

But in *Il.* 9.699, ὁ δ᾽ἀγήνωρ ἐστὶ καὶ ἄλλως, as predicate of Achilles, it clearly means "arrogant."

λυγρός, λευγαλέος, "grievous," as epithets of death, old age, delusion, pain, sorrow, wound, battle. But when they are predicates of persons λυγρὸς ἐών (*Il.* 13.119, etc.) λευγαλέοι τ᾽ ἐσόμεσθα (*Od.* 2.61)–the meaning is "weak."

στονόεις, πολύστονος, "causing groans," as epithet of arrows, pains. On the other hand, as predicate, *Od.* 19.118, μάλα δ᾽ εἰμὶ πολύστονος, "I am full of sadness." Compare *Od.* 17.102, 19.595, εὐνήν, ἥ μοι στονόεσσα τέτυκται, "a bed full of sorrows."

πολυδάκρυτος, "tearful," as epithet in πολυδακρύτοιο γόοιο (*Od.* 19.213, etc.). But, as predicate, in *Il.* 24.620 πολυδάκρυτος δέ τοι ἔσται, "by you he will sorely be mourned."

ἐρατεινός, "lovely," epithet of cities, lands, rivers, and such good things as the company of friends, manhood, ambrosia. But it acquires a grim ironic meaning as predicate in *Od.* 9.230, οὐδ᾽ ἄρ᾽ ἔμελλ᾽ ἑτάροισι φανεὶς ἐρατεινὸς ἔσεσθαι.

ἄλαστος, "unforgotten," "unforgettable," as epithet of grief. But in *Il.* 22.261 the vocative ἄλαστε addressed by Achilles to Hector, is very nearly a predicate and has quite a different meaning. I would understand it in an active sense: "haunting," "giving no rest," "pursuing like a curse."[5]

5. Adjectives used both as epithets and predicates without any obvious difference of meaning

There are some adjectives which are mainly epithets but are also used as predicates without any appreciable difference in meaning. This usage is relatively rare; and when it does occur we often find in the context a reason for it. The poet himself seems to explain it.

Consider the following:

ἄλκιμος, "strong." There are, we have seen, various epithets for "strong" which are rarely used as predicates and then almost always in a concessive phrase. ἄλκιμος stands out in being both a frequent epithet and a full predicate. Let us now consider the predicative instances:

Il. 13.278:

ἔνθ᾽ ὅ τε δειλὸς ἀνήρ, ὅς τ᾽ ἄλκιμος, ἐξεφαάνθη

6.521–22:

δαιμόνι᾽, οὐκ ἄν τίς τοι ἀνήρ, ὃς ἐναίσιμος εἴη,
ἔργον ἀτιμήσειε μάχης, ἐπεὶ ἄλκιμός ἐσσι.

Od. 1.301-02:

> καὶ σύ, φίλος, μάλα γάρ σ᾽ ὁρόω καλόν τε μέγαν τε,
> ἄλκιμος ἔσσ᾽, ἵνα τίς σε καὶ ὀψιγόνων εὖ εἴπῃ.

Od. 22.226-32:

> οὐκέτι σοί γ᾽, Ὀδυσεῦ, μένος ἔμπεδον, οὐδέ τις ἀλκή,
> . . . .
> πῶς δὴ νῦν, ὅτε σόν γε δόμον καὶ κτήμαθ᾽ ἱκάνεις,
> ἄντα μνηστήρων ὀλοφύρεαι ἄλκιμος εἶναι;

Cp. *Il.* 15.570, *Od.* 10.552-53.

These passages bear on the very idea of strength and of courage. They reason it out. There is an attempt to draw out the meaning of the word ἄλκιμος, the adjective which to the poet's mind was the most likely to convey a full sense of quality.

But why? Why, for instance, ἄλκιμος and not καρτερός, which would have equally well fitted the hexameter in most of these cases? It is that the noun ἀλκή (*ἄλξ), from which it derives, presents a particular transparency of meaning. It is an action noun (for example, in *Od.* 22.305-06, οὐδέ τις ἀλκή γίγνεται οὐδὲ φυγή); it suggests a characteristic activity (cp. ἀλαλκεῖν, ἀλκτήρ); its positive value is proved by the negative forms ἄναλκις, ἀναλκείῃσι. Hence, unlike its synonyms ἴς, βίη, κράτος, σθένος, it never shades off into the sense of "brute strength." It is not used of the elements (cp. ἴς ἀνέμοιο, κράτος . . . σιδήρου). There is in it a notion of animal or human capacity, whence it often recurs as object of knowledge and experience (cp. μεμνημένος ἀλκῆς, μνή-σασθε δὲ θούριδος ἀλκῆς, δεδαηκότες ἀλκήν).

The predicative instances of ἄλκιμος thus rest on sure foundations. They acquire, in their context, a pregnant significance. The poet appears aware of the implications.

ἀμύμων. A very frequent epithet conveying a native perfection in people or things—with proper names of characters, with nouns signifying human relation (mother, father, son, etc.), profession (charioteer, seer, etc.), with anything implying achievement in craftsmanship or nature (handiwork, a bow, the island of the Sun, etc.).

Now this sense of perfection in the epithet expresses something naturally present. It does not have any moral meaning. And yet it lends itself to moral implications. These are fully realized where ἀμύμων is used predicatively. Consider *Od.* 19.329-34:

> ὃς μὲν ἀπηνὴς αὐτὸς ἔῃ καὶ ἀπηνέα εἰδῇ,
> τῷ δὲ καταρῶνται πάντες βροτοὶ ἄλγε᾽ ὀπίσσω

> ζωῷ, ἀτὰρ τεθνεῶτί γ᾽ ἐφεψιόωνται ἅπαντες·
> ὃς δ᾽ ἂν ἀμύμων αὐτὸς ἔῃ καὶ ἀμύμονα εἰδῇ,
> τοῦ μέν τε κλέος εὐρὺ διὰ ξεῖνοι φορέουσιν
> πάντας ἐπ᾽ ἀνθρώπους, πολλοί τέ μιν ἐσθλὸν ἔειπον.

Notice the contrast with ἀπηνής, "harsh," "cruel," which is always predicative or emphatic and never a mere epithet. This contrast or connection imparts to ἀμύμων itself a predicative force. Hence an insistence on the concept itself: on moral perfection. As if the simple predicate were not enough, the meaning "perfect" is immediately transferred to activity of mind, to the "thinking of blameless thoughts."

Compare *Od.* 1.232-33:

> μέλλεν μέν ποτε οἶκος ὅδ᾽ ἀφνειὸς καὶ ἀμύμων
> ἔμμεναι . . .

See the whole passage, especially 229-30. The house of Odysseus was about to be rich and flawless, and this is contrasted with its present foul state.

Another predicative instance occurs in *Od.* 14.508-09:

> ὦ γέρον, αἶνος μέν τοι ἀμύμων, ὃν κατέλεξας,
> οὐδέ τί πω παρὰ μοῖραν ἔπος νηκερδὲς ἔειπες·

Eumaeus's judgment "faultless is your story" is immediately related to a quality of thought and of speech: "you said not a word that was wrong."[6]

πεπνυμένος, "spirited," "wise" (cp. πέπνυσαι, πεπνῦσθαι, *Il.* 24.377, 23.440). It recurs most often as epithet of Telemachus about to speak (*Od.* 1.213, 230, etc.) and of others in the same way. It must be for similar reasons the epithet of heralds (*Il.* 7.276, 9.689, *Od.* 18.65, cp. *Il.* 7.278, *Od.* 2.38) as well as of Oucalegon and Antenor, great speakers (*Il.* 3.148). This is, clearly, a special epithet connected with speech.[7]

It is on the strength of this basic connection that πεπνυμένος is often used as a predicate. See *Od.* 3.20, 328: ψεῦδος δ᾽ οὐκ ἐρέει· μάλα γὰρ πεπνυμένος ἐστί and compare *Od.* 4.204-06, 8.388, 18.125, 19.350-52–all predicative or emphatic instances in which the connection with speech is either expressly brought out or is implicit in the fact that a man is called πεπνυμένος for having just spoken wisely. (Hence a more general meaning, without any connection with speech, in *Od.* 4.190, 3.52, *Il.* 23.570.)

Here again we can trace the poet's touch, though in a different way than in the case of ἄλκιμος and ἀμύμων. What extends the predicative function of πεπνυμένος is reflection on the characters as they speak and thereby reveal their qualities. This is a fundamental Homeric trait. Words, spoken words, are in Homer a touchstone of intelligence. Compare *Od.* 11.367: σοὶ δ᾽ ἔπι μὲν μορφὴ ἐπέων, ἔνι δὲ φρένες ἐσθλαί.

6. General conclusions

The incapacity of the Homeric epithets to be predicates or pointed attributes at once illustrates their nature and establishes their syntactic function. We may thus redefine the epithet with greater assurance: it integrates a thing with a quality insofar as such a thing is visualized in a certain act or state of being, and this without any literal or pointed connection with the contents here expressed.[8]

To this characteristic of the Homeric epithet corresponds a reciprocal characteristic of the Homeric predicate. Whereas the noun-epithet phrase is self-contained, the predicate is quite relative to the context. I doubt that Homer could have such a sentence as "Achilles is good" without any further specification. Consider the instances given above of predicates meaning "sweet," "agreeable." We find ἐθέλω δέ τοι ἤπιος εἶναι or πᾶσιν γὰρ ἐπίστατο μείλιχος εἶναι, "I wish to be good to you," "he knew how to be kind to all": the quality needs its immediate term of reference, needs to be strongly connected with the occasion; it is not expressed as an absolute endowment standing above the passing action. Hence the "dative of interest" which we so often find with such predicates, or some further assertion such as two or more predicates which support and explain one another. For example, Il. 24.156-57, 185-86:

> οὔτ' αὐτὸς κτενέει ἀπό τ' ἄλλους πάντας ἐρύξει·
> οὔτε γάρ ἐστ' ἄφρων οὔτ' ἄσκοπος οὔτ' ἀλιτήμων.

Cp. 11.649, 654, 9.341, Od. 15.212, 9.515.

Quality is not expressed as an absolute. Insofar as epithets and predicates are concerned, it presents itself (with the former) in a concrete image and (with the latter) in a sense of relation or connection with a given circumstance. If we thus look at Homer's representation as a whole, we find a world of permanent images which emerge in the course of daily acts and, on the other hand, faculties, susceptibilities, dispositions portrayed insofar as they immediately fit the occasion and affect one another. This is made clear when epithets and predicates are used side by side.

Consider Alcinous's wondering address to Odysseus in Od. 11.363-65:

> ὦ Ὀδυσεῦ, τὸ μὲν οὔ τί σ' ἐΐσκομεν εἰσορόωντες,
> ἠπεροπῆά τ' ἔμεν καὶ ἐπίκλοπον, οἷά τε πολλούς
> βόσκει γαῖα μέλαινα πολυσπερέας ἀνθρώπους....

Alcinous, we might suppose, could have left out the reference to the earth; he could simply have said, "you are honest," "you are truthful." But this would not be Homeric. Ready-made moral categories would have to be presupposed. Rather than a thinly expressed judgment we have full-scale representation. The noun-epithets "black earth," and "wide-scattered men" convey a sense of hazardous possibilities that might well be realized in the present circumstance. The same kind of polarity is similarly brought out in other passages—not by anything the poet might say, but by the significance of epithets and predicative expressions succeeding one another: cp. *Od.* 1.196-99, 347-49, 5.182-87, 6.120-26, 7.210-12, etc.

15. THE MEANING OF THE EPITHETS

The concrete value of the epithets naturally affects their meaning. They cannot be understood as isolated words detached from the phrases where they belong, separated from their frames of reference. This is especially apparent, of course, in those epithets which exclusively refer to one thing. Take, for instance, πολυκληίς, εὔσελμος, which recur only as epithets of ship. If we knew them only as isolated relics from the body of Homeric poetry, we should hardly know what to make of them. But, as it is, they derive their full significance from their constant connection with ship. The literal meaning "many-benched" or "well-benched" is but a necessary constituent of the image they serve to convey. Homer has familiarized us with them. They evoke, even by themselves, the idea of ship. They might conceivably have become nouns in their own right with the meaning "ship." [1]

The epithets πολυκληίς, εὔσελμος may seem extreme cases. They are, however, symptomatic. Quite generally the Homeric epithets draw strength and meaning from their concrete and necessary connection with certain nouns. What they lack in meaning as isolated words they gain in power of association. It is as if they both qualified a thing and were qualified by it. As a result, they do not signify qualities which are applicable to whatever may seem fit, but rather elicit some property which inheres in the things themselves.

Take even such a broad meaning as that of swiftness. How does it come up in Homer? How is it expressed as an adjective? Through synonyms which vary according to what they are construed with. For things have different ways of being swift. A hero, a bird, a ship are all swift, but they are seen as different images of swiftness. Why is this? Because this swiftness is part of their nature, not a quality which they show on certain occasions. Hence any particular epithet for "swift" also conveys some substantive sense of the being or thing which is meant to be swift. Say ποδάρκης and the very word evokes Achilles; so ποδήνεμος or ἀελλόπος evokes Iris; ἀργός or ἀργίπους a dog. In a similar way θοός will most likely make one think of a ship; κραιπνός of a storm or of a wind. Even ταχύς and ὠκύς are not general terms for "swift," but they inevitably come to mind with some image of a hero or of running feet or of horses, deer, arrows.[2] They cannot be applied loosely, to an action noun, for instance, as when we say "swift journey," "swift action."[3]

Why, we may ask, these necessary connections between epithet and noun? Why do we never find in Homer κραιπνὸς 'Αχιλλεύς, for example, or καρπάλι-μος δ' 'Αχιλλεύς, which, metrically, would have been quite possible? Why are these epithets found only with "foot," "wind," "storm"? Or, again, why not ποδάρκης as well as ποδώκης, for horse? Or why not, say, κραιπνὸς ὀϊστός?

Many such combinations might, no doubt, have been possible, but they do not occur. The reason must lie in some sense of affinity between the noun and the adjective. How this affinity was originally conceived we cannot know. We only have before us the phrase itself. It is through consideration of the given phrase rather than through etymological research that we may recover, I think, some of the epithet's force. In other words, the connection, say, between κραιπνός and its nouns is made meaningful and convincing by the recurrences themselves. We are made to realize that there is perhaps some reason why "foot," "wind," "storm" have a common way of being swift; compare "wind-footed Iris," "storm-footed Iris." Or, again, the fact that ποδώκης is shared by Achilles and horses may give us pause. In any case, the epithet is filled with substantival connotations, with image-making suggestions.

We touch here upon an essential difference between the Homeric epithets and ordinary adjectives. When we say "swift ship" we usually imply "especially swift." We unwittingly oppose swift to slow. Not so in Homer. The quality is for him intrinsic to the thing itself. It follows that the Homeric epithets are not classifiable into abstract categories of meaning. What overlies the literal meaning is rather a sense of form, configuration, mode of being.

In studying the meaning of the epithets, we shall thus look at the concrete connection between a thing and its quality, between the qualitative identity thus established and the kind of activity or condition which brings it to view. What stands out is some concrete element in the thing itself to which we may trace back such particular polarities of meaning as "long" and "short," "black" and "white," "good" and "bad"; and this concrete element may be appreciated by ordering the epithets according to broad determinations like size, dimension, form, color, and function.

16. ASPECTS OF THINGS

1. βαρύς and παχύς as epithets of hand

βαρύς is the normal Greek word for "heavy"; but in its material sense it is used by Homer only as an epithet of hand.

We find βαρείας χεῖρας, χεῖρα βαρεῖαν in phrases which mean "lay the hand upon . . . " (*Il.* 1.89, 219). Such phrases convey a sense of pressure. Compare *Il.* 11.235=17.48: a hero *pressed* his spear βαρείη χειρὶ πιθήσας, "trusting his hand." Conversely we find the same epithet of a hand releasing its pressure: *Il.* 13.410, 21.590, βαρείης χειρὸς ἀφῆκε, "released from the hand"; in 23.687 of hands clashing against one another; cp. *Od.* 18.56. In all these instances there is the effect of a hand that exerts or releases its impact.

Compare now παχύς, "thick," "massive." It is also in Homer an epithet of hand and most frequently so, but always dative and almost always instrumental, as in εἵλετο χειρὶ παχείη (*Il.* 7.264, cp. 5.309, 8.221, 10.454, etc.).[1] In such instances the hand is seen in its act of holding, touching, seizing.

It would be difficult to give an adequate translation of either of these epithets. For instance, in *Il.* 1.219, ἐπ' ἀργυρέη κώπη σχέθε χεῖρα βαρεῖαν, we could hardly translate "heavy hand": see pp. 13–14 above. For the same reason we could hardly render χειρὶ παχείη in the passages quoted as "thick hand"; for, in doing so, we should hardly avoid pointedness of meaning. What the Homeric phrase conveys is the sense of a close, enveloping hold. This is intrinsic to any hand that firmly clasps an object, and it is so, of course, also in the case of Penelope (*Od.* 21.6).[2]

Notice the equal metrical value of βαρύς and παχύς. They could be interchanged, but they hardly ever are.[3] There is in their different connections with hand a basic appropriateness. What strikes us is an intrinsic quality of the hand in two distinct and basic types of action: pressing and holding. "Heavy hand," "thick hand" have no explanatory or narrative function. They do not even have the purpose of completing the sentence and cannot really be parsed word by word as complements to the verb. They are internal to the action itself, they are relevant to nothing else but the passing act. Hence the difficulty of translating them and, at the same time, doing justice to their concrete connection.

2. Height: μακρός and αἰπύς

μακρός is the usual word for "long" in Greek. In Homer it also means "long" as, mostly, an epithet of spear; but it also means "high" as epithet of mountain, tree, column: furthermore, it means "deep" as an epithet of wells (*Il.* 21.197).

To Homer the sense of a straight outline was here more important than that of a vertical or horizontal position. To appreciate this, try to realize the shaft of a well along with that of a spear, a tree, a column. Long, high, deep merge together into a reality of shape. We may thus be better able to understand μακρός as epithet of a mountain shaken up by divine action: cp. *Il.* 8.199, 13.18. The trembling shape is well characterized by the epithet.

For a similar reason we often find μακρὸν Ὄλυμπον as accusative of direction (*Il.* 1.402, 2.48, etc.): what stands out is a soaring shape which is seen and approached.

In this last connection we may differentiate between μακρός and the synonymous αἰπύς. Why do we so often find μακρὸν Ὄλυμπον at the end of a line rather than αἰπὺν Ὄλυμπον?[4] The question is, again, one of appropriateness in meaning. It is μακρός which conveys a high mountain in its concrete connection with the act of going, coming, arriving.

As for αἰπύς (and αἰπεινός, αἰπήεις, αἰπός), it means "steep" as well as "high": see especially *Od.* 3.293. Even as epithet of a mountain which is approached and reached, it brings out the sense of climbing, ascending: cp. *Od.* 19.431. It is therefore found with cities and their names: *Il.* 2.573, 538, 869, 6.35, etc. Notice, especially in the *Catalogue of Ships,* the recurring form of such a sentence as, for example, "they who held (or inhabited) lofty Dion." We are presented with the image of towns rising on sheer rocky heights in sites which appear impregnable; hence αἰπύς, αἰπεινός also as epithets of the walls of Troy around which men die fighting (*Il.* 6.327, cp. 11.181, *Od.* 14.472).

In this sense αἰπύς also differs from ὑψηλός, which, rather, gives us a view of airy eminences as of snow covering the tops of high mountains (*Il.* 12.282) or of a cloud vanishing and revealing them (*Il.* 16.297); compare ὑψηλός with δόμος, θάλαμος (*Il.* 22.440, *Od.* 1.126, etc.): a house or a room, with its walls and ceiling, produces a *feeling* of height; cp. ὑψηρεφής, ὑψόροφος.[5]

There is thus in αἰπύς a sense of steepness, danger; whence the phrase αἰπὺς ὄλεθρος, "sheer death." In this light we may better appreciate *Od.* 11.278, ἀψαμένη βρόχον αἰπὺν ἀφ' ὑψηλοῖο μελάθρου. There is no need, with Merry and Riddell, to take αἰπύν predicatively, translating "having fastened high a noose from the lofty beam." This would give us a non-Homeric descriptiveness: αἰπύν as epithet of βρόχον is itself suggestive of deadliness, ὑψηλοῖο as epithet of chamber is itself suggestive of "high-roofed." The pregnant meaning is due to a sense of position which the epithets arrest in an image.

3. Depth, density

The meaning of depth often merges with that of substance, texture. This happens when the adjective, which we normally translate as "deep," is so intimately connected with the name of a thing that it draws its meaning from the thing's substance; and we thus have a noun-epithet phrase.

Consider the adjective βαθύς, "deep," applied to sand being touched (Il. 5.587), to a field being ploughed (Il. 10.353), a cloud broken through (Il. 20. 446), a standing crop swept by the wind (Il. 2.147). Compare Il. 16.766, 15.606, 11.306, 415. The material so affected in these instances is called "deep" insofar as it is soft, penetrable, malleable.

Take now Od. 12.214, ὑμεῖς μὲν κώπῃσιν ἁλὸς ῥηγμῖνα[6] βαθεῖαν τύπτετε . . . and Il. 1.532, εἰς ἅλα ἆλτο βαθεῖαν. Compare Il. 13.44 (with it 13.352), 21.213, 239. The meaning, I assume, is not "deep sea" (ἅλς is usually the shallow sea), but the opening or enclosing seawater, "deep" only insofar as you can plunge or emerge. In support of this, note the rarity of "deep" in reference to sea. We never find such a sentence as, for example, βαθέην περόωσι θάλασσαν. Indeed Homer never seems to apply to sea the attribute "deep" in a purely dimensional sense. We find at the most μεγακήτεα πόντον, μέγα λαῖτμα θαλάσσης, πολυβενθής mostly of λιμήν.

Depth is here one and the same with penetrability. In connection with a vital organ it is also vulnerability, sensitivity. Hence, just as concretely, βαθύς can be epithet of mind or φρήν—the midriff, that sinewy inner region which in Homer is a seat of feeling and thought. Thus in Il. 19.125, τὸν δ᾽ ἄχος ὀξὺ κατὰ φρένα τύψε βαθεῖαν · Notice the sharp grief and the deep, penetrable, sensitive φρήν. The point of incidence is brought into focus—a point in which a sense of depth is realized inwardly.

Compare πυκνός, πυκινός, "thick." It is used in a quantitative sense of things thickly set close to one another (Il. 7.61, cp. 13.145. 4.281); but multiplicity yields a sense of mass; and the same adjective can apply to one single object which has an inner complexity, as when Athena is said to "enter [penetrate] Erechtheus's thick house" (Od. 7.81, cp. 7.88, Il. 10.267, 12.301=Od. 6.134, 23.229). What does "thick house" suggest in all these instances? It is the sense of something compact, rich, full; the governing verbs themselves (to enclose, to protect, to break open, to attack) support this sense. This is what a house ought to be in its fullest meaning.

What πυκνός implies is thus the contents of a thing. Like βαθύς, it can refer to φρήν, to the midriff, to the mind's inner complexity, as in *Il.* 14.294, ἔρως πυκινὰς φρένας ἀμφεκάλυψεν. Enveloping love here suggests something solid as its object. Homer's concrete perception of mind makes the expression possible and gives the adjective the value of an epithet. For πυκινός makes one image with mind. It cannot be arbitrarily translated as "grave," "prudent." We are rather shown the mind as pregnant matter.

Hence in *Il.* 2.55, πυκινὴν ἠρτύνετο βουλήν (cp. 6.187, 3.208, 212). Thoughts, counsels, guiles are here woven, articulated, as if they were matter worked into fullness of form; and the material sense of the verbs gives us some insight into the epithet's meaning. Again, no partial translation like "judicious" or "cunning" would be adequate. We rather have a notion of intrinsic weight: a thought or a plan insofar as it is fully or positively conceived. [7]

The epithet's concrete value and the difficulty of rendering it are especially significant in Andromache's οὐδέ τι μοι εἶπες πυκινὸν ἔπος, addressed to dead Hector (*Il.* 24.744). How incongruous it would be to translate, "'to me you said not a wise word.'" What Andromache means is simply a "word," but a word in its fullest strength.

We may compare ἀδινός, which is also used both of things set thickly next to one another (as in *Od.* 1.92, 4.320, μῆλ᾽ ἀδινὰ σφάζουσι; cp. *Il.* 2.87, 469) and of one thing which makes a compact whole (as in *Il.* 16.481, *Od.* 19.516, ἀμφ᾽ ἀδινὸν κῆρ); and, just as πυκνός is referred to a word (*Il.* 24. 744), so is ἀδινός referred (and most frequently so) to a cry: *Il.* 18.316, 22. 430, etc.

But ἀδινός implies a sense of time: sheep continually slaughtered, a lamentation which is begun (ἀδινοῦ ἐξῆρχε γόοιο), the beating or throbbing heart. With πυκνός we have instead something self-contained and perceived all at once: close ranks, a god's mind, a final word.

Most characteristic of ἀδινός is the reference to voice. Its range is here extensive, as it qualifies adverbially any crying, groaning, sighing, wailing (*Od.* 16.216, 18.124, etc.). What stands out is the strong, protracted sound—in grief as it happens, but not necessarily so (*Od.* 10.413). This serves to explain Σειρήνων ἀδινάων in *Od.* 23.326. Can the epithet refer to the Sirens themselves and not to their voice? I think it can. For the Sirens are nothing but voice—a perpetually haunting song whose words hardly matter, as they sing of anything that happens under the sun (*Od.* 12.191).

Through the noun-epithet phrase a quantitative and a qualitative sense merge into one; and in the case of ἀδινός (with the suggestion of time) what prevails is a sense of intensity. I would therefore disagree with Buttman, [8] who traces a development from "dense," "numerous" to "strong," "violent," "loud." We should not take ἀδινός in the abstraction of any isolated meaning, but try to realize how different conceptual notions are merged all at once in the concrete noun-epithet image.

4. Fullness, bloom

Thickness may appear as all one with full-blown substance, as in the meaning of πυκνός in *Il.* 14.349, where earth brings to light a hyacinth: πυκνὸν καὶ μαλακόν. The lush evidence of things appealed to Homer. Adjectives meaning "dry" (ἀζαλέος, δανός, ἰσχαλέος) are never used in the poems as epithets; and the same generally applies to "hard," in spite of the many things mentioned which are naturally hard.[9]

Consider now θαλερός, which is referred to voice as well as to things which we may regard as naturally florid.[10] It is the reference to voice which concerns us here in that it differs from our own usage and may give us some insight into Homeric perception.

θαλερός is so used as an epithet always in the sentence θαλερὴ δέ οἱ ἔσχετο φωνή, "and checked was his [or her] flourishing voice," of voice failing through violent emotion (*Il.* 17.696, 23.397, *Od.* 4.705, 19.472).

Why the epithet? Because what stands out is not any message, but voice pure and simple in its elemental and sensuous nature, valued most keenly when suddenly missed and cut off. See how the epithet with its positive and joyous ring maintains its rightful place in spite of the occasion marked by the whole sentence. The poet cannot but keep in focus the existential value of things, even where the context might be thought to be most against it. Compare *Od.* 10.457, 398.

We find the same trend in θαλερός applied to tear, as in *Il.* 2.266, θαλερὸν δέ οἱ ἔκπεσε δάκρυ. Cp. 6.496, 24.9, 794, *Od.* 4.556, etc. The tear is seen in itself and by itself, quite apart from the grief of the context. In such a light a tear is like a dewdrop emerging from the eye.[11]

Similar associations are suggested by τέρην, referred, like θαλερός, to a falling tear: *Il.* 16.11, 3.142, 19.323, *Od.* 16.332. But compare the epithet's other frames of reference: skin, flesh when wounded, mangled, threatened in *Il.* 13.553, 4.237, cp. 14.406; leaves crushed, plucked in *Il.* 13.180, *Od.* 12. 357, 9.449.

What is this common quality of leaf, flesh, tear? It is a soft, sensuous texture which gives way. It is something intrinsic to the nature of the thing perceived, and quite apart from any superficially describable likeness. Thus a tear has its momentary bulk. It gathers into full, rounded form before it vanishes. Never mind the small size; what the epithet brings out is the thing itself—the effluence, the lymphous drop. Compare πυκνὸν . . . δάκρυον in *Od.* 4.153.[12]

We may now try to explain λειριόεις in *Il.* 3.152, the passage in which the

Trojan elders, ceaselessly talking, are compared to the cicadas that shed their "lilylike voice." The epithet is also used of a warrior's flesh in *Il.* 13.830. Again we have a common reference to voice and flesh, sensuous softness being true of both.[13]

The epithet thus presents voice as something palpable. This sense of voice is very Homeric: a divine voice is *shed* around Agamemnon (*Il.* 2.41); the cry of Nausicaa and her companions *surrounds* Odysseus (*Od.* 6.122); Hector's voice is *scattered* over the plain like matter broken up into fragments (*Il.* 16.78). Voice itself has the epithet ἀτειρής, "not to be worn away," as of something materially solid. And the epithet θαλερός gives us, as we have seen, something of the same sensation.

Now the song of the cicadas possesses this palpable quality in the highest degree. It fills the landscape. It is deep, uninterrupted.[14] Entering within its range is like penetrating invisible matter. The place has its sound just as it may have zones of heavy perfume through which one passes.

But why lilylike? It is possibly because the lily, unlike other flowers such as the violet or the rose, does not primarily suggest color, but density, depth, softness. Compare the epithet πυκνός, applied by Homer to the hyacinth (*Il.* 14.349) and by Hesiod (*Op.* 584) to the cicada's song.

What stands out is thus the thick flood of sound. In order to appreciate λειριόεις, we must give up the notion of anything refined or exquisite. This beauty is of a different kind. It is hardly a matter of taste. It consists in a vital fullness.[15]

5. Form: part and whole

I here understand *form* in a visual, tangible sense. I also understand it in a positive sense: the form or shape of a thing must be felt as a value in itself.

Homer is filled with such a sense of form. Take, for instance, such epithets of ship as "even," "well-made," "well-benched," "hollow." A ship so presented is what a ship must be. We are presented with a qualitative ship-image. The very way a thing is named fills us with a satisfying sense of what it is. The feeling of beauty is not directly expressed, but it is always implicit.

Let us see how the noun-epithet phrases carry out this mode of representation by bringing out the whole and part. In "well-benched ship," for instance, "ship" represents the whole, "bench" represents the part, and "well" infuses a sense of quality. We thus have "lovely-cheeked" of a woman, "swift-footed" of a man; "high-necked" of a horse, "broad-fronted" of an ox, "many-ridged" of a mountain, "rich-clodded" of the earth, etc. Here is a comprehensive representation of things. It subjects them to a persistent sense of form which is always coherent with itself. Let not habit blunt us: the noun-epithet phrases turn things into images. Why, for instance, "lovely-cheeked

Briseis"? Because our sense of form is enhanced. Quality is made palpable by being focused on so distinctive a feature.

What we miss in detached impressions we thus gain in the strong sense of evidence. We have configuration, not description. For the epithet brings into refinement of form a substantival element which is already inherent in the name, and the result is an intimately compact image.

Here then is another aspect of Homer's concreteness. The epithets are no adventitious matter. This perception of the whole and part is deeply rooted in the Homeric representation of things even quite aside from the noun-epithet phrases. We find it in the pervasive tendency to present a thing in the evidence of some vital constituent part wherever the passing act brings that part into view. See, for instance, how the idea that Athena beautifies Odysseus is expressed in *Od.* 6.235 (cp. 8.19, 23.162): ὡς ἄρα τῷ κατέχευε χάριν κεφαλῇ τε καὶ ὤμοις. What stands out is head and shoulders. Note how this is expressed: the parts of the body are not separated from the whole (as they would be by saying "beauty on his head and shoulders"), but they are quite integrated with it, both Odysseus himself and his parts being expressed in the same case-form.

The same construction is applied to the branch of a tree in *Il.* 1.236-37, to a promontory in *Il.* 2.395-96. Similarly Homer will not say of a god that he came "down from Olympus," but "down from the peaks of Olympus" (*Il.* 1.44, 2.167, etc.); he will not say, "he walked along the sea" but "he walked by the shore of the roaring sea" (*Il.* 1.34, cp. 327, 350, etc.); he will not say simply, "to cross the sea," but use such a phrase as "to sail over the sea's broad shoulders" (cp. *Il.* 2.159, 8.511, etc.), "to pass over the sea's great chasm" (*Od.* 5.174, 9.260, etc.) or, most often, sea with its epithet (see p. 75).[16]

6. Workmanship, function

A sense of achievement often replaces that of the whole and part: for example, "well-made" of ship instead of "well-benched," "well-founded" of a town instead of "well-walled," "well-streeted." Here again there is a large frame of reference—from, say, εὐκαμπής of a sickle to εὔορμος of a harbor.

These epithets naturally apply mostly to man-made things. Workmanship appealed to Homer as much as the congruence of the whole with its parts. Think of how he dwells on Odysseus making his raft or Hephaestus working at Achilles' shield. Achievement is all one with the thing itself.

Most striking in this respect are epithets of this kind but lacking the εὐ-prefix, meaning not "well-made," but simply "made," "achieved," "completed." Such are κολλητός, ποιητός, τυκτός, τετυγμένος applied to things which range from a cup to a wall or house; similarly πλεκτός of a chord, a basket, a fillet; στρεπτός of a tunic. In *Il.* 23.741, for instance, we have ἀργύρεον κρητῆρα τετυγμένον. How shall we explain "wrought krater"? In a concrete and not a descriptive sense. In other words, the epithet does not give us any information about the krater, but simply presents it before our eyes as a man-made thing.[17] This is indeed the striking fact about a krater's existence. In our way of taking things for granted and always looking for some pointed detail, we should hardly mention anything so seemingly obvious. But Homer sees the krater as a fine thing in that it is an object achieved and displayed before us. It did not exist before being made, and now it is superbly present. There is beauty in the very fact of achieving.

It will be objected that Homer points to the functional side of what is well made. Indeed, function or adequacy to a purpose characterizes the things so mentioned. Shall we then say that Homer has a utilitarian view of things? No, not at all. It is the visual form which comes to the fore. It is significant that there is no word in Homer which means merely useful (χρήσιμος, ὠφέλιμος). Usefulness is thus secondary to form, an ingredient of beauty. This is also shown by the epithets. For "shield," for instance, we have ἀμφιβρότη, "man-covering"; πάντοσ' ἐίση, "even on all sides"; ὀμφαλόεσσα, "embossed"; φαεινή, "shiny." There is no generalized meaning of safety, which would be most plausible in the case of a shield. What stands out is visual: a shape or an effect of light. Even for the meaning "protective" we are made to see a surface that covers a man's body. The bare idea of practical utility seems rare in the epithets. In the later part of the *Odyssey* (which is narrative in tone) we have ἀλεξάνεμος of a cloak (14.529), κυνῶν ἀλκτῆρα καὶ ἀνδρῶν of a javelin (14.531, 21.340).

7. Loveliness

The sense of form or beauty [18] is also expressed by epithets which, coming from the root -ερ or connected with ἵμερος, imply love, desire, delight.

We must especially note the frame of reference. Consider the following:

ἐραννός. Only of a city: *Il.* 9.531, 577, *Od.* 7.18.
ἐπήρατος. A city, a place: *Il.* 18.512, *Od.* 13.103, etc.; Aphrodite's garments: *Od.* 8.366; a banquet: *Il.* 9.228.
ἐρατεινός. A city, a region: *Il.* 2.532, 571, 3.239, etc.; manliness, love: *Il.* 6.156, *Od.* 23.300; a banquet: *Od.* 8.61; ambrosia: *Il.* 19.347; a river's streams: *Il.* 21.218; young people: *Il.* 3.175; a girl: *Od.* 4.13.
πολυήρατος. A city: *Od.* 11.275; youth: *Od.* 15.366; marriage: 15.126, cp. 23.354.
ἐρατός. Only the gifts of Aphrodite: *Il.* 3.64.

ἱμερόεις. Marriage: *Il.* 5.429; song, dance: *Od.* 1.421, *Il.* 18.603, etc.; parts
   of the body: *Il.* 3.397, 14.170.
ἱμερτός. Only of a river: *Il.* 2.751.

What stands out is the reference to cities. These epithets thus compete with
others meaning "well-founded," "well-situated" (εὖ ναιετοώσῃ, εὖ ναιομένη,
ἐΰκτιτος, ἐϋκτίμενος). The former, however, and most notably ἐρατεινός, are
most often directly applied to the proper name, the latter to the common
noun for "city," "citadel." Hence the frequence of ἐρατεινός in the *Catalogue
of Ships:* for example, *Il.* 2.591, "those who inhabited lovely Arene." Hence
also the phrase ἐϋκτίμενον πτολίεθρον, as object of conquering: *Il.* 13.380,
4.33, etc. Although these distinctions should not be pressed, yet they have
some significance. The epithets with the -ερ root would seem to convey a particular sort of beauty: the appeal of cities in that they are inhabited, loved,
admired. A city becomes a pole of attraction. This explains how it shares these
epithets with such ideals as youth, manhood, love. For such things have no
distinctive feature that objectively stands out. What makes them concrete is
the emotion which they inspire.

Conversely, and for the same reason, none of these epithets refers to a plain
single object. Homer will not say, for instance, "lovely cup," using ἐρατεινός
or any of its synonyms. The images which these epithets suggest are of too
complex a nature.

Here are trends which have their concrete poetic logic. Deviations can usually
be explained on grounds which are no less concrete. Take δῶρ᾽ ἐρατά in *Il.*
3.64. Unlike its kindred epithets, ἐρατός here refers to "gifts." But what gifts?
Not objects, but Aphrodite's gifts. So ἐπήρατος in *Od.* 8.366 for Aphrodite's
garments. We are at once reminded of ἐρατεινός, πλυήρατος, as epithets of
love, youth, manhood, marriage.

Compare, in *Od.* 4.13, παῖδ᾽ ἐρατεινήν. Most unusually the epithet is referred to "daughter," "girl." But who is the girl? She is Helen's daughter. The
association with Aphrodite is implicit in the epithet and made palpable in
the line following: "Hermione who had the looks of golden Aphrodite."

Or take, in *Il.* 3.397, στήθεά θ᾽ ἱμερόεντα. The epithet has elsewhere an ideal
frame of reference; singularly it here refers to body. But how? To breast,
and to Aphrodite's breast. Compare *Il.* 14.170: Hera wipes off every stain
ἀπὸ χροός ἱμερόεντος, and she does so in a quest of love. The epithet is
again appropriate not in any pointed way but because of a range of associations which are both sensuous and ideal.

8. Color: concreteness in color[19]

Here again quality is part and parcel of a thing's substance. Color is not so much a superficial pigment as an essential aspect of what we see, no less than size or form. We might call it a native complexion of things, inevitably present. Hence Homer hardly ever casually mentions the color of any object— a cloth, for intance, that might happen to be red or yellow or blue.[20]

How color thus emerges out of matter is conveyed by the poet himself in *Il.* 7.61-66 " ... their ranks sat close together, bristling with shields and helmets and spears. As a ripple spreads over the sea when the west wind rises afresh, and the water darkens beneath it; so were seated the ranks. . . . " Compare *Il.* 4.275-82: "As when from a height a goatherd sees a cloud coming over the sea . . . blacker than pitch does it seem . . . , so did the serried ranks move, darkening bristling with shields and with spears." The poet here catches color in the making. The vividly perceived condensation produces blackness. We are thus placed face to face with nature, removed from any conventional description of things.[21]

This rich sense of color is embedded in the language. Take *Il.* 14.16, ὡς ὅτε πορφύρῃ πέλαγος. What does the verb πορφύρω mean? As Leaf remarks, it refers both to the heaving and coloring of waves. Hence πορφύρεος as epithet of wave (*Il.* 1.482, *Od.* 13.85, 11.243) and of the sea itself (*Il.* 16.391).

In the light of these remarks, we may look at other epithets of the sea. In each case a concrete passing aspect is singled out and boldly given permanent status.

Take οἴνοπι πόντῳ, οἴνοπα πόντον, especially frequent of sea crossed over by ships (*Il.* 7.88, *Od.* 1.183, etc.). Why wine-colored? It is the effect of that heaving movement and turbulence which is also expressed in πορφύρεος. Compare ἰοειδής, "violetlike," *Il.* 11.298, *Od.* 5.56, 11.107. Texture and color merge into one.

Or take πολιῆς ἁλός, πολιὴν ἅλα. Why white? It is the foaming sea by the shore (*Il.* 1.350, 15.619, etc.); or the splashing sea plied by oars (*Od.* 4.580, 9.104, etc.); compare λευκαίνω in *Od.* 12.172. A similar effect perhaps in ὑπεξαναδὺς πολιῆς ἁλός (*Il.* 13.352; cp. *Od.* 4.405) of foaming water around an emerging body.

Or consider ἠεροειδέα πόντον, ἠεροειδέϊ πόντῳ, always of high seas traveled in far-off journeys or as the site of remote islands (*Od.* 2.263, 5.281, etc.). Here again something concretely experienced: color merged with air, mist, or that featureless space which sometimes seems to break the horizon between sea and sky.[22]

It might be asked, Why do we not find *blue* sea? The sea is blue to us. But it is blue only when looked at from a distance as one general whole. Plunge into it, touch it, look down at it from a sailing boat, and it is not blue at all but of varying shades—translucent, green, purple according to depth, light, movement. Homer does not look at it as a mass to be surveyed and described, but simply mentions it and pictures it at a point of contact—in immediate connection with human acts or with the impinging storm.

There is generally the same concentration of sense impressions in any adjective suggestive of color and used as an epithet. We have a concrete image, not specious terminology which assigns each several thing to one currently accepted determination of color (as when we say "blue sky," "green fields").

Consider in this respect the epithet "white" (λευκός) of water mentioned in the moment of flowing (*Od.* 5.70, *Il.* 23.282; cp. *Il.* 2.307, ἀγλαὸν ὕδωρ). Water, however, is called "black" (μέλας) in phrases which imply the idea of water drawn from the depth of a river, well, or sea (cp. *Il.* 16.161, 2.825, *Od.* 4.359, 6.91, 12.104, 13.409), or where we have the effect of an encompassing submerging wave (*Od.* 5.353, *Il.* 23.693; cp. *Od.* 4.402, *Il.* 21.126, 202). In such instances "white" approaches the sense of "translucent," black that of "deep," "covering." Color is but part of a wider sense.

This is so even where the frame reference seems obvious. Such is the case of "white" applied to outspread sails, arms stretching out, bones laid bare, milk pressed out or curdled, a boar's teeth exposed (cp. *Il.* 1.480, 5.314, *Od.* 1.161, *Il.* 4.434, 11.416, etc.). We have, as it were, a flash of white: not an idle color term but a moment of bright exposure.

Earth, on the other hand, or mainland (*Od.* 14.97, 21.109) are called black. The blackness is here all one with the thick compact mass. There is a similar concrete feeling about "black ship": we are made to see a dark solid shape out at sea.

These epithets have a much richer meaning than mere "black" and "white"; and this is an effect of the noun-epithet relation. Each thing to which they apply bestows upon them something of its character. When the poet says γαῖα μέλαινα, that black is earthy, that earth has its portion of black. The respective abstractions of quality and object are fused and made concrete in the reality of an image.

This nondescriptive fixation of images also accounts for the comparative scarceness of color terms. If description prevailed, we should doubtless have a greater variety. But the lack of variety is made up for by pregnant meaning. This is eminently poetic. *Od.* 10.94, for instance, λευκὴ δ᾽ ἦν ἀμφὶ γαλήνη, "white sea-calm was all around" gives us a sense of luminous stillness. Even more so, about Olympus in *Od.* 6.45, λευκὴ δ᾽ ἐπιδέδρομεν αἴγλη; compare Shelley's "white radiance of eternity."

9. Materials and color

If color in things implies a sense of their substance, the reverse is also true: material implies color. Homer may not have any specific words for brown, yellow or gray, but when he says "bronzed," "golden," "silver" he also implies the respective colors. Consider Telemachus in Menelaus's palace telling Pisistratus (*Od.* 4.71-73):

> observe . . .
> the flash of bronze through the echoing halls,
> and of gold and amber and silver and ivory.

It would be quite unlike Homer to describe the colors of objects in Menelaus's palace; but it is obvious that this material splendor is filled with color. Compare the presentation of Alcinous's palace in *Od.* 7.84-94.

We may thus better appreciate the epithets of material which Homer so often applies to cup, krater, cauldron, sword, etc. Take, for instance, the recurring lines (*Od.* 1.136-37, etc.) which present a handmaid "with a golden jug pouring water over the silver bowl." Why golden? Why silver? Certainly not for the case of curiosity or to point out the preciousness of the material (the very repetition of the lines excludes this). No, this juxtaposition of gold and silver has a rich, sensuous effect. The epithets highlight the act of pouring water, giving it brilliance, color.

A metallic luster, where it occurs, is what gives the greatest conspicuity to any object. It strikes us immediately. No less than the epithets μέλας or λευκός, it translates color into a more encompassing sphere and thus removes us from descriptive interest. Hence many epithets which generally mean "shiny." Note especially some instances which differ most widely from ordinary modern usage: φαεινός of garments (*Il.* 3.419, *Od.* 6.74, etc.) and not only of metals; σιγαλόεις, of masonry (*Od.* 16.449, 19.600, etc.) as well as of cloth (*Il.* 22.154, *Od.* 6.26); παμφανόων, of wall (*Il.* 8.435, *Od.* 4.42, etc.). Things are here seen in the radiance of their material—a radiance which (through the noun-epithet connection) acquires in each case its striking distinction. Thus σιγαλόεις, found as it often is with "garments," acquires the sense of a silky gloss. This impression of a shining material is rendered more explicitly in *Il.* 18.595-96, where the dancers portrayed on Achilles' shield wear χιτῶνας . . . ἐϋννήτους, ἧκα στίλβοντας ἐλαίῳ. Note the adverb ἧκα, which is elsewhere used for gentle movement, soft breath, whispering voice. What stands out is a soft, even glow. The finely spun material has a radiance which outmatches any particular dye.

10. Vegetation and color

Similar remarks may be made about epithets of the vegetal world. The color of plants is submerged in efflorescence, just as that of man-made objects is in the radiance of their material.

It is interesting in this respect that the adjective χλωρός is not at all generalized in the meaning "green." It is quite rare: referred to cut wood still green or fresh (*Od.* 9.320, 378; cp. 16.47), twice to honey (*Il.* 11.631, *Od.* 10.234), and elsewhere in the phrase "green with fear," "green fear" (*Il.* 15.4, 7.479).

There are, on the other hand, many epithets with the general meaning "flourishing," "blossoming":

Il. 6.148, *Od.* 5.63, ὕλη τηλεθόωσα. Cp. *Il.* 17.55, *Od.* 7.114, 116, 11.590, 13.196.
Il. 10.467 (cp. 17.53), ἐριθηλέας ὄζους. *Il.* 5.90, ἀλωάων ἐριθηλέων.
Od. 12.103, ἐρινεός . . . φύλλοισι τεθηλώς. Cp. *Od.* 6.293. Of dew: *Od.* 13.245; cp. 5.467.
Il. 2.506, *Od.* 6.291, ἀγλαὸν ἄλσος.
Od. 7.128, πρασιαὶ . . . ἐπηετανὸν γανόωσαι.

Flourishing, luxuriant rather than green. But at the same time, these instances imply the idea of green insofar as it applies to nature. Again, the noun-epithet phrases give us a condensed view, a concrete fullness; and color is not something apart; it merges with the vital material, with the blossoming form. Think of the fact that English *green* and Latin *viridis* go back to a root which means "to blossom."

We find the same concreteness in other related instances. Homer does not say "green meadows" but "grassy meadows," πίσεα ποιήεντα, *Il.* 20.9, *Od.* 6.124. So of valleys: *Od.* 4.337=17.128. Compare λεχεποίης (*Il.* 2.697, 4.383); ὑλήεις (*Il.* 10.362, etc.), δενδρήεις (*Od.* 9.200, 1.51), ὄρος καταειμένον ὕλη (*Od.* 13.351, 19.431).

Especially suggestive is εἰνοσίφυλλος, "leaf-shaking," of mountains (*Il.* 2.632, 757, *Od.* 9.22, 11.316) and even more so ἀκριτόφυλλος (*Il.* 2.868), "with leaves indistinguishably blending." These suggest the infinite shades of shimmering green on a mountain slope.

Similarly we do not find in Homer the vague blue of mountains seen in the distance, but ὄρεα σκιόεντα (*Od.* 5.279, 7.268, *Il.* 1.157). I take the effect to be a visual one, as of a dusky shape on the horizon—no matter how we explain the shade (whether of forests or valleys or the mountain's position).

All these are not epithets of color, but color is present in their evocation of blossom, grass, leaves, forest, meadow. Indeed, these epithets would not be so felicitous were it not so. They derive some of their strength from the fact that the language ignores abstract terms of color. For they inevitably make up for this seeming deficiency. Green is as old as nature, but Homer sees it otherwise than we do—as an integrating element which need not be mentioned on its own account. After all, it is grass and leaves and forest which make green what it is.

17. HUMAN DISPOSITIONS

The epithets of persons require a category apart because the characters are obviously preeminent in the poems. We find, nevertheless, the same basic trends of concrete meaning.

1. Concrete as opposed to purely qualitative meaning

There are many epithets of heroes which we usually translate as "valiant," "courageous," "strong," "goodly," "great." Such translations, though unavoidable, are inadequate. Take, for instance, μεγάθυμος or μεγαλήτωρ. What these epithets convey is the nature of a man in the heroic sense—that is to say, a human animal perfectly formed. It should be remembered that θυμός and ἦτορ are felt in Homer to be vital organs of all living creatures and not only as those centers of moral feeling which we call "spirit" or "heart." Hence the un-Homeric ring which a literal rendering of these epithets would have: "magnanimous," "great-hearted." No, what we have here is the large frame of a man—something that is inevitably so, an identity rather than a quality.

Clearly such a meaning, to be effective in its own way, must avoid all particular point. It is as solidly self-contained as it is unobtrusive. It simply accrues to the hero's figure the moment it is presented to us. It is figurative, visual, plastic, even where we might translate it as having a moral attribute.

Qualities of strength or character are expressed otherwise than through the epithets. In the τειχοσκοπία, for instance, Odysseus and Menelaus have no epithets where their demeanor is portrayed (Il. 3.210, 211, 213, 223, 224), but they do where they are simply presented in an immediate act (3.205, 206, 216). Especially significant is 200-02:

> οὗτος δ᾽ αὖ Λαερτιάδης πολύμητις Ὀδυσσεύς,
> ὃς τράφη ἐν δήμῳ Ἰθάκης κραναῆς περ ἐούσης
> εἰδὼς παντοίους τε δόλους καὶ μήδεα πυκνά.

Odysseus has his epithets when Homer points him out where he stands, the moment he is perceived; but his subtlety of mind requires a different kind of expression.

Shall we say that the epithet is so worn out by usage that its meaning must be expressed in some other way? Not at all. The same literal, conceptual meaning is seen on two different levels—as part of an image and as a form of activity. We might rather say it is the person's name which is worn out and so deprived of transparent meaning that it needs an epithet to give it new life.

2. Classification and meaning

The concrete meaning of a hero's epithets may be best shown by the impossibility or difficulty of classifying them according to conceptual meanings of quality, such as "wisdom," "strength," "nobility," "greatness."

What stands out are not qualities as such but features, attitudes, dispositions arrested in solid form. Consider the following categories:

1. ποδάρκης, μεγάθυμος, πολύμητις, βοὴν ἀγαθός, καλλιπάρῃος, etc. What these bring to the fore is an essential part or element of the human organism. Swiftness, courage, wisdom, beauty are hardly seen in themselves, but rather insofar as there is an organ or limb to give them body. We may include here ἀγήνωρ, ἀγαπήνωρ, whose ending -ήνωρ, "man" has a function similar to -ήτωρ, -θυμος.[1] Compare chapter 16, section 5.

2. κορυθαίολος, αἰολοθώρηξ, χαλκοκορυστής, ἐυμμελίης, τανύπεπλος, etc. The stress falls upon a part of armor or dress. What one wears is felt as an extension of one's body, whether in effectiveness or appearance. This category is therefore similar to the preceding one.

3. ἱππόδαμος, πλήξιππος, σακέσπαλος, ἐγχέσπαλος, ἑκήβολος, etc. A typical act is here arrested, often with its object, in a visual image. We have the presentation of a god or warrior bent on his task. Compare the idea of function, pp. 119-20.

4. κρατερός, ἴφθιμος, ἄλκιμος, ἀγαθός, ἀμύμων, ἀγανός, φαίδιμος, etc. These have a general meaning and application. They are joined both with a proper name and with a common appellative. We have, for instance, φαίδιμος υἱός as well as φαίδιμος Ἕκτωρ, πατρὸς ἀμύμονος as well as Ἀχιλῆος ἀμύμονος. Remarkably frequent is the reference to the nouns meaning "son," "daughter," "child," "man," "woman." The sense of excellence is joined to that of a basic human function, a basic human identity. "I bore a child," ἀμύμονά τε κρατερόν τε, says Thetis in Il. 18.55. What we see is a son in his full potency. The same applies to other forms of identity: for example, πότνια μήτηρ, θαλερὸς παρακοίτης. Compare ἀγλαός, which, though not used with a proper name, is very frequent with υἱός, τέκνα. Again, the

quality merges with an image, and we can hardly assign any distinctive qualitative meaning.

5. δῖος, διίφιλος, διοτρεφής, διογενής. An intrinsic state or condition is
pointed out rather than such quality as we may term "divine." There is a kinship between heroes and gods. We may put patronymics in the same category.

Now this kinship is not idealized into a quality, but broadened into a sense
of resemblance in ἀντίθεος θεοείκελος, ἰσόθεος, etc. This is not to say that
these epithets do not suggest admiration or wonder; but this is implicit in a
sense of natural status, and the epithet is not allowed to become a common
expression of praise; an exception is, possibly, θεῖος in *Il.* 16.798: see Leaf's
note on this line.

6. κλυτός, κλειτός, and their derivatives. These epithets, like those of the
preceding group, point to a positive concrete status or condition. They do not
convey glory in a moral sense. What stands out is the fact of being named,
heard about, and, therefore, being present, existent, notable. [2]

None of these epithets is a qualifying attribute. As far as meaning is concerned, they present various ways of bringing out the full positive presence
of characters and people. If, on their basis, we were to characterize the Homeric hero, the resulting characterization would be intolerably vague and
stale. Nor would an abstract analysis of meaning in each particular instance be
very helpful: ἄλκιμος, for instance, points to strength as well as courage,
ἴφθιμος also to beauty; and wisdom, on the other hand, shades off into shrewd-
ness, craft, skill, and therefore again into practical strength. It is typical of
this situation that the epithet δαΐφρων should be translated now as "wise"
now as "warlike."

3. Unobtrusiveness and perspicuity

Why is it that we find so often such a line as τὸν δ᾽ ἠμείβετ᾽ ἔπειτα μέγας
κορυθαίολος Ἕκτωρ, but not, say, τὸν δ᾽ ἠμείβετ᾽ ἔπειτα μέγας μένος ἄσχετος
Ἕκτωρ, which might have been quite appropriate from a narrative, prosaic
point of view? Or why so often the line-ending πόδας ὠκὺς Ἀχιλλεύς, but
very rarely μεγάθυμος Ἀχιλλεύς? It is because the presentation of these heroes
in a passing act must be as vivid as it is unobtrusive.

The lack of meaningful characterization in the epithets, which might be
regarded as a defect, is really most effective poetically. The hero, as he is
shown in action, is left free of all burdening qualification. At the same time
he is not a mere name. He is there before us in the might of his nature. That he
should be swift of foot, or a tamer of horses, or that his helmet should gleam
in the sun—these are nothing but inevitable facts of his existence. They only
enliven his outline with their passing touch, and do not predetermine at all his

character or course of action. How typical of Homer, how poetically right is the fact, for instance, that Achilles should be swift-footed but that his swiftness is never illustrated or made an issue in the poems. This is an exquisite irrelevance. Time and again the quick and vital image of the hero is impressed on our mind, and yet his behavior is something else, free to develop on its own account from instance to instance. The name, the epithet confer existential weight, without conditioning the dramatic and moral values of the action.

There is, of course, one great exception: Odysseus and his epithets, which have so intimate a bearing on his character: πολύτλας, ταλασίφρων, πολύμητις, πολυμήχανος. An inward dimension is here uncovered and embodied in a man. What stands out is this embodiment, quite apart from the occasions of suffering and wisdom. There is a coincidence between the mettle of the man and the continuous burden of the action, regardless of any point or message. This is why, again, these epithets are difficult to translate, in spite of the transparent meaning. Suffering, patience, daring, resourcefulness, wisdom, craft are all included. [3] They make us think of Odysseus himself rather than of any particular virtue. In the same way we have περίφρων Πηνελόπεια, a solid instance of what Penelope happens to be, rather than any such qualification as "prudent," "chaste," "faithful."

4. Lack of derogatory epithets

The concrete meaning of these epithets is naturally alien to such abstract polarizations as "good" and "bad," "strong" and "weak," "courageous" and "coward": see p. 112 above. What these epithets underline is the full, positive presence of a person. Hence the lack of derogatory epithets.

Personal epithets generally meaning "evil" are remarkably rare. They are found mostly with mythical figureheads that are not integrated into the vital action of the poems. There is ὀλοόφρων of Atlas (*Od.* 1.52), Aetes (*Od.* 10.137), Minos (*Od.* 11.322); στυγερός of Eriphyle (*Od.* 11.326), ἔκπαγλος of Laomedon (*Il.* 21.452). We have ἄγριος Κύκλωψ, in *Od.* 2.19, but where Polyphemus is mentioned with his own name he has the epithet κρατερός (*Od.* 9.407, 446), ἀντίθεος in *Od.* 1.70; compare the murderous Antiphates as κλυτὸν ᾿Αντιφατῆα in *Od.* 10.114. Nor is the epithet δολόεσσα of Calypso (*Od.* 7.245), Circe (*Od.* 9.32) necessarily derogatory; cp. πολυφάρμακος (*Od.* 10.276). As for the various epithets of Ares meaning "baneful," "destructive," they may be explained in that the god is very nearly identified with the idea of war. [4]

In reference to the more distinctly Homeric characters, epithets of blame are hard to find. There is ὑπερφίαλον Διομήδεα in *Il.* 5.881, where the reading ὑπέρθυμον should perhaps be preferred. In *Il.* 19.325, ῥιγεδανῆς ῾Ελένης, in *Il.* 24.39, ὀλοῷ Ἀχιλῆι: both instances occur in impassioned speech, acquiring significance from the anomaly.

This reluctance to blame is due to the positive nature of the epithets. It also explains those instances in which the epithet appears contradictory, ill-suited to a character that is admittedly a villain. The most notable case is *Od.* 1.29: μνήσατο γὰρ κατὰ θυμὸν ἀμύμονος Αἰγίσθοιο. A Parryist may see in this nothing but a variation of *Od.* 4.187: μνήσατο γὰρ κατὰ θυμὸν ἀμύμο-νος Ἀντιλόχοιο. But there is a deeper reason why ἀμύμονος Αἰγίσθοιο does not offend us or even surprise us, but has on the contrary a satisfying Homeric ring. It is that Aegisthus is here nothing more than an object of remembering, thinking; and names of persons governed by such verbs normally have the epithet: cp. *Od.* 1.65, 5.11, 10.199-200, 14.170, *Il.* 2.725, 24.509. *Od.* 10.199-200 especially, Κύκλοπος . . . μεγαλήτορος, appears to be a forcible parallel. Thus, in the case of Aegisthus, the epithet ἀμύμων simply lets us linger on the name which the mind of Zeus summons up. We see Aegisthus as a man's or hero's image. Any supplementary and intrusive indication of the character's depravity would be out of tune. It would detract from Zeus's self-contained mental act, diverting our attention.

This, of course, does not prevent the poet from saying Αἴγισθον δολόμητιν in *Od.* 3.198, 307 (cp. 4.525, 1.300), and ἀνάλκιδος Αἰγίσθοιο in *Od.* 3.310. For these passages are quite different. They come (*Od.* 3 and 4) in Nestor's and Menelaus's long narrative accounts, which lie outside the mainstream of the poem, or (*Od.* 1) in Athena's speech which draws an ideal comparison between Telemachus and Orestes. There is in all a narrative insistence on the role of Aegisthus, who is also called πατροφονεύς. We are thus far removed from the Homeric representation of single acts caught in the moment of their immediate occurrence.

It is ἀμύμονος Αἰγίσθοιο, which is more thoroughly Homeric. The phrase "blameless Aegisthus" has its own poetic logic. It is an ultimate and flagrant proof of what we have seen to be characteristic of Homeric expression—namely, the faculty of so drawing an image as to make it perfectly self-contained and existentially relevant only to the momentary act, quite apart from the narrative and moral ramifications of the story.[5]

18. CONCLUSIONS ON MEANING

1. A common trend

There is in the epithets a pervasive kinship of meaning due to the way they elicit quality from the mere aspect of a thing. There is a similar appeal in, say, "swift-footed Achilles" and "taper-leaved olive." No matter what the object may be, it is the consistency of its nature that yields a sense of excellence or well-being.

Think of dimension. Take, for instance, the epithet "long." Homer does not say that anything is more or less long. "Long" is hardly ever used for the sake of measurement. Rather, it is applied to things which appear to be intrinsically long. Such things must have first given to human eyes a sense of length; hence a sense of reality and effectiveness in the very fact of being long. A long spear, or a long-shadowed spear, is exactly what a spear must be.

Or take form, shape. It inevitably conveys beauty. The epithets are never used to say that anything is more or less beautiful or well-made. The very adjective καλός does not suggest any narrow discrimination of taste. No, beauty is one and the same with the intrinsic nature of a thing, one and the same with what must have first given a positive aesthetic impression. It is thus hardly differentiated from craft, growth, shapeliness, luxuriance.

Even what is intrinsically evil or ugly must be given its due insofar as it is a phenomenon visualized in its own right. We thus have, for instance, "tearful, man-destroying, evil-echoing, much-rushing war" as well as "faultless, much-sporting dance." Evil, no less than good, has its concrete outline. It is tightly held in an image. It is not so much a theme of loathing as a deadly clash or a cry.

2. Fullness

This concreteness of the epithets may also be taken as a sense of fullness. Any partial or one-sided qualification is quite alien to them. We thus shall not find in Homer anything like Virgil's *putris glaeba* (*G.* 1.44), *arguto pectine* (*Aen.* 7.14), *aestas pulverulenta* (*G.* 1.66), or Hesiod's θέρεος καματώδεος (*Op.* 584, 664). "Crumbling clod," "shrill shuttle," "dusty, toilsome summer"—these do not give us the solid, full-blown image of a thing. They present us, rather, with something curious, minute, picturesque, pointedly significant.

For a similar reason we shall find nothing in Homer like ἀνόστεος, "boneless," of the polypus in Hesiod, *Op.* 524. It smacks of meticulousness or irony to characterize anything through the lack of an essential organ or detail. The Homeric epithets, on the contrary, never curtail, never deny. If they are composed with *privative alpha*, it is always to affirm more strongly what they refer to: compare ἀμύμων, ἀπειρέσιος, ἀπείριτος, ἀπείρων, ἀτειρής, ἄφθιτος, ἀθάνατος, ἄμβροτος, ἄαπτος. So ἀτρύγετος of the sea: "unvintaged," "not to be vintaged," "desolate," "immense." Where the *privative alpha* is felt as negation, we have not an epithet but a predicate: ἄβλητος, ἄβρομος, ἀγέραστος, ἀελπής, ἄναρχος, ἄναυδος, etc.

3. Expressiveness

It must be understood that the epithets are forms of pure expression. This is to say that their primary purpose is to express simply and fully the identity of whatever they refer to.

This should put us on our guard from taking too narrow a view of the epithets. We should not say, for instance, that the suitors are called "splendid," "brave," "godlike" because they are people of high rank. Similarly it is stale, false—or, at best, a misleading half-truth—to say that the epithets point out the heroic nature of the subject matter, that they apply to gods and heroes as being different from ordinary mortals, that they imply princely or divine connections, that they are found with man-made objects that are particularly costly, such as the furnishings of a king's palace or the weapons and armor of warriors. No, the epithets are not a conventional blazonry. All that I have said so far should dispel this view. Here are additional considerations supporting my point:

1. Epithets of gods, goddesses, heroes, heroines are also applied to slaves— as in the case of Eumaeus (*Od.* 14.121, 16.461, 17.508, 21.234, 22.157), Philoitios (20.185, 254, 21.240), Euryclea (19.357, 491, 20.134, 21.381; cp. 2.347, 20.147-48), Chryseis (*Il.* 1.143, 310, 369), Briseis (1.184, 323, 346, 2.689, 19.246, 24.676; cp. 19.282), Melantho (*Od.* 18.321). So *Od.* 6.239, ἀμφίπολοι λευκώλενοι; 19.60, δμωαὶ λευκώλενοι.

2. The same kind of form-enhancing epithet applies to tools and ordinary objects as well as to heroic materials. Note the following:

Od. 11.121, 129, etc., εὐῆρες ἐρετμόν.
Od. 13.224, εὐεργέα λώπην.

Od. 22.386, δικτύῳ ... πολυωπῷ.

Il. 13.599, ἐϋστρεφεῖ οἰὸς ἀώτῳ.

Il. 21.30, ἐϋτμήτοισν ἱμᾶσι.

Il. 23.115, σειρὰς τ᾽ εὐπλέκτους.

Il. 18.568, *Od.* 9.247, πλεκτοῖς ἐν ταλάροισι.

Od. 2.354, 380, ἐϋρραφέεσσι δοροῖσι.

Od. 18.368, δρέπανον ... εὐκαμπές.

Od. 21.6, κληῖδ᾽ εὐκαμπέα.

Il. 23.114, ὑλοτόμους πελέκεας; 23.118, ταναήκεϊ χαλκῷ.

Il. 18.595-96, χιτῶνας ... ἐϋννήτους.

Od. 14.529, χλαῖναν ... ἀλεξάνεμον.

Od. 14.24, δέρμα ... ἐϋχροές.

Od. 3.463, ἀκροπόρους ὀβελούς.

Od. 5.234-37: tools with which Odysseus builds his raft. The raft itself has its epithet, πολύδεσμος (5.22, 7.264), just as the great ships have theirs.

3. Compare the epithets of various animals. The lion, the eagle, and the horse have of course their epithets, but so has the goat, the sheep, the hare. It is the same with the vegetal world: not only great lofty trees have their epithets, but also celery (*Il.* 2.776) or simple grazing grass (*Od.* 6.90). Here, as elsewhere, the epithets do not mark any special degree of dignity, importance, greatness; they simply evince an object, giving it the flavor of its presence.

This is not to say, of course, that there are no special epithets for gods and heroes. Religious and heroic attributes are found in any tradition. What characterizes Homer, on the contrary, is the extension of the epithets on a grand, pervasive scale. Henceforward the beauty or dignity of form need not be something solemn. It is no longer confined to time-hallowed things. It is secularized, universalized. Shapeful rhythms of outline and function are seen at work in the world at large. They make up the prevailing patterns of what we touch, feel, or see. Hence the vast range and, at the same time, the stylistic uniformity of the epithets.

4. Significance

I here understand "significance" as a meaning which we may read into a certain word in relation with the context. Such a meaning is necessarily vague. It lies outside the word's literal acceptation. It is equally far removed from any pointed or deliberate reference. It must be distinguished, on the other hand, from that concrete poetic meaning which I have been discussing. For it is not inevitably present in the vivid poetic image itself. It intervenes insofar as the image stands in relation to other images. When, for instance,

Banquo observes in Macbeth's castle "this guest of summer, the temple-haunting martlet," the bird's image is wonderfully self-contained, but we cannot help feeling a contrast with the imminent crisis.

Homer's powerfully juxtaposed scenes are often fraught with this implicit significance. The epithets, for their part, bring it out within the scope of a single sentence. For the epithets, we have seen, simply affirm the existence of a thing. By doing so, they give it independent status as an image. But such an image is not static. Through the action of the poem such an image is seen in a necessary, and not accidental, connection with the act or situation which brings it into view. Hence comes an existential, nonnarrative relation between the noun-epithet image and its immediate context. Take, for instance, the line "So spoke divine swift-footed Achilles." The lack of narrative connection between the epithets and what Achilles is going to say only enhances the existential relation: the hero's unimpeachable figure on the one hand, and the precariousness of his words or actions on the other.

Since acts and situations are reduced to essential moments, this vital relation is seldom lacking in the poems. It is, of course, more or less remarkable from passage to passage. In the verse just quoted it might pass unnoticed; and yet it is implicit in all the instances of the same verse, making them similarly forcible.

There is the same kind of relation where a hero with his positive epithet is the object of a deadly blow, as, for example, in *Il.* 4.474, "Ajax struck Simoeisius-the-flourishing-yeoman. . . . " The ensuing simile (4.482 ff.) "he fell as a poplar falls . . . " only makes this implicit value of the epithet more palpable. There is of course no intention to bring out any effect; but there is an inescapable logic in the nature of things, the suggestion is unavoidable, and what stands out is fresh life crushed to the ground. The poet's representation is such as to make the truth of this contrast implicitly relevant, and we are justified in seeing it there.

Or take *Il.* 1.310, "he placed on the ship Chryseis-of-the-beautiful-cheeks"; cp. 1.143, 369. There is no intention to point out Chryseis' beauty and to set it in contrast with her experience. But images speak for themselves. Chryseis speaks not a word, she is a passive object taken and given back; yet she is seen in the full figure of a girl and has an epithet which is also applied to goddesses. The contrast may give us pause.[1]

5. Pathos

A poignant sense of impingement is inevitably produced when anything violently affected is presented by a noun-epithet image which brings out its sensuous material. Consider the phrase θαλερὴ δέ οἱ ἔσχετο φωνή, "checked was his [or her] flourishing voice" (*Il.* 17.696, 23.397, *Od.* 4.705, 19.472).

Or θαλερὴ δ᾽ ἐμιαίνετο χαίτη, "and soiled was the flourishing mane" (*Il.* 17.439; cp. 4.146–47, 17.51). Or χρόα λειριόεντα δάψει, "will rend the lily-like skin" (*Il.* 13.830–31; cp. 4.237, 5.858, 6.27, 8.452, 11.573, 13.180, 435, 553, 649, 14.406, 15.316, 16.805, 21.398, 22.321, 23.805, *Od.* 2.376, 4.749, 13.398, 430, 19.263).

Compare pp. 117–18 above. In such instances, the noun-epithet phrase simply composes a thing's image, giving it full exposure. There is no particular emphasis, no particular point. At the same time, however, a thing so exposed is seen in its inherent frailty through the act expressed in the sentence. We cannot help feeling an affecting contrast between the full-blown human voice and the experience which checks it, between the glossy hair or fine skin and the impinging blow. The pathos comes from the language, from the style itself; or, which is the same thing, from a certain mode of perception and representation. The epithets, which simply express and do not comment, here play their poetic role. Hence no cloying or surfeiting effect. We are presented again and again with a purely existential condition. It is as though the moment itself produced the sense of something tender or beautiful but bare and vulnerable. This contrast of values is more explicitly rendered, but without epithets, in *Il.* 16.794–99, 18.24, 19.284–85, 22.402–04; there is a deliberate touch that shifts the attention to the character in question.

Consider now the same kind of expression over a longer stretch. The river Scamander in *Il.* 21.1–382 is an instance in point. "They are filled with corpses my lovely streams (καλὰ ῥέεθρα)," Scamander cries under the onslaught of Achilles (218). Later he is attacked by Hephaestus' fire (342–82); and throughout the passage the phrase recurs like a refrain rendering the endangered current (352, 354, 361, 365, 382, cp. 345). The poet does not point to any transgression or profanation. Indeed, if anything, he takes the side of Achilles and Hephaestus. All the same, his form of expression—and not least the epithets—cannot but do justice to the situation. The fair-flowing, silver-eddying river is continually set before us in its fullness (cp. 1–2, 8, 15–16, 130, 206, 212, 228, 268, 304, 326). Those waters are inevitably beautiful and awesome, though disturbed, polluted, blighted. All the more are we made to feel the violation worked upon them.

Or consider throughout the *Iliad* the city of Troy with its epithets "lofty," "windy," "sacred," "lovely," "well-walled," "well-built," "well-founded," "of-the-large-streets." Notice especially how often it has such an epithet as an object of "conquering," "destroying": *Il.* 2.12, 113, 133, etc. The idea of a city's greatness and its destruction is worked into the language. Hence (inevitably though unwittingly) a tragic ring in the epithet, which is itself so positive. This is especially remarkable in the lines (*Il.* 6.448–49, 4.164–65)

ἔσσεται ἦμαρ ὅτ᾽ ἄν ποτ᾽ ὀλώλῃ Ἴλιος ἱρὴ
καὶ Πρίαμος καὶ λαὸς ἐϋμμελίω Πριάμοιο.

They would hardly be so haunting were it not for the epithets, which so un-
obstrusively affirm the city and its king even in the face of doom.

6. Life-giving earth

This significance of the epithets has been much debated in connection with
Il. 3.243–44. Helen, pointing out to Priam the Achaean warriors, wonders
at the absence of her brothers Castor and Polydeuces, thinking that they either
did not join the expedition or do not wish to appear on the spot because
ashamed of her; to which the poet adds:

... τοὺς δ᾽ ἤδη κάτεχεν φυσίζοος αἶα
ἐν Λακεδαίμονι αὖθι, φίλῃ ἐν πατρίδι γαίῃ.

but them now held the life-giving earth
in Lacedaemon, there in their native land.

John Ruskin remarks on these lines:

Note, here, the high poetical truth carried to the extreme. The poet has to
speak of the earth in sadness, but he will not let that sadness affect or
change his thoughts of it. No; though Castor and Pollux be dead, yet the
earth is our mother still, fruitful, life-giving. These are the facts of the
thing. Make what you will of them.[2]

Matthew Arnold commented on these remarks of Ruskin as follows:

This is a just specimen of that sort of application of modern sentiment to
the ancients, against which a student who wishes to feel the ancients truly,
cannot too resolutely defend himself. . . . It is not true, as to that particular
passage, that Homer called the earth φυσίζοος because "though he had to
speak of the earth in sadness, he would not let that sadness change or affect
his thoughts of it", but consoled himself by considering that "the earth is
our mother still, fruitful, life-giving". It is not true as a matter of general
criticism, that this kind of sentimentality, eminently modern, inspires Homer at all.[3]

And Milman Parry, after illustrating Düntzer on the influence of the meter
on the epithet, says,

The consequence of this scholarly indifference to Duntzer's theory is that
everyone has continued to be guided by his personal inclination in the

interpretation of the epithets. Some can use this approach with intelligence; others use it so as to bring us back to the days when indications of the weather were found in the epithets of the sea, and when Ruskin explained φυσίζοος αἶα (*Il.* 3.243) by saying: "The poet has to speak. . . ."[4]

Ruskin is right. The passage quoted comes from a chapter on the "pathetic fallacy," in which he elaborates on the fact that great poets express feeling in the pure representation of an object. Now such a principle applies to Homer, and not least to his noun-epithet images. For it is around these solid images of existence that the fluid, brittle action constantly revolves. Hence a silent tension, an implicit polarity. It is impossible not to feel an intimate, though unspoken, relation between the dead and the life-giving earth. Compare chapter 11, section 6.

As for Arnold's criticism, how can we not import our own sentiment into what we read or perceive? Nor need we force upon Ruskin the alleged consolatory intention. We are, rather, to make what we will of the Homeric words. What strikes us may thus be tragic rather than palliative: the fact that though earth is life-giving, yet the individual being lies mercilessly buried in it. Or both implications are true: the thought of earth's bounty and that of mortality are complementary. There is, in any case, an affecting resonance. It gives us pause. This is proof of how vital is the noun with its epithet.

As for Parry, his comment begs the question and leaves us in the dark. If we explain away the phrase as epic idiom for saying merely "they were dead," we might as well deny the feeling which runs through the whole passage. For what shall we say of Helen's wondering words and the presentation of her dead brothers which immediately follows? Surely we must not read this as a purely factual account. There is an inevitable contrast between what Helen believes and what has actually happened, between delusion and reality, between the vivid present and encompassing death.[5]

7. Places

Names of places with their epithets may be similarly significant. Take, for instance, *Il.* 20.390-92, where Achilles cries out over slain Iphition:

> Here is your death, and your birth on the lake
> Gygaean, where is your father's domain,
> by fish-rich Hyllos and eddying Hermos.

Why these epithets? What do they add to the meaning? What is their purport and significance?

Notice, first of all, that the epithets of places never give us in Homer any curious description, but simply focus on points of arrival, departure, passage, habitation, activity. This is to say that they solidly implant an act or condition where it rightfully belongs.

On the other hand, the action of the poems is such as to bring these places into a vital and pregnant relation with its development. It thus happens that places stand out in themselves and are, at the same time, dynamically related to what is happening. The epithets give them a self-contained existential evidence, and the action (which brings them into view) an inevitable relevance to the surrounding drama.

Hence there is pathos in the passage quoted above, "Fish-rich Hyllos" and "eddying Hermos" are there as they always were, with their epithets giving them their vital identity untouched by Iphition's death; and yet it is the tragic moment which gives them recognition. While the war is raging, the fair outlying world pursues its existence.

In the same spirit we may read the many instances in which a place-name with its epithet gives the provenance of a hero falling or fighting far away in Troy. Hippothoos, for instance, in *Il.* 17.301, falls "far from rich-clodded Larissa." Cp. 5.44, 479, 543, 6.13, 13.793, 16.288, 17.350, 611, 19.329, 20. 385, 485, 21.87, 141, 154, 157. Here are pregnant juxtapositions: on the one hand, the solitary hero in Troy and, on the other, distant but intimately associated places which are summoned up at a crucial point and yet are impassively self-existent. The effect is quite unintentional, but all the more significant in that it is inevitably rooted in the scheme of things. Virgil breaks the purely existential and implicit relation when he writes about Antor (*Aen.* 10.782):

> caelumque
> aspicit et moriens dulcis reminiscitur Argos.

Or about fallen Umbro (7.759-60):

> te nemus Aegitiae, vitrea te Fucinus unda,
> te liquidi flevere lacus.

Or read the *Catalogue of Ships,* paying attention to the place-names with their epithets and bearing in mind the same kind of associations. In *Il.* 2.559-61, for instance:

> Those who inhabited Argos and Tiryns-the-walled-one,
> Hermione and Asine that-command-the-deep-bay,
> Troezen and Eionae and vine-rich-Epidaurus.

These epithets simply give focus to a place insofar as it is inhabited and left behind by the Achaeans venturing to Troy. Far from having any geographic or eulogistic purpose, they do so by bringing out some feature which makes a place what it is to the beholder's eye: a field, a rock, a sea-washed shore. The many instances have a cumulative appeal. It is the whole of Greece which imaginatively stands out, as people leave to die. Here again is a juxtaposition both natural and tragic, unwittingly touched off by the poet by no other means than appropriateness of representation.

Quite a different effect but one due to the same forceful implication of the epithets may be found in *Il.* 1.154–57, where Achilles, in his quarrel, declares that he has nothing against the Trojans:

> for they never drove away my cattle and horses,
> never in rich-clodded man-nourishing Phthia
> did they plunder my crop, for many in between
> shadowy mountains there are and the sounding sea.

Suddenly the focus shifts; the war, the quarrel with Agamemnon loses its edge, as the epithets make us linger on Phthia, on the intervening mountains and sea, regardless of the present clash. War seems an encroachment.

19. TIME

1. Relation between the use of epithets and the duration of the action

There are two outstanding characteristics of Homer: the abundance of epithets and the clear concentration of the action within a span of days.[1] These two characteristics are, I believe, intimately connected with each other.

The Chadwicks, taking into account such characteristics in their survey of literature, remark: "This concentration of the action upon a brief period is doubtless to be connected with fulness of detail."[2]

But how is this connection to be conceived? We must not take it in an external and superficial sense, in the sense that the brevity of time must be compensated by abundance of treatment in order not to impair the size of an epic poem. This is not so, at least as far as Homer is concerned. The bulk is here internal to the action. There are no digressions: how many opportunities there might have been to lengthen the narrative by giving the past history of many of the characters! Nor is the Homeric fullness a question of mere detail: in the account of a banquet, for instance, we find only the essentials of eating and drinking, but no varied description of food and drinks.

We must look into the connection between fullness and concentration in time. What is it that in Homer fills the lapse of time? It is, of course, the action. But this action is not presented as a story *about* something that happened; it is, rather, broken up into single acts, into single moments of actuality. The use of epithets is symptomatic in this respect.

2. The epithets and the general action

The story is enacted, dramatized as it takes place, and the single sentences represent single moments of action moving forward. The noun-epithet phrases —which appear static and crystallized into patterns when divorced from their context—have a dynamic function as elements of these succeeding sentences.

They give body to a moment of time; and the moment is engrossed, drawn forward by its very weight.

Take the beginning of the *Iliad* as an illustration. We have a first moment of action "when they first stood apart in strife the lord of men Agamemnon and divine Achilles." The two men are solidly implanted where they are by names and epithets; at the same time the strong verb gives us the sense of a momentary dramatic position. The weight of bodies hangs in a transient stance. We are simply told a fact; and yet there is also existential suspense. This inevitably summons up what follows.

We next find Chryses. The golden scepter and the chaplets of far-shooting Apollo in his hands are one and all with his sudden appearance by the ships. Thanks to the epithets we have an immediate and compact representation which gives him power as an image. We cannot but expect him to speak out and impart a decisive thrust to the action.

We next see him rejected. "Along the shore of the wide-roaring sea in silence he walked; much then he prayed lord Apollo-to-whom-fair-tressed-Leto-gave-birth." Again, the epithets hold us to a pregnant moment. They do so by fixing the solitary spot and the god in magnetic juxtaposition. Once more the very presence of Chryses is prophetic of imminent development.

In such a way the whole action of the poem is seen as a succession of moments, whence the often observed fact that the Homeric narrative is continuous, that it is rectilinear, that it tolerates no interruptions.

This continuity of the action, however, should not be taken for granted as a habit of composition. It is an aspect of Homer's concreteness. It springs from the need to look at events in the actuality of their taking place. Nor would this kind of composition have any merit, if literally understood; it might merely signify an account of facts strung one after the other. No, what gives quality to the composition is the resilience of each sentence—the way in which fullness of representation is inextricably combined with a quickening movement. Hence the cumulative richness of experienced moments.

We should thus qualify the remark of the Chadwicks that concentration in time is connected with fullness of detail. As far as Homer is concerned, we must not take the term "detail" in a purely descriptive or digressive sense. We rather have a fullness which makes room for any successive moment in a vital series. The noun-epithet phrases, we have seen, are necessary ingredients of this fullness.

3. The epithets and the days

Since the successive sentences represent continuous moments of actual time within the action, it follows that the time-span so traced must coincide with the sequence of certain days. Without the division of the action into days, we

142

should have an intolerable accretion of moments indefinitely pursued hanging in a temporal void. In the absence of historical or mythical dates, the reference to the time of nature is indispensable. But we have seen that the epithets contribute to the body of any single sentence in representing an actual moment of time. This is thus tantamount to filling a parcel of any successive day or night. It is plain, therefore, that there is an intimate connection between the use of epithets and the division of the action into days.

It is not enough, however, to see this connection in purely logical terms. The surrounding day is something felt in its pervasive presence. In order to realize this, we must give each noun-epithet phrase its proper weight and let it linger within the easeful flow of the sentences. As the verse advances step by step, the edge of what is yet in store recedes, unfolding the waning day.

Take, as an example, the beginning of book 8 of the *Odyssey:* "When the early-born rose-fingered Dawn appeared,/up from bed arose the sacred might of Alcinous,/up rose divine Odysseus raider of cities./Alcinous' sacred might led the way/to the Phaeacian assembly ... /There sat they on the well-polished stones/near by." Here Alcinous orders that a ship be made ready for Odysseus' return. The story thus resumes a little later: "The youths went, as he bid, to the shore of the unvintaged sea./Then when down they came to the ship and sea,/the dark ship they drew out to the water's depth,/in the dark ship they set the mast and the sails,/into the loops-of-leather they adjusted the oars/all in due order and they spread the white sails."

Insofar as each act is visualized, we see it taking its place in the daylight air. We are not simply told a story. No, what is done is also a happening in its own right. And the Greek lines give us the cadence of each instance as it rises and subsides, yielding to what comes next. The initial daybreak is like a starting point which imparts the first movement of these phases. Hence the succeeding moments, whose incessant rhythm we hear, up to the night in which Odysseus tells his adventures.

The epithets, where they occur, establish points of focus, arrest, momentary suspense. Would such a style be possible if a certain day were not taken into account, if we had a general survey of Odysseus' life stretched out in indefinite time? Such a style would be quite out of place in this case. It would be ridiculous to give such prominence to Alcinous or Odysseus rising up from bed, walking, sitting down. We should have the impression of something too obvious even to be mentioned; or it would be as if Odysseus or Alcinous had nothing better to do. Least of all would there be any reason for Homer's noun-epithet phrases.

4. Visual perspective and progression in time

Let us draw some conclusions of a more general order.

The noun-epithet phrases hold us to the visual or tangible aspect of an act or state of being; on the other hand, the dynamic nature of the Homeric sentences is such that their mere contiguity produces progression in time. Here, as in any narrative, we have two distinct elements: the solid presence of things and the passage of time. But in Homer the noun-epithet phrases are so integrated with each sentence that these two elements of solidity in things and of transience in time are inextricably bound to each other.

Consider now the consequences of such a mode of expression over the whole length of the poems. The narrative, we might say, is implicit in the existential presentation; it flows naturally from sentence to sentence. Or, inversely, we might say that existence is always implicit in the narrative. On the one hand, we have a cumulative extension of moments laid out in their own right as if the plot were a mere excuse for their presentation; and, on the other, a plot laid out with extraordinary simplicity as if these cumulative moments were there to give it its cadence and its volume. Through the plot these moments take their disposition in time; through these moments the plot acquires its texture and substance. Hence a bare plot which brings into view a world picture. We have at once a visual display and a progression in time.

This is why, for instance, we are familiar with "windy Troy," "many-fountained Ida," "the well-built walls," "the close-fitting gates," "deep-eddying Scamander," etc., although we are never given any description of the city or of its surroundings. It is that these things are so mentioned only insofar as they integrate a certain act, giving it body and focus; only insofar as they are instantly seen, touched, visited, or presented as points of departure or arrival, defence or attack. As always in Homer, the happening is gathered into the scenery, the scenery into the happening.

It is as if the action (which is time) drew with it in its course the features of things (which are elements of space), and as if, vice versa, the features of things clung to the action, preventing it from wandering off into a thin narrative of its own. Thus, in the *Iliad,* while the scenery of the place inevitably and almost unwittingly becomes part of the action, the action itself remains solidly centralized between Troy and the sea. Nothing happens but it is seen in its field of vision; no place is brought into view but it is a theater of action. The treatment is both expansive and progressive. There is always a space, an opening perspective wherein things stand out before they make room for what follows, lit up by the epithets which thus produce moments of visualization within the narrative.

5. Homer and Virgil

A glance at Virgil as a foil to Homer in this respect might help to drive home my point.

Look at the designations of cities in the *Aeneid*—Troy falling, Carthage arising, Rome looming in the future. These are mentioned with a view to their fortunes, with a sense of their history or as terms of hope, memory, pride, regret. If they are qualified at all, they have a pointed attribute. For in this long perspective of time they become symbolical of some fate, they assume an ideal identity. Compare the way in which a city is presented as sending her sons to war: for example, *Aen.* 10.172, 179, 184. How could Homeric epithets be here at home in their function of crystallizing a point of focus to the immediate action?

The same perspective of time is an important element in the presentation of characters. Why such pointed qualifications as *pius Aeneas, contemptor divum Mezentius, fidus Achates*? One basic reason is that these people are seen in their long careers, in their persistent behavior. Or why the usual scarceness of epithets with warriors and their arms in the battle scenes? It is that the focus lies somewhere other than in the momentary clash: what matters more is a protracted effort or a sense of the whole campaign. We see Turnus, Pallas, Aeneas, Mezentius engaged in incredible feats, producing victories and defeats which affect the course of the whole war. This is not the case in Homer, not at least in the same way. Why so? Even Achilles must await his moment, shaped by his epithets into the same kind of image as anyone else holding his ground. And the long-shadowed spear has its way of being hurled, the well-balanced shield its own way of being held up, the horse-haired crest its own way of waving in the wind: these things keep even the mightiest hero in a sort of natural stance.

There is hardly a passage in Virgil which might not lend itself to this sort of analysis. A good example is Aeneas watching Carthage being built, his actual view merging with the idea of how people set about bringing their ideals to fulfillment (*Aen.* 1.419–38). Compare Odysseus in Phaeacia, wondering (*Od.* 7.43–45) "at the harbors and well-balanced ships . . . at the long walls, lofty, palisade-crowned, a marvel to see." Here, as elsewhere, the objects so rendered in their noun-epithet phrases give focus, substance, extension to a gaze which expends itself in the present without any ulterior motive. Odysseus is absorbed in perception. He is wholly receptive to the moment. If he were to contrast his own homelessness with the rich, settled city laid before him, the language would be altogether different. Why so? Because in the broader survey of time the thought of personal or public fortunes would blur the light of the present; consequently the aspects of things would be left out of focus, and the noun-epithet phrases would have no reason to occur.

6. Historical considerations

It would be facile to attribute these differences between Homer and Virgil to their respective ages. On this strength, primitive simplicity might be opposed to later philosophical thinking. Or it might be maintained that Homer's stress on single acts is only natural in a society which lacked historical records, while Virgil's synthesis is at home at the height of the Roman Empire. Or, again, we might be told that Homer's composition is what we should expect in recitation before an audience, whereas Virgil's vast survey is characteristic of a literary artist who spends years at his work.

These explanations are most limited in scope. They may enlighten us on the conditions surrounding each work, but not at all on the actuality of the work itself. While generalizing about the environment, they ignore the moment of perception which lies at the source of the poetry. As for the aesthetic problem, they do no more than transpose it from the poet's mind to some abstract historical entity.

We should thus look at Homeric poetry as an achievement *sui generis.* It is not to be explained as a stage in culture and poetic craft. It is, rather, a new departure. Nowhere else does there seem to be such visual focus on so extensive a scale. If one looks at the great ancient epics of the East, one will find in this respect something closer to Virgil than to Homer. Heroes are idealized and their whole lives are taken into account; cycles of myth or history occur wherein nations or tribes are seen in their comprehensive destinies. Myth, religious symbolism, narrative scope naturally preclude Homer's kind of representation, which rests on lingering, self-developing moments.

How then shall we explain in historical terms Homeric expression seen in this light? What conditions favored this breaking of any narrative contents into moments of pure visualization? If historical considerations are called for, they should be such as to have some intrinsic (and not merely circumstantial) connection with the poet's mode of representation—namely, with his mode of perception and expression. In other words, we should look at the intellectual climate of the age and country.

The Ionia of the ninth and eighth centuries B.C. provides a most fitting background. For this was an open vantage-place situated between the remains of Mycenaean civilization and the rise of the city-states, between mythical memories and imminent human discoveries—a vantage-place where art was about to conspire with philosophy in the perception of nature. In such an atmosphere, we imagine, gods and heroes might be visualized in the light of common day; and all narrative complexities might be intuitively reduced to make room for the rendering of balance, position, form as actually perceived in the sensible world.

For consider the artistic and philosophical implications in Homer's mode of representation. What they portend is no less than the idea of time in its immediate and sensuous manifestation. There is in Homer a new sense of time in the making: acts and states of being caught in their realization rather than described; each fact felt in its incidence, each incidence in its cadence. Hence a rhythm which is meaning as well as sound, a beat which is filled with the pulse of life: time made palpable in things.

While the subject matter of the poems ostensibly harks back to the Mycenaean past, the form of expression continually quickens the material into actuality. Homer is here a forerunner. What is ultimately the same kind of perception lies at the source of much that is vital in early Greek art— in the *kouroi,* for instance, those bodies held in a moment of supreme poise, in which the mass is relieved of any static weight, each part and limb animated by a life of its own. Here, as in Homer, it is as if time penetrated the solid material. We have a materialized instance rather than a statue whose subject matter is taken for granted.

What we call (in the artistic sense) a shape, a form, an image arrests any fleeting thing at a point of focus, in such a way that we still feel the moment of suspense, the precarious rest between past and future. Time is made manifest in existence, existence in time. Homer makes us strongly aware of this coincidence on a massive scale. Here the epithets come into play. Where they occur, they help contain a single act or state in its sudden immanence. They mark a stillness within the movement, an intransitive quality within the transitive action. Hence a natural poise in their use. They can neither exaggerate nor curtail. They aim neither at sublimity nor minuteness. They simply let a thing rise to its occasion; and in this they concur with the very logic of perception.

PART III: THEORIES OF THE EPITHET

20. DEFINITIONS OF THE EPITHET

1. Rhetorical approach

Aristotle, our earliest evidence on the subject, uses the term *epithet* to describe a certain figure of speech. In the opening chapters of *Rhetoric* III he deals with it along with compound words, *glossai,* metaphors, and similes.

We do not find here any definition of the epithet, but Aristotle's meaning is clear. The most important passage in this respect is that in which Alcidamas is blamed for his excessive use of epithets (III.3.3). The examples quoted are not only "wet sweat," but also such phrases as "with a precipitous movement of the soul" or "to clothe the body's shame." These are opposed to saying simply, "sweat," "precipitously," "put on one's clothes." What we normally call "noun-epithet phrase" is here an instance of a larger group. Why, we may ask, is such a sentence as "he clothed the body's shame" an epithet? The reason is that there is, at bottom, a plain meaning which may be expressed as "he dressed"; and the extensive periphrasis may be considered an extension of it, an epithet which substitutes for the shorter expression. In the same way the epithet "earth-shaker" might be found in place of the name Poseidon.

Epithet is thus for Aristotle any form of expression which, in designating a thing, swerves away from the direct objective statement. It appears to be called κόσμος in *Poetics* 22.7; and it implies ornamentation, amplification. We may compare Demetrius's term ἐπιφώνημα (2.106-08) for any part of a passage which is supposed to add adornment rather than give the required meaning: such is Sappho's sentence "low on the earth is the purple flower," following the representation of the trampled hyacinth.

It is as if, in saying anything, there existed two clearly distinct modes of expression which we may call the plain and the ornamental. It is the basic function of speech, Aristotle tells us (*Rhetoric* 3.2.1-2; cp. *Poetics* 22.1-2), to be perspicuous, to make a meaning clear, and this is achieved by the use of familiar, ordinary words (κύρια); words which are in any way strange or rare (ξενικά) serve only to provide pathos, color, solemnity. The latter attract attention: people wonder at the unfamiliar, while the familiar passes unobserved. Epithets are thus conspicuous among the so-called ξενικά.

This rhetorical sense of "epithet" is well established. The term is thus applied in English to any strong, unusual expression of praise, abuse, characterization. It so recurs in Shakespeare. In *Othello* I.i.13-14, for instance, we read "with bombast circumstance / horribly filled with epithets of war." We find here the broad Aristotelian sense. These epithets are statements, utterances. We are given the feeling of a flaunting speech filled with bloody imagery. There is, of course, no question about war and its attributes.

2. Grammatical approach

Quite opposed to the rhetorical viewpoint is the grammatical one: the epithet regarded as a natural element of the language, as a part of speech. What stands out is not a stylistic feature but a class of words. This presupposed, of course, a classification of the vocabulary according to form, meaning, and syntax. The epithet as a distinctive word could be conceived only within the general framework of the parts of speech.[1] Interestingly, in this case the rhetorical interest preceded the grammatical.

We find the term *epithet* first used in a grammatical sense in Dionysius Thrax (first century B.C.). He gives to the parts of speech a classification which is quite close to our own. The epithet (or adjective), however, is not a category by itself; it is a subdivision of the noun and is called ὄνομα ἐπίθετον. Dionysius distinguishes in this connection some twenty-four kinds of noun. The epithet comes third in the series after the proper name (κύριον) and the appellative (προσηγορικόν; for example, "man," "horse"):

> The epithet is placed beside a proper name or an appellative, with the same frame of reference; and it expresses praise or blame. It may be taken in three ways: in relation to the mind (as in "wise," "licentious"), to the body (as in "swift," "slow"), to external circumstances (as in "rich," "poor").[2]

Apollonious Dyscolus, again, uses the same term, ὄνομα ἐπίθετον, though his classification of nouns differs from that of Dionysius.[3] Similarly the Latin grammarians from Varro to Priscianus do not offer any separate treatment of the adjective. We find the term *nomen adjectivum* corresponding to ὄνομα ἐπίθετον.

This treatment of the epithet as a noun is very significant. Steinthal writes:

> No one in antiquity, perhaps, even thought of considering the ἐπίθετον, the adjective, as a separate part of speech. . . . Neither Aristotle, nor the

Stoics, nor the grammarians could find any such cue in their reflections on language. The Aristotelian category of ποιόν could not suggest any division between δικαιοσύνη and δίκαιος. For there were only two possibilities: either to see the former as ποιότης just as well as the latter, or to conceive the δικαιοσύνη as πρᾶγμα or οὐσία νοητή, and in this case δίκαιος was applied to the οὐσία which was inherent in δικαιοσύνη. . . .

Equally removed from this separation between epithet and noun were the Stoics who saw in every ὄνομα a ποιότης. Our common notion of a thing possessing its characteristics would sound strange to them. Every characteristic, every ποιότης is a σῶμα; a blending and compenetration of many σώματα into a unity.

As for the grammarians, the very term ἐπίθετον, *adjectivum,* implies that there is no stress on the opposition between a thing and its quality. The ἐπίθετον designated, like any other noun, a σῶμα, a πρᾶγμα, an οὐσία '; λευκόν is what is white, the white thing, the white color, and in this respect it does not differ from any other ὄνομα.[4]

It is the testimony of the grammarians which is important here. Just as the epithet is a noun, so is the noun—any noun—an expression of quality as well as substance. "It is the function of nouns to attribute particular or common qualities to things," say, for instance, the followers of Apollonius and Herodianus, and this is echoed by Priscianus.[5] ποιότης, *qualitas* are here the key words, not only in reference to abstract nouns: such a noun as "man" or "horse" also expresses quality—the quality which constitutes a man or a horse. Apollonius cites in this connection a noun-epithet phrase of Homer (*Il.* 3.229): οὗτος δ' Αἴας ἐστὶ πελώριος. The pronoun here points to the fact that Ajax is there (ὕπαρξις), while the name with the epithet introduces the idea of ποιότης.[6]

By regarding the epithet as a noun, the ancient grammarians avoid the rhetorical pitfalls. For they naturally keep out of the picture the perplexing questions of style which do not lend themselves to systematic treatment. It is the language itself which offers its evidence; and this evidence has its inherent truth, which must necessarily have a bearing on literature as well as on common speech. It might be objected, of course, that this avoidance of stylistic questions is quite negative and that grammatical generalities will hardly serve to explain the Homeric epithets. Nevertheless, an important principle is here established which is too often ignored or taken for granted. Its poetic implications may be further developed.

We may wonder now at our custom of opposing the noun and the adjective. How and when did this opposition come about? I think that it may be traced back to the influence of Scholastic philosophy. Aristotle did indeed oppose the subject to its predicates (*Categories,* chap. 5); but he did so on the grounds of pure logic. With his solid empiricism, he did not try to force the facts of language into a logical scheme. He dealt with each subject matter on its own merits. Thus, when treating the epithets in his *Rhetoric*, he had chiefly in view the oratory of his time. When, on the other hand, he turned to the parts of speech, he focused on the basic elements of ὄνομα, ῥῆμα, σύνδεσμος. He lets the various phenomena come within the purview of his philosophy of nature. His very logic, we might say, is concrete. It is applied to the ways of thought and not to reality as a whole. Not so with Scholasticism. The facts of language, among others, were here seen as manifestations of *a priori principles*.

We thus find in Scholasticism the term *nomen substantivum,* to which is opposed the *adjectivum.*[7] See how Aquinas uses these terms. In *Summa* I, 39, 3-4: "Nomina substantiva significant aliquid per modum substantiae, nomina vero adjectiva significant aliquid per modum accidentis quod inhaeret subjecto"; in *Sententiae,* I.9.1: "Substantivum autem significationem suam habet absolutam; sed adjectivum ponit significationem suam circa subjectum"; in *De Potentia,* 9.6: "Nomina substantiva significant per modum substantiae, adjectiva vero per modum accidentis." It is plain how the opposition of these terms was thence introduced into grammar and into our way of thinking.

What are we to make of the epithet or adjective viewed in this way? What is *significatio per accidens*? What, more particularly, is *accidens* in this sense? The word *accidens* implies something that happens fortuitously, unexpectedly. Hence the adjective is not only something added to the substantive, but imputed to it, secondary, adventitious. It is opposed to the *substantivum,* whose meaning is self-contained, absolute, necessitated by its own nature. We have a central substance to which we may attribute this or that attribute.

Aquinas's language also implies, it is true, that the meaning expressed by the adjective *inheres* in the substantive or subject; but once this opposition between them was brought out and emphasized, the path was clearly laid open for an even wider divergence. The alleged secondary value of the adjective might be presented as subjective, imaginary, arbitrary—as something imputed but not necessarily there. At the same time, however, this subjective element of the adjective might be stressed and exalted at the expense of the objective *nomen substantivum:* here was room for the indeterminate, for infinite qualification and nuance laid over the dull reality of objects taken for granted. This happened most obviously in the Romantic age.[8]

These considerations, if pursued at length, would carry us quite beyond the problem of defining the epithet. But they are relevant to it. For the notion of qualities removed from things throws us off balance. It undermines our perception of quality and identity expressed in one form. How recompose this unity? The epithet claims here its rightful place. In order to justify it theoretically, we must realize the necessity of its function in the expression. Failing this, it comes to be viewed as something superfluous or quite arbitrary.

3. Ambiguities

Ambiguities necessarily arise: the term *epithet* used on the one hand for a figure of speech, as in Aristotle's *Rhetoric,* and on the other for a certain class of words, as in the grammarians. These two acceptations interfere with each other. We find in the term itself a disturbing ambivalence.

This ambiguity is already shown in Quintilian's passage, 8.6.40: "Ornat enim ἐπίθετον, quod recte dicimus appositum, a nonnullis sequens dicitur." Cp. 8.6.10, *adpositum=epitheton.* Quintilian here discusses the epithet, like Aristotle, along with the figures of speech; and yet, at the same time, he treats the epithets as a class of words: *sequens* and *adpositum* are forerunners of the later *adiectivum.* His examples of the epithet are merely adjectives: *dulcis musti* and *dentibus albis* (8.2.10), *umida vina* (8.6.40).

The ambiguity is blatant where Quintilian says, "Ornat enim ἐπίθετον. . . . " Aristotle similarly uses the word κόσμος, Demetrius ἐπικοσμεῖν, but not with such a narrow frame of reference. What strikes us here is that *ornare* should be imputed to the epithet, and that the epithet should, at the same time, be treated as something very close to a part of speech.

The same kind of ambiguity comes up again in the later grammarians. In their treatises they tend to treat the epithet in the section concerned with the parts of speech and then again among the various tropes.[9] The instances given are adjectives. What is said about their function often echoes the definition of Dionysius Thrax: "laudandi vel vituperandi gratia."

No less significant in this respect are the various translations and renderings of ἐπίθετον. They follow upon Quintilian's *sequens adpositum.* We thus find in Diomedes (Keil, 1:323): "Quaedam mediae potestatis quae adiecta nominibus significationem a coniunctis sumunt . . . a quibusdam adiectiones dicuntur"; in Charisius (Keil, I.533), "appellationes consequentes, adiecticiae" or (273) "dictio vocabulo adiecta." It is in Priscianus that *adiectivum* appears to be firmly established (2.27; Keil, 2:59ff.).

While the Latin grammarians continue to treat the epithet as a kind of noun, it is also clear that there is a rhetorical influence in their definitions. Note how the term *dictio* creeps in instead of the ordinary *nomen*; note also that the Greek term ἐπίθετον is often kept along with its Latin equivalents, as if the translations were not self-explaining.

This ambiguity of the term *epithet* is an inevitable one, due as it is to the impossibility of confining to a certain part of speech or discourse the baffling concept of quality. For how could the epithet be so singled out? How could qualities be expressed apart from things? We may here see how right were the ancient grammarians in taking the epithet as a noun, in thus positing an encompassing unity of quality and substance. The breaking of this unity opened the way to inconsistencies. Qualities removed from things came to be regarded as arbitrary additions, as rhetorical effects.

4. Epitheton perpetuum

For the sake of greater accuracy, the term *epithet* was further specified by
the ancient commentators of the Latin poets. We find: *epitheton perpetuum,
naturale, generale, familiare, firme et perpetuo appositum.* [10]

Porphyrio has some interesting instances of *epitheton perpetuum.* On Horace, *Carm.* 1.37.29, "deliberata morte ferocior," he writes: "Deliberata utrum
pro cogitata positum est—an vero 'de qua plerique deliberant, id est dubitant,
ut sit hoc perpetuum epitheton mortis." Cp. on Horace, *Carm.* 4.14.18, 1.34.9,
Epod. 3.17, 5.15, *Sat.* 1.1.36. Servius uses *generale, familiare* besides *perpetuum:* see his comments on Virgil, *Ecl.* 3.33, 6.13, *Aen.* 2.223, 4.178, 6.279.
He specifies the sense of *epitheton naturale,* commenting on Virgil's Neptune
angered at the storm in *Aen.* 1.127, "prospiciens summa placidum caput
extulit unda." He writes, "Quaerunt multi quemadmodum *placidum* si graviter
commotus, quasi non fieri possit ut irascatur ventis, propitius sit Troianis.
Epitheta enim naturalia sunt, alia ad tempus; et *placidum* ut naturale Neptuni
est, ita graviter ad tempus ob factam tempestatem."

Perpetuum, naturale is thus opposed to what is *ad tempus.* This is to say
that what is naturally permanent is opposed to what is merely temporal,
occasional, circumstantial. Such an epithet brings out a quality which is inherent in the thing itself. Thus, in Virgil's passage, the god maintains his
native sovereign calm, angry though he is. Servius, with his sense of the epithet, does justice to the situation. Neptune's *placidum caput* stands its own
ground. It is unconditioned by the storm. If also presented *ad tempus,* it
is only because of its inherent gravity: "graviter *ad tempus ob factam tempestatem.*"

It should be emphasized that *epitheton perpetuum* does not at all imply
an epithet which is constantly found side by side with a certain noun. In the
instances of Porphyrio and Servius we mostly find epithets which are rare
or unique in the combinations which are pointed out; *deliberata* or *libera* said
of death, for instance. What we have is an inherence of meaning, even if the
word is used once only. This is why *perpetuum* is also *naturale, generale,
familiare, firme et perpetuo appositum.* There is no notion of an epithet sanctioned by usage and so frequent as to become almost meaningless.

Such a term as *epitheton perpetuum* thus has its intrinsic justification. It is
a way of asserting more explicitly what the classification of ἐπίθετον as
ὄνομα in the ancient grammarians implies. Compare the term *positivum* in
Macrobius (*Sat.* 1.4.9), used both for what we call "substantive" and to
designate the epithet or adjective in its positive aspect as opposed to comparative and superlative. What we have in *perpetuum* and in its synonyms is the
sense of a substantive idea which retains something of the ancient conception
of the noun.

The same cannot be said of a term which is very commonly used today: *epitheton ornans*. I cannot find any trace of it in any ancient author. It seems to have been first used at the beginning of the last century. We thus find it in Doering's commentary on Horace, *Carm.* 1.4.4, "canis . . . pruinis." Orelli is more explicit: on Horace, *Carm.* 1.28.22, "Illyricis obruit undis," he remarks that *Illyricis* "defendi potest si habemus pro simplici epitheto ornante seu poetico"; on Horace, *Ep.* 1.16.7–8, "rubicunda . . . corna," he writes, "Est quod dicunt epitheton ornans, id est perpetuam aliquem et communem ποιότητα exprimens, non statum singularem moxque transeuntem in alium."

Though loosely used as synonymous with *perpetuum*, *ornans* really points to something quite different, or even opposite: a dispensable weak embellishment. This at least is the way in which it is currently used; for no trouble is ever taken to explain what *ornare* means, and we are put into the habit of taking epithets for granted, of considering them a mere conventional ornament. The chief trouble lies in the fact that this term is used for poetry. "Epitheton ornans seu poeticum," says Orelli. And the definition has been taken over, as if it were the poet's role to express agreeable superfluities.

5. Further subdivisions

The definition of the epithet as ornamental rightly gave pause to scholars. It was clearly inadequate. The attempts to clarify it, however, did not dwell on a criticism of the concept of ornamentation. Rather, the ornamental criterion was accepted as it was, and the epithets themselves were further subdivided according to loose semantic functions. It was decided which epithets were ornamental and which were not. Or the epithets as a whole were classified into certain fields of meaning. Homer obviously lent himself to this kind of analysis. Here was an abundant use of epithets covering all sorts of objects, and these distinctions could throw light on whatever favorite semantic trends might thus be advanced or defended.

Thus, for instance, Meylan-Faure [11] illustrates the epithets as "distinctive" (for example, patronymics), "descriptive" (for example, "foot-lifting horse"), "laudative," "moral." Düntzer [12] sets apart the "determinative (*Bestimmende*) epithets" (for example, patronymics) and divides the others into two classes: (1) "stress-epithets," (*hebende*) such as "great," "glorious," and (2) "characterizing epithets" (*wesentliche*), which give a thing's essential trait, as in "cold snow," "evil war." Or the subdivision is based on relevance to the context; and, accordingly, the epithets are ornamental or necessary in varying degrees. Thus Bergson [13] distinguishes the epithets between those that are necessary to the intelligence of the context ("determinative"), those that introduce a certain tone or nuance ("qualifying," "affective"), and those that have nothing to do with the context ("ornamental").

But how can we explain the epithets by thus removing them from their living sentences and looking at them in a sort of neutral abstraction? And how can we oppose a purely poetic (or concrete) meaning to a meaning which is "necessary to the intelligence of the context"? Does not every word contribute to the understanding of a poetic passage, and in a way which is neither exclusively affective nor ornamental nor mechanically required to bring out the sense? Take, for instance, "swift-footed Achilles." The epithet, to use Düntzer's terminology, is at once *hebend* and *wesentlich;* it at once stresses and characterizes, it bestows a quality which is also a distinction. We have before us the image of Achilles in its integrity. Moreover, in doing this, the epithet also contributes to the meaning. It confers a necessary weight to whatever Achilles might be doing and to the moment he does it. Here is a force of suggestion which cannot be ignored unless we take language to be merely a system of signs.

6. Milman Parry and the function of the epithet

All ambiguity is swept away by Milman Parry. He wastes no time in making nice semantic distinctions or in trying to find how the principle of ornamentation may be made consistent with meaning. The epithet now finds its place in a sharply defined system whose basic element is the formula defined by Parry as "an expression regularly used, under the same metrical conditions, to express an essential idea." [14]

The "essential idea" is here taken in a most rudimentary sense: the mere designation of a thing or of an act. This neglect of meaning, however, is compensated for by stress on meter. All the words which occur in a formula are justified and enhanced insofar as they serve to make up the satisfying flow of hexameter verse.

In this system the epithet has the most obvious metrical value. Whereas other words serve mostly to complete the sentence, the epithet appears to be a dispensable luxury. This is, however, a luxury which continually recurs in Homer. Its very frequency appeared to reflect a habit, an assimilated stylistic device; and it was the study of the epithets which first led Parry to postulate a system of formulas so complex that it could be regarded only as traditional.

What then is for Parry an "ornamental epithet"? What is it that makes an epithet "ornamental"? It is its use in versification. The "ornamental epithet" is thus given its unique characterization. It constitutes a metrical abstraction. It is neither a part of speech nor a rhetorical figure in the ancient sense. It is also something peculiar to Homer or to poetry which is alleged to come from oral tradition.

Parry's ruling is here categorical. Having defined the epithet in general most unobtrusively, [15] he divides all the epithets into two main classes: (1) *particu-*

larized (that is, functional, relevant to the occasion, as, for example, "left" in "left hand") and (2) fixed (for example, "heavy" in "heavy hand," with no particular relevance to the context). It is the latter which, of course, claim Parry's attention, whence the equation: fixed=ornamental=required by the meter=traditional.

Again and again Parry returns to this basic assumption. For instance: "The use of the fixed epithet, that is, of the ornamental epithet, is entirely dependent on its convenience in versification." [16]

This peremptoriness is characteristic. For Parry's noun-epithet phrase is a metrical unit at a fixed place in the hexameter, its necessity guaranteed by the fact that there are no other metrically equivalent units that might replace it in expressing the same "essential idea": any attention to a particular meaning in a certain passage would undermine the forthrightness of the formula.

The view of a conventional hexametric language here comes to a head. The result is a denial of meaning, poetic language being no more than finely worked fabric laid over the few "essential ideas" of the epic subject matter. Did this constitute progress in respect to previous views of the epithet? Whatever the case may be, there is something refreshing in such a radical position. The ground is cleared. We are now faced with a more fundamental problem. Such questions arise as: Is there any connection between rhythm and meaning? Can rhythm be so deprived of meaning? Is meaning only meaning insofar as it is particularized? Is not poetic fullness suggestive of meanings other than those that can be literally explained in a narrative sense?

21. INTERPRETATIONS OF THE EPITHET

1. Ornamentation and meaning

The flaws inherent in the preceding definitions of the epithet come up in the work of interpretation. We find, on the one hand, the weak notion of ornamentation; and, on the other, the attempt to find meaning in what is merely pointed, relevant to narrative or discursive details.

There are good examples of this twofold tendency in Stanford's commentary to the *Odyssey*.[1] On *Od.* 6.1, ὡς ὁ μὲν ἔνθα καθεῦδε πολύτλας δῖος Ὀδυσσεύς, he comments, "The first *Epithet* is fully operative, the second is conventional." According to this interpretation the fact that Odysseus is weary after his ordeal at sea justifies the epithet πολύτλας, "much-suffering," while δῖος, "divine," has no such justification and is merely conventional or, which is the same, ornamental.

What need is there to imply that Odysseus was tired when falling asleep? This burdens the passage with a futile and wholly unpoetic propriety. No, we find the noun-epithet phrase in *Od.* 6.1 because the hero is centrally exposed (cp. 7.1, 133 etc.). What needs to be stressed is precisely the lack of point.

Stanford reflects here a trend which harks back to the ancient Scholiasts. Here are some examples,[2] first of epithets supposed to be ornamental:

Sch. A on *Il.* 2.45, ἀμφὶ δ' ἄρ' ὤμοισιν βάλετο ξίφος ἀργυρόηλον: Agamemnon's sword is here said to be "silver-studded," elsewhere "gold-studded" (cp. 22.29-30). . . . Such words are not used in their proper sense (κυρίως) but in obeisance to poetic usage (κατ' ἐπιφορὰν ποιητικῆς ἀρεσκείας). Just as the poet expands on corslet and shield (11.19-28, 32-40), so he there adorns the sword (11.29-30).

Sch. T on the same passage: The epithet is either redundant (παρέλκει) or the sword has silver studs mixed with golden ones.

Sch. b T on *Il.* 15.170-71, νιφὰς . . . ὑπὸ ῥιπῆς αἰθρηγενέος Βορέαο. How can snowy Boreas be "born in a clear sky"? The epithet is therefore redundant, as in *Il.* 6.377, πῇ ἔβη Ἀνδρομάχη λευκώλενος.

Sch. b T on *Il.* 6.377, πῇ ἔβη Ἀνδρομάχη λευκώλενος: The epithet is the poet's (πρός ποιητοῦ), not the character's.

Sch. A b T on *Il.* 8.1, ἠώς κροκόπεπλος: This is said when there is much darkness and little light. But it is a poetic periphrasis (ποιητική περίφρασις).

Sch. A on *Il.* 6.160, δῖ᾽ Ἄντεια: The epithet is added for ornamentation (κατὰ ποιητικὸν κόσμον), as in the case of δῖα Κλυταιμνήστρη (*Od.* 3.266).

We may oppose to these the instances of pointedness. Consider the following passages:

Sch. b T on *Il.* 1.53-55, ἐννῆμαρ . . . λευκώλενος Ἥρη: Rightly does Hera suggest to Achilles that he seek the causes of the plague. . . . For Hera is the air; and Achilles, who was also a physician, having been a pupil of Chiron, perceived that the air was corrupted by the plague. Hera is said to be white-armed because the air is transparent, bright. . . .

Sch. b T on *Il.* 1.329, τὸν δ᾽ εὗρον παρά τε κλισίῃ καὶ νηῒ μελαίνῃ: Through "black ship" the poet denotes the gloom of Achilles' situation.

Sch. b on *Il.* 3.16, Τρωσὶν μὲν προμάχιζεν Ἀλέξανδρος θεοειδής: Why does the poet call "godlike" a man so outrageous? For this is an epithet of praise and glorification. The objection would be well-taken if Paris were praised in all respects. But the poet praises his outward shape; and the truth of this praise makes the reproaches more credible, when they are made. Also our hatred of Paris is increased in that he so shames his own beauty.

Sch. A b T on *Il.* 3.75, Ἄργος ἐς ἱππόβοτον καὶ Ἀχαιΐδα καλλιγύναικα: Paris calls Achaea a land of beautiful women, supposing it to be so through his love for Helen.

Sch. b T on *Il.* 13.66, τοῖν δ᾽ ἔγνω πρόσθεν Ὀϊλῆος ταχὺς Αἴας: The Telamonian Ajax, being himself strong, did not notice the help of the god, but the Locrian Ajax was weaker and quick in noticing it.

Sch. T on *Il.* 13.553, εἴσω ἐπιγράψαι τέρενα χρόα νηλέϊ χαλκῷ: because Antilochus was young; thus in *Il.* 11.115, ἀπαλὸν δέ σφ᾽ἦτορ ἀπηύρα.

Sch. H.M.Q. on *Od.* 3.442, μενεπτόλεμος Θρασυμήδης: Rightly does Nestor use the epithet for Thrasymedes and not for his other sons (as in 414); for Thrasymedes served in the army with his father and thus had valor.

Sch. P on *Od.* 4.718, ἐπ᾽ οὐδοῦ ἷζε πολυκμήτου θαλάμοιο: "Much-wrought" applied to the chamber is not a mere epithet, for it refers to Odysseus' toil in building it (23.192).

The ineptness of these pointed explanations is especially glaring in the case of the "illogical epithet" [3]—this is to say, an epithet which seems to run counter to the required sense, most notably where a wicked character appears to be glorified:

Il. 6.160, δῖ᾽ Ἄντεια: Sch. b T explain "although divine" and refer to certain critics who read Διάντεια.

Il. 11.138 (cp. 123), Ἀντιμάχοιο δαΐφρονος: Sch. b: "*courageous* is said

ironically; for he incited others to fight in spite of his own bad disposition. . . ."
Zenodotus read here κακόφρονος instead of δαΐφρονος.

Od. 14.18, ἀντίθεοι μνηστῆρες, explained by Sch. Q.V. as "opposed to the
gods." Similarly Sch. E. M. V. on *Od.* 1.70, ἀντίθεον Πολύφημον.

Od. 1.29, ἀμύμονος Αἰγίσθοιο: Sch. H.P.V.: "Either he was a fine man before he committed adultery or the epithet refers to his lineage" (Compare
Stanford: "Here referring to physical beauty since Aegisthus was far from
blameless." [4] Bentley, it is said, wished to read μνήσατο γὰρ κατὰ νοῦν ἀνοή-
μονος Αἰγίσθοιο.). [5] See chapter 17, section 4.

2. The epithet "by nature"

Refreshingly positive at this point is the view of the epithet "by nature."
We are given a cue by Sch. A on *Il.* 8.555, where the stars are said to be bright
"around the shining moon." To the objection that the brightness of the
stars is here inconsistent with that of the moon, the Scholiast replies: "The
moon is not said to be bright on a particular occasion, but universally."
Similarly, Sch. b and T refer to the interpretation "bright by nature."

The Scholiasts occasionally use the term "by nature" in this sense. See their
notes on *Il.* 1.432, 4.434, 9.14, 15.630, 16.161. See especially Sch. B.H.Q.
on *Od.* 9.425, ὄιες . . . δασύμαλλοι. He cites other instances from the animal
and vegetal world to show how the epithet brings out properties which are
intrinsic to each being.

Eustathius and Apollonius Sophista attribute the interpretation "by nature,"
φύσει, to Aristarchus, and this in connection with the "shining moon" of
Il. 8.555. [6] But Aristarchus seems to have condemned a similar use of the epithet referred to characters. [7] Thus the happy intuition was not carried through.
What stood in the way was the need to assign the characters a certain role and
judge them accordingly.

Eustathius seems to come closest to a comprehensive view of the epithet
"by nature." In his comment on *Od.* 1.29 he writes:

Neither in the *Odyssey* nor in the *Iliad* does the poet ever wish to seek
blemishes or to satirize, except when there is absolute necessity to do so.
Therefore the Homeric Zeus calls "blameless" the scoundrel Aegisthus,
not drawing the epithet from his vices, but from whatever quality he might
have had, and he did have birth, beauty, intelligence, or anything else you
might name. Nor was it for the poet to attribute a nagging attitude to great
Zeus.

Or on ἀντίθεοι μνηστῆρες (*Od.* 14.18):

If the poet wants to show the wickedness of the suitors he does so very
strongly: he thus calls them "overbearing" later on. But he calls them here

"like gods" because of what happens to be their birth or beauty or wealth
or manliness; and this is very Homeric, just in the way Paris is called "godlike." For the poet naturally praises and gives no blame unless he can help it.
Thus in the same passage he calls the hogs "well-grown," and later he so
calls the goats, just as, earlier, the seals.

Eustathius's sympathetic attitude does justice to the epithets. What for
Eustathius is Homeric benevolence we might interpret as Homeric objectivity.
For here is an imaginative equanimity prompted by the sheer presence of
things. In this sense all the Homeric epithets are used "by nature."

3. The metrical impasse

The interpretation of the epithet "by nature" was not followed up in its
poetic implications. The problem remained open: How give a generally valid
theory of the Homeric epithets, which continued to be interpreted either in
a punctiliously pointed fashion or merely explained away as "conventional,"
"ornamental," or (which in this terminology amounts to the same thing)
"poetic"?
The "ornamental" interpretation was the one chosen. All pointedness,
deliberate meaning, or nuance were rightly excluded; but how was the ornamentation to be explained? In the absence of any philosophic poetic principle, the ornamentation was attributed to metrical need. Thus Düntzer writes,
on the one hand, that "the epithet used by the poet has no relation to the
fact expressed in the sentence" and, on the other, he shows how the poet
"could use variously characterizing epithets of the same sense but of different
metrical lengths and coin forms which corresponded with the needs of his
verse." [8] This is a prelude to Parry, who saw in Düntzer's work "the most important step since Aristarchus towards the understanding of the fixed epithet in Homer." [9]
The effect of this metrical approach was far-reaching. Research concerning
the epithet turned to such questions as its place in the hexameter, possible
shifts of place, length, effect of initial vowel or consonant on the length of the
preceding syllable; and, in the case of epithets having the same frame of
reference, the uniqueness of an epithet's metrical value or the existence of
metrical equivalents. [10] The same artificiality was shown by Düntzer's opponents. They were thrown off balance by the specious plausibility of the
metrical proofs, and, in their defence of the epithet's meaning, they stressed
points which were either obvious or farfetched. [11]
Research was here sadly deadlocked. Metrical value was extolled *in spite* of
meaning, meaning vindicated *in spite* of meter. We have compartments which
are alien to each other, both meaning and meter interpreted in their poorest

and most literal acceptation. How could poetry arise from such incompatible elements? The question was never asked.

4. Milman Parry and Homeric verse

Milman Parry brought the metrical interpretation to its significant conclusion. We can hardly speak, in this case, of the epithet's metrical suitability. Meter is, rather, a raison d'etre. It is the whole of Homeric language which is metrically conceived.

There is no need here to praise Parry for such ideas as that of epic economy, breadth of range and simplicity of form, extrusion of duplications in expressing the same thing. It would be captious to expend one's efforts in finding instances where Parry's system breaks down. Exceptions only confirm a prevailing trend.

What must be rejected is the presumption of the whole system; what must be rejected is the claim that this system gives us in any way an account of how Homeric poetry came into being. What we are presented with is but a description of facts or alleged facts. Parry surveys in its surface the outcome of expression, not expression itself. We are shown a series of ready-made results, but we are offered no glimpse into any creative process or really poetic reason.

It might here be urged that I am misunderstanding Parry's objective, that he was concerned with Homeric verse-making and not with aesthetics. This is not so, however. There is in Parry the continuous implication that an expression is correct in that it follows a certain mold established by tradition. He does not admit the possibility of other choices. The determinism which he posits in the technique of verse-making also applies to the mind of the poet. As I read Parry, a question continually arises: Could such and such an idea, such and such a meaning have been expressed otherwise? If the meter excludes any other epithet of a different quality in any other part of the hexameter, could not the whole hexameter have been worded differently? From Parry's point of view the question is futile. He writes:

> One cannot speak of the poet's freedom to choose his words and forms, if the desire to make this choice does not exist. Homer had inherited from his predecessors a language whose several elements were used solely in accordance with the needs of composition in hexameters. [12]

The hexametric rules are thus extended to the imagination. We might speak of a hexametric mind.

This is far from the truth. In all poetry there is a sense of inevitability which is all one with felicity of expression. Noun-epithet phrases, whole lines must have fluttered in the poet's mind to find their full realization at the right moment and in the right context. What is uttered arises against the indefinite margin of what remains unuttered. We cannot do justice to any given expression if we take it for granted. Though we shall never be able to explain all the reasons why an idea is expressed in a certain way rather than in another, yet we must bear in mind that range of possibilities which by the very fact of its being neglected contributes to the full, final realization.

It should not be thought that these are only theoretical questions. Theory is here intimately linked with interpretation. For, in Parry's view, an alternative mode of expression is the substitution of one formula for another as a means of smoothing out a statement; or, similarly, any choice of the poet is a product of association with some other formula, an automatic solution wherein sound opens the way to meaning. Parry leaves no room to spontaneity of choice: to the fact that words are suggested by a mode of visualizing the matter at hand.

It is in this question of alternative expressions that Parry's central flaw resides. There is a perversity which vitiates the method of interpretation. In order to illustrate my argument, here are a few typical instances of Parry's interpretation.

Dealing with subject noun-epithet formulae occupying the end of the hexameter, Parry points to the line-endings ἀκόντισε Τυδέος υἱός and ἀκόντισε φαίδιμος Ἕκτωρ, remarking that, where convenient, the poet can replace the hero's name and epithet with another formula by saying ἀκόντισε δουρὶ φαεινῷ. And he adds:

> This stylistic need to eschew the repetition of a name where it would be awkward is the cause of another artifice, a series of formulae which do no more than elaborate the idea of the verb. Examples of such formulae are χάλκεον ἔγχος, and δουρὶ φαεινῷ. . . . In the same way . . . alongside of κόρυθ᾽ εἵλετο φαίδιμος Ἕκτωρ (twice), we have λίθον εἵλετο χειρὶ παχείῃ (twice), δόρυ δ᾽ εἵλετο χειρὶ παχείῃ, ξίφος εἵλετο χειρὶ παχείῃ, etc.[13]

Look now more closely at the two instances of Hector seizing a stone: Il. 7.263-65:

> ἀλλ᾽ οὐδ᾽ ὣς ἀπέληγε μάχης κορυθαίολος Ἕκτωρ,
> ἀλλ᾽ ἀναχασσάμενος λίθον εἵλετο χειρὶ παχείῃ
> κείμενον ἐν πεδίῳ. . . .

Il. 11.354-56:

> Ἕκτωρ δ᾽ ὦκ᾽ ἀπέλεθρον ἀνέδραμε, μῖκτο δ᾽ ὁμίλῳ,
> στῆ δὲ γνὺξ ἐριπὼν καὶ ἐρείσατο χειρὶ παχείῃ
> γαίης . . .

It is quite perverse to interpret the phrase χειρὶ παχείη as a substitute for φαίδιμος Ἕκτωρ. No, the phrase has its meaningful place by setting in relief a hand's strong act—to the clasp, the clutch. The mentioning of Hector's name, and even more so his name and epithet, would destroy the picture, quite apart from the awkwardness it would introduce.

Nor should we take for granted the phrase χειρὶ παχείη. Numberless line-endings could be imagined. We might have had, for instance, λίθον εἵλετο δαίμονι ἶσος or λίθον εἵλετο τόν περ ἐσεῖδε or λίθον εἵλετο κείμενον ἐγγύς. It will rightly be said that such endings are very poor by comparison. But this is precisely the point: Why is it that χειρὶ παχείη is so good in this case? See pp. 113-14 above.

Or take in Od. 6.122 ἀμφήλυθε θῆλυς ἀϋτή, the cry of girls heard by Odysseus —an expression suggested, according to Parry, by ἀμφήλυθεν ἡδὺς ἀϋτμή in Od. 12.369 or vice versa.[14] One expression is thus derived from the other, without the slightest feeling that both might be due to a certain way of per-ceiving things. If we sought a reason for the felicity of this assonance, Parry would again point to the rhythmical pattern and its place in the hexameter.

But we may look at the matter in quite a different light. Nothing is more intrinsic to poetry than giving body to such intangibles as sound or perfume. This is frequent in Homer: sound in Il. 4.436, 8.63, 12.289, 338, 15.312, 16.633-37, etc., perfume in Il. 14.173-74, Od. 5.59, 9.210; cp. Il. 1.317. The phrase ἀμφήλυθε θῆλυς ἀϋτή springs from the same kind of sensuous per-ception as Il. 2.41, ἔγρετο δ᾿ ἐξ ὕπνου, θείη δέ μιν ἀμφέχυτ᾿ ὀμφή. Cp. Il. 10. 535, 11.466, Od. 11.605, 16.6, 19.444.

Nevertheless, Homer could say "I hear a cry" rather than "a cry comes to me" (cp. Il. 13.757, Od. 2.297, etc.). Why then did he choose the latter? Because this cry is fully exposed in itself and by itself—something, as it were, emerging from nowhere in a solitary spot. Hence Odysseus wonders about its nature, imagining (in the lines following) shouting nymphs in mountains, meadows, streams. Compare the way in which the divine voice spreading around Agamemnon in Il. 2.41, Odysseus' cry in Il. 11.466, or the sweet smell in Od. 12.369 are similarly rendered and similarly give rise to anxious surmise.

We may now better understand the epithet. Why does it occur? One reason is that this cry is presented in full focus and rightly has an epithet eliciting its full, natural identity. For θῆλυς may suggest "fresh," "soft," "lush," "crescive," as well as meaning "feminine": cp. θῆλυς ἐέρση, τεθαλυῖα τ᾿ ἐέρση (Od. 5.467, 13.245) and θαλερός referred to voice: cp. p. 117. R. Fitzgerald translates "that was a lusty cry of tall young girls."

Anything like ὡς ἄρα κουράων που ἐτήτυμον ἔκλυον αὐδήν would have been quite inadequate. It would have left that cry entirely out of focus as some-thing matter-of-fact, casually heard, hardly appropriate to association with the nymphs mentioned immediately after. There are thus many reasons why the poet used the expression he did.

Or take a more general topic. Meter, according to Parry, so tunes the poet and his audience to certain formulas that epithets occur only in certain case-forms even where the meter might allow otherwise. He writes:

> Why, we may ask, does Homer, without one exception, call Odysseus δῖος only in the nominative case? . . . This limitation of the epithet to a single case is too widespread to be the work of chance. Achilles is qualified by the same epithet, δῖος, 55 times in the nominative and twice only in an oblique case. Odysseus is πολύμητις 81 times, but only in the nominative.[15]

Parry overlooks here a most obvious and important fact. If these epithets are much more frequent in the nominative case, the reason is that when a character is presented as subject, he is most often central to the field of vision and thus most likely to have the epithet. The epithet's meaning is here neither particularized nor ornamental; it is concrete; it embodies, it centralizes the hero.[16]

Nor should statistics mislead us. The noun-epithet phrases quoted by Parry often occur in a line which, when the occasion arises, is repeated throughout the poems. Thus the number of instances is by no means as significant as it seems. This has been pointed out by Norman Austin, who writes as follows about Parry's statistics: "What his tables obscure . . . is that the purpose of many nominative formulas is solely, or almost exclusively, to introduce speeches. Were Odysseus not such a speechmaker the πολύμητις formula would virtually drop from the tables."[17]

Parry's concept of a hexametric language is so set forth as to make us forget that, after all, Homer's language has its syntax just like any other language. The choice of phrases is ultimately dependent on a need for perspicuity in the relations which bind meanings to one another. This obvious syntactic fact has its poetic implications. The poet sharpens into keener outline those balances which ordinary speech observes as a matter of course. (See chapter 13, section 4.)

5. After Parry

Parry's system, posthumously, appeared to win the day. Its panoply of instances abstracted from the poetry, its specious rigor, its assurance, its clarity of presentation eventually produced a shattering effect. The success was further facilitated by intellectual trends which characterize our age: the subjection of criticism to anthropological and sociological interests, all those varied forms of study that go under the loose name of structuralism. Parry was, in his way, a forerunner.

The concept of formula thus conditioned research in Homeric style. It appeared to give the precision of an exact science to any inquiry into the fluid facts of poetry. Language, art, cultural history were here compounded into one crystallizing factor which would be immediately apprehended, as if a magic key had been put into the hands of scholars. If deftly used, such a key could now open the way to many secrets in the epic matter: obscurities of diction, repetitions, and contradictions suddenly appeared explainable and natural.

The definition of formula, how a formula acquires vogue or is modified, to what extent the language of Homer is formulaic—such questions occupy the work in the field. And since the central factor is here the hexameter verse, the dominant concern is the relation between word and meter from the viewpoint of technique in versification. Research has thus become more and more abstruse. It is made so by the very nature of the problems: for example, how does a formula correspond to the cola of the hexameter, how far can it shift from one place to another? This learning is airtight, esoteric, technical. Its practitioners at times seem to write for one another and not for the general scholar, let alone the reading public interested in Homer.

But Parryism contained within itself the source of its own disruption. Once you admit any uncertainty about which phrases are formulaic or not, the whole system begins to be undermined. Hence the current distinction between "hard" and "soft" Parryism—a distinction which is not so much a matter of opposing schools as of a natural tension within the scholarly mind. For the contrast is inherent in the matter itself: on the one hand, a sense of poetry or language and, on the other, the rigid concept of formula. No different is the case of any critical study: analysis arresting spirit in some typical form. But in the study of Homer these polarities are brought out in sharpest opposition.

Hence the brave attempts of J. B. Hainsworth and of A. Hoekstra. Formula is their great subject, Parryism their starting-point; they work from within the system and yet they contribute, unwittingly perhaps, to the destruction of Parry's formidable edifice and thus show how precarious the formulas really are.[18] The formula, by being shown in its fluidity, inevitably loses its edge. It appears and disappears. These scholars are both fascinated by it and struggle against it. The idea of a poet at work vies with that of a craftsman working with tools he has inherited.

Parry's legacy, however, is a heavy one. The formula so occupies the scholar's mind that it naturally turns his attention away from seeking any value of expression intrinsic to distinctive words and phrases. What still matters most is the formula's role in the verse, the words being merely its ingredients. Hence, insofar as the epithets are concerned, a disregard which might seem strange to those unacquainted with the situation. This is well shown in the alleged declension of noun-epithet phrases. Thus A. Severyns (whom Hainsworth mentions as a forerunner in pointing out the suppleness of the formula) tells us, for instance, that περικλυτὸς Ἀμφιγυήεις appears in the genitive as περικλυτοῦ Ἡφαίστοιο.[19] Similarly, Hoekstra posits a declension of the phrase "sweet wine."[20] The epithet is thus treated as no more than a suffix or prefix which must be inevitably dragged along by the noun in the various case-forms—that is to say, in the changing relations brought out by the sentence.

The impression thus given is a false one. A survey would show that Hephaestus in the vast majority of cases has no epithet at all, that the genitive phrase adduced by Severyns recurs only twice, and that the full epithetic designation is mostly found where Hephaestus, in a simple sentence, is presented as subject of such simple acts as "to speak," "to do," "to go." The same might be said about Hoekstra's example. Wine has an epithet mostly in the accusative, when fully exposed as object of verbs which mean "to pour," "to libate," "to drink," "to bring," "to give"; for it is in these cases that the sweet, cheering, red, sparkling substance of wine is most evident.

It is as we should expect. The epithet has its syntactic function. The alleged declension (or conjugation) of formulas—which Parry himself excluded[21]— would subject the poet to the intolerable burden of declining his imagery, as if a poetic image were something quite static and not one and the same with the perception of a certain act or mode of being.

The value of single words is also impaired by the Parryism of those who take a more literary approach. Accepting the formula as Parry conceived it, they exalt Homer's achievement *in spite* of formulaic constraints; and they point out poetic felicities insofar as formulas are transposed or adapted to diverse contexts for the sake of some artistic effect.[22] We may admire their interpretation of single passages, but the implications of this method are surely wrong. Homer, at least, hardly benefits from them. For while it is admitted that the core of Homer is formulaic and traditional, the best poetic qualities are sought in those parts which are most removed from the formulaic and traditional. But, as Rosenmeyer writes, "the Homeric formula is not an instrument, it is an ultimate object . . . , it is the poetic reality itself."[23]

The noun-epithet phrases—which are the most stable feature of Homeric diction—are, again, the most expendable element in this kind of treatment. And yet they are deeply characteristic of Homer. Here is something that stands out over and above the narrative contents of any passage. Such lines as "when the early-born rose-fingered dawn appeared" or "at once speaking out he addressed winged words" are among the high points of Homeric poetry, although they are lines alleged to be most uncontroversially formulaic and traditional. We should try to recover these "formulas" in their original value, look at them as if newly discovered. From an aesthetic point of view, it does not make the slightest difference whether they are traditional or not. If so, we should accept Parry's findings as they are, but thoroughly reinterpret them in the new light of a poetic principle. The noun-epithet phrases, which so engrossed him and to which he gave such prominence, are a stimulating challenge in this respect.

As it is, the challenge is not met, with few exceptions.[24] In works more specifically concerned with epithets we most often find mere illustrations of Parry's law of economy or remarks on the epithet's relevance to historical data.[25] Or what we see emphasized is some kind of literal appropriateness which has nothing poetic about it: for example, the supreme king Agamemnon is ἄναξ ἀνδρῶν, the beautiful Paris is θεοειδής, the huge Ajax is πελώριος, Menelaus or Diomedes is βοὴν ἀγαθός because shown to shout louder than others.[26] Or, in a way which is reminiscent of the Scholiasts, efforts are made to extract a pointed meaning from the epithets wherever the context allows it: thus Mark W. Edwards distinguishes epithets which are "significant" from those that are "fillers" padding the verse, and he explains, for instance, "Priamid Hector" of *Il.* 23.182–83 as "Priam's son though he be," "Achilles dear to Zeus" of *Il.* 24.472 as a sign of the hero's superiority to "lesser men bustling about him."[27]

Such lines of interpretation leave us cold. They hardly seem to touch the spirit of the epithets. Descriptive relevance, literal appropriateness, one-sided pointedness introduce a minute obtrusive interest which jars with the grand Homeric outline. We are almost made to regret Parry's indifference to meaning. His metrical schemes may tune us to their music; and, if they do, it is because he is so heedless of any point in any particular word. We might be cheated into thinking that the flow of rhythm is sufficient to itself, words and their meanings a mere veil to the story's musical rendering.

Indeed, Parry's chief strength lies in the fact that his method is so widely applicable: the array of instances is in itself impressive; and, by the same token, the weakness of other approaches to the epithet lies in their meagerness and partiality, in the strained and fragmented method of their application.

This is also (and most notably) the case of many attempts which are explicity anti-Parryist. In reaction to Parry, a certain symbolism is imported into the epithets—a symbolism which must necessarily be quite arbitrary and made to fit selected occasions.

Critics so inspired give up the fabric of language. The imperviousness of the formulas deters them from looking further into the sentences. There exists, they say, the great epic subject matter with its far-reaching implications and complexities; and here may be found suggestions of meaning which the epithets perchance embody but which may escape the careless reader or even the scholar who is too concerned with the interpretation of single passages.

Such is the intent of W. Whallon when taking this approach. He remarks, for instance, that "when Zeus weighs the lot of Achilles against that of *Horse-taming* Hector (*Il.* 22.211), we may be reminded of the horses of Peleus that take Patroclus to his death but themselves escape, being captured by Hector, whose body they will afterwards drag behind the chariot of Achilles." [28] Or take J. T. Sheppard, who sees ascending phases of orchestration which the epithets mark throughout the poems—for instance, διίφιλε, of Achilles in *Il.* 1.74, is a prelude to 9.117-18, 16.169 and gives us a foretaste both of the glory and the grief which come to Achilles from the love of Zeus. [29]

We find in these interpretations a new kind of pointedness, different from that which is noticed, say, by Mark W. Edwards. It is more ambitious, more complex. On slender threads a metaphoric construction is built over the text, in a way which may remind us of the early allegorical interpretations of Homer. And if so much emphasis is laid on this alleged value of a few epithets, what do these critics think of the vast majority of epithets which do not lend themselves to their analysis? Their view of the latter must necessarily be a poor one.

Post-Parryism thus leaves the epithets in a troubled state. The student of Homer is perplexed. He cannot take what he reads at face value. The epithets, he is told, are no more than a stopgap or else they need a key to be understood.

In these circumstances, it might be interesting to see how major classicial scholars respond to Parryism. It is extraordinary how they have generally accepted Parry's theory or acquiesced in it. [30] People whose task it is to expound the meaning of words are seen subscribing to a theory which seemingly invalidates the very premises of that task.

Let us take as an example C. M. Bowra with his vast knowledge of poetry. How does he reconcile his poetic taste with the theory of formula, particularly in connection with the epithets? What strikes us is an unresolved ambiguity. On the one hand, Bowra notes the vividness and charm of the epithets; [31] on the other, he takes an apologetic tone in justifying them. He gives positive instances, but remarks on the dullness of their repetitiveness. "The noun-adjective combinations," he writes, "may be negative in their effect, but so far from being an obstacle in story-telling, they are a help, because they allow the action to proceed along broad simple lines." [32] Hence the idea of ease in versification: "In so far as a noun qualified by an adjective takes longer to say than an unaccompanied noun, it helps the poet and enables him to think ahead. . . ." [33]

Criticism here struggles with ill-assimilated notions of the "oral" poet, whence the explanation of the epithet as a "breather"—an explanation often invoked. [34] But how impute this sluggishness to the poet? If there be a stop, it must be a contemplative pause focused on the object of representation, and not a negative one determined by the need to rest and think ahead.

At this point, the questions of interpretation become questions of aesthetics. The problem is how not to let the principle of poetry be submerged by Parry's formulas, but rather bring these formulas under its sway. Scholars appear caught in the meshes of this problem. Hence their tentative and uncertain language. This contrasts with Parry's clarity—a clarity which, on the other hand, is achieved at the high cost of ignoring the question of poetic value.

6. The epithets and the common reader

Parry dwells at length on the way in which the beginner gradually comes to accept the epithets and ends up hardly questioning their meaning, taking them for granted, becoming indifferent to them, accepting them as a necessary convention of epic.[35]

This view does not do justice to the common reader; and by *common reader* I mean that vast anonymous body of people whose love of literature constitutes the leaven from which taste is formed and criticism eventually grows. Their appreciations might be regarded as a silent aesthetics which is no less real for being unpublished.

The attitude in respect to the Homeric epithets is a case in point. They naturally stir that kind of delight which Proust's Robert de Saint-Loup felt in enunciating them. In a similar way all unprejudiced and sympathetic readers of Homer, who may know nothing of epic tradition, naturally appreciate the epithets. They hardly undergo the painful experience posited by Parry. They are not puzzled at first and disappointed later. Their initial wonder does not fade into nothing. Even without reading Homer in the original Greek, even through an artless or literal translation, they are attuned to the epithet's expressive value. The same is true of children who have Homer read to them. I remember my first impressions of the *Iliad,* how impressed and delighted I was by such phrases as "swift-footed Achilles," "white-armed Hera," "the resounding sea." I realized how good they were without knowing why.

Here is a basic response. It is, of course, immediate, uncritical; but the instinctive quality of the response should make it all the more interesting and significant to the philosophic critic. The question thus presents itself: How explain the truth of this response? How find its reasons in the ways of perception, feeling, thought? How put it in terms of cause and effect? What matters here is not the interpretation of single passages, but the appreciation of the epithets as a whole.

There are many thinkers, critics, and scholars who have answered these questions with sympathetic insight. Their views often stand in contrast with the one-sided interpretations I have reviewed so far. I shall give a few examples.

Let us begin with a good grammarian. Kühner comments thus:

> In order to make visual (*veranschaulichen*) and bring out the meaning of a substantive, as well as to give speech a greater fulness, the poets very often attach the so-called *epitheta ornantia*.[36]

Wherefore this need to visualize? It is the need to go beyond the mere practical report or designation of an object, to give us the thing in itself and by itself, its sensuous or ideal presence. We touch here on an essentially poetic quality. This is how S. E. Bassett puts it:

> A thing entirely undescribed, or without any characterization, is only a fact. It is not a component of a picture of life. Therefore by an epithet Homer marks some easily recognized feature of a familiar object, and thus deepens the impression that it is real. [37]

This visualization is thus tantamount to a fresh sense of reality. A thing—whether directly observed or imagined—is seen in some vital feature which gives it life. The Homeric epithets, which are so free from the narrative idea of the context, do this all the time. By doing so, they put into permanent form that sense of the truth of things which we sporadically glean in our own experience. G. Santayana expresses this unfolding experience in connection with the Homeric epithets:

> This process, which novelists and playwrights may go through deliberately, we all carry on involuntarily. At every moment experience is leaving in our minds some trait, some expression, some image, which will remain attached to the name of a person, a class, a nationality. Our likes and dislikes, our summary judgements on whole categories of men, are nothing but the distinct survival of some such impression. These traits have vivacity. If the picture they draw is one-sided and inadequate, the sensation they recall may be vivid, and suggestive of many other aspects of the thing. Thus the epithets of Homer, although they are often far from describing the essence of the object—γλαυκῶπις᾽ Αθήνη, ἐυκνήμιδες᾽ Αχαιοί—seem to recall a sensation, and to give vitality to the narrative. By bringing you, through one sense, into the presence of the object, they give you that same hint of further discovery, that same expectation of experience, which we have at the sight of whatever we call real. [38]

Striking and important is the connection here established between immediate experience and the Homeric epithets, which are so often regarded as components of formulas quite removed from life.

The same idea is touched upon by Erich Auerbach. He points out how Homer deals with Odysseus' scar in *Odyssey* 19, giving it its full evidence; and then he goes on to say,

> Even the Homeric epithets seem to me in the final analysis to be traceable to the same need for an externalization of phenomena in terms perceptible to the senses. Here is the scar, which comes up in the course of the narrative; and Homer's feeling simply will not permit him to see it appear out of the darkness of an unilluminated past; it must be set in full light, and with

it a portion of the hero's boyhood. . . . To be sure, the aesthetic effect thus produced was soon noticed and thereafter consciously sought; but the more original cause must have lain in the basic impulse of Homeric style: to represent phenomena in a fully externalized form, visible and palpable in all their parts, and completely fixed in their special and temporal relations.[39]

The Homeric epithets, however, are not indiscriminately applied to anything that comes into view. There is a spontaneous selection. There is an intrinsic appeal in the perceived object. It is a perspicuity, a value of form which has nothing to do with any external interest. Anyone who responds to this visual appeal is no punctilious or inquisitive observer seeking an ulterior motive in what is presented to his view. He simply looks at things insofar as form and position give them prominence. He has something of what Ruskin calls the *innocence of the eye.*[40] F. Dornseiff mentions, in this regard, the "calm lingering look,"[41] and quotes from an essay on the *Odyssey* of Hugo von Hofmannsthal: "The slightest act, a daily happening, a pasturing animal, a rolling sea-wave, a weapon, a tool, a wound—upon each of these things rests for a moment the eye of a god, and the glance of this divine eye becomes our own."[42]

All these interpretations remove us from the world of formulas. A Parryist might put us on guard, forbidding us to take words at their face value. Let us then quote, finally, a statement which similarly stresses perception and is especially valuable in coming from a scholar who has deeply studied the influence of meter on the Homeric language. K. Meister writes about the epithets: "The explanation of this stylistic feature must in the first place be sought in the poet's urge to give and stir up perception; only secondarily are the epithets utilized to fill empty spaces of the hexameter."[43]

What the general reader is dimly aware of, what the passages quoted above articulate, points the way to the Homeric scholar. The important task is to see in what way this principle of perception which the epithets embody penetrates the texture of the poems.

How does perception come into account? What qualitative difference does the epithet make in a sentence? How does rhythm or meter subserve the need so to express a perceived object? Or, more generally, what are the relations between rhythm and expression, between expression and meaning? Such concerns might clear the path of criticism, removing us from abstractions as well as from any literal or rhetorical interpretation.

The problem of the epithets seems to crystallize at a sensitive point much that is pertinent to the appreciation of art. It is the problem of why and how an object of perception is singled out, mentioned, exposed. Here is something fundamental and yet delicate—not a matter of facile emphasis or stress, but of touch, accent, modulation. By highlighting the slightest object in its moment of emergence, an epithet impresses upon the occasion a sense of general existence; by receding and occurring elsewhere, it lets the same object subserve a larger purpose or design. The noun-epithet phrases thus introduce a purely contemplative moment. There is profound logic in their distribution and in the part they play—no less, say, than in a composition of Rembrandt the sudden light which gives existential evidence to drapery or brocade, while a high drama unfolds in an impalpable atmosphere.

22. AESTHETIC REFLECTIONS

1. "Oral Poetry"

Much of what I have said might be opposed by the objection that I have not sufficiently taken into account the nature of "oral poetry"; and this is especially so in view of the claim that this kind of poetry requires a new aesthetics. The interpretation of the epithets as formulaic metrical elements is strictly related to this claim: they are regarded as a vital need for the "oral poet" in his task of instantly shaping verse before an audience. A poet who writes and composes at leisure, it is said, needs no such device.

The problem before us is, therefore, whether this difference of conditions is such as to warrant a new kind of aesthetics.[1] What stands out in this difference is the relation between poet and audience. We may thus put the question more precisely: Is the relation between the "oral poet" and his audience *so* different from that between *any* poet and his public? And again (since aesthetics is a matter of perceptions): Does this difference affect the poet's mind so radically?

The keen sense of a relation between poet (or orator) and audience is of course an ancient one, coming up as it often does in Plato, Aristotle, and generally in Greek criticism. To the ancient Greeks, after all, literature was largely an everyday performance enacted before their eyes. What the theorists of oral composition have done is to transform this concrete inevitable relation between speaker and hearer into a grand abstraction. Anthropology and history are now brought into the picture. The audience becomes the tradition, the depositary of myth and folklore, the spirit of the age; and the poet is made into the spokesman of the tribe: he embodies in his work the rich threads of a tradition which is the common property of his milieu.

In this picture the force of attraction weighs heavily on the side of the audience. It is a collective entity which stands supreme. As for the poet, a wall of traditional preconception is interposed between his mind and the actual world. His activity is molded beforehand. Instead of poetic expressions we have formulas, instead of poetic thoughts we have themes, instead of poetic conceptions we have mythologies. That these schematizations would appeal to his mind is of course taken for granted, hardly worth mentioning.

Is there room here for a new aesthetics? Is there room for any aesthetics at all? The very term "oral poetry," as Douglas Young once remarked, is a contradiction in terms, since poetry is a thing of the mind. Should we then posit a collective mind, a collective aesthetics? This is hardly possible. The poet's working mind cannot be circumvented. We should end up artificially construing on a collective scale what is true of the individual.

Thus, in spite of everything, the theorists of "oral poetry" are bound to take into account the poet's individual act. Let us look at their general ideas on the subject and see whether we find in them any cue to a new aesthetics.

2. Milman Parry and the theory of "oral poetry"

In our inquiry into Parry's system in the light of aesthetic ideas, it will be convenient to treat it under different headings.

Historical method

Parry begins by saying:

> The literature of every country and of every time is understood as it ought to be only by the author and his contemporaries. . . . The task, therefore, of one who lives in another age and wants to appreciate the work correctly consists precisely in rediscovering the varied information and complexes of ideas which the author assumed to be the natural property of his audience.[2]

The relation between poet and audience is here made into the prime concern of scholarship. But how can we know the mind of an audience, let alone an audience so far removed from our time? The difficulty is admittedly a colossal one.

But, quite apart from the difficulty, what of the critical approach? It is certainly untrue that a work of literature can be understood as it ought to be only by the author himself and his contemporaries.

As for the author's contemporaries, there are all too many instances of their failure in recognizing the artist in their midst. The crux of the problem, however, is the poet's understanding of his own work. Parry, in his historical approach, ignores that a poetic statement is independent, its significance often lying beyond the poet's own intentions. This is a well-known truth. It is mythically expressed in the ancient image of the poet as a prophet as well as in Plato's idea of a divine madness in which wisdom is unaware of itself.

We find what is essentially the same principle in modern criticism—in Albert Béguin, for instance, who writes,

> The birth of authentic poetry is an event, a fact which is singularly indepen-
> dent of the idea construed about it, before or after, by him who enjoys the
> favor of producing it. It is perhaps not paradoxical to argue that, face to
> to face with the mystery which is the genesis of a poem, the author is as
> helpless as the reader.[3]

Or in Northrop Frye:

> The assertion that the critic should not look for more in a poem than the
> poet may safely be assumed to have been conscious of putting there is a
> common form of what may be called the fallacy of premature teleology. It
> corresponds to the assertion that a natural pehnomenon is as it is because
> Providence in its inscrutable will made it so.[4]

This is the truth which Shelley beautifully expounds in his *Defence of
Poetry,* blending ancient and modern feeling—in the concluding passage for
instance:

> Poets are the hierophants of unapprehended inspiration; the mirrors of the
> gigantic shadows which futurity casts upon the present; the words which
> express what they understand not; the trumpets which sing to battle, and
> feel not what they inspire; the influence which is moved not, but moves.
> Poets are the unacknowledged legislators of the world.

This is, after all, why we continue to interpret the classics from age to age, in
ways not necessarily less valid than the previous ones.

This inner meaning, moreover, does not belong only to the contents of a
poem. It lies also in the vocabulary—in that mentioning of things to which
Parry pays special attention. For how could we realize, for instance, the concreteness of Homeric words without being able to compare the evidence
of more abstract languages? Without a long remove, Bruno Snell, say, could
not have appreciated the value of Homer's verbs for *seeing* nor could Parry
himself have come to his conception of Homeric style.

Far from identifying with Homer's audiences, we should disregard them as
much as possible. We could then achieve a different kind of historicity from
Parry's by realizing in present-day terms what in Homer resists the test of
time and thus restoring a fresh value to expressions which seem different, remote, foreign.

Originality

The "oral poet" is supposed to use a traditional style, the "literate poet"
an individual style. In relation to the poet's mind, the differentiation

between the two is based on Parry's concept of originality. He writes, for instance,

The poet is thinking in terms of the formulas. Unlike the poets who wrote, he can put into verse only those ideas which are to be found in the phrases which are on his tongue, or at the most he will express ideas so like those of the traditional formulas that he himself would not know them apart. At no time is he seeking words for an idea which has never before found expression, so that that question of originality in style means nothing to him.[5]

Or:

One oral poet is better than another not because he has by himself found a more striking way of expressing his own thoughts but because he has been better able to make use of the tradition. He strives not to create a new ideal of poetry but to achieve that which everyone knows to be the best.[6]

This Parry applies to Homer. There is no originality, he maintains, except perhaps in formulas which might not be thought to make up sets of analogous cases or conform to standard measures; such an instance might be that of equivalent noun-epithet phrases where a rarer epithet replaces a more common one—for example, πελώριος or πολύτροπος for δίφιλος. He concludes at a certain point, commenting on the epithets of six major heroes in the nominative case:

The poet (or poets) of the *Iliad* and the *Odyssey* was so thoroughly steeped in traditional formulae that he never once, for the nominative case of the six names in question, created of his own accord an epithet revealing the personal stamp of his thought. Traces of originality remain, perhaps; but of an originality that does no more than rearrange the words and expressions of the tradition without important modifications. The poet's greatest originality in the handling of epithets would have been to use some noun-epithet formulae a little more or a little less frequently than other poets. All the epithets of the *Iliad* and the *Odyssey* we call "Homeric". But the entire investigation which we have just carried out has not turned up a single epithet which can be called "Homeric" as the epithets of Pindar have the right to be called "Pindaric".[7]

There is in Parry a misapprehension of what originality really means. Original is for him equivalent to "new," "novel," "singular," "striking"; an original word is one which is newly coined or used in an unusual way. Similarly, an individual style is said to be one in which each word subserves the immediate purpose of the author—whether in driving a particular point or in bringing out a general effect.[8]

But no poet, not even the most modern, is truly original in this way. Rarely does any writer coin a new word or use an old one in a strikingly new sense. Even phrases or sentences come mostly from common usage. It is when he attempts to be singular, it is when—as Parry puts it—he strives to create a new ideal of poetry, that he is often least spontaneous and original. The line "To be, or not to be: that is the question" is strongly Shakespearean, though the words are most common and the sentences themselves may be taken from everyday life or current philosophy.

What then is originality? It is a fresh quality of realization. We feel a sensation in an original way when it strikes us with particular truth. We cry out "beautiful!" at a visual impression that comes sharply on the spur of its occasion, as if we had discovered beauty for the first time; and the old worn-out word acquires then a new resonance. In such circumstances the word is, in its way, original. The same applies to poetry on a far more complex scale. A poetic expression is original in that it corresponds to a moment of imaginative realization. It does not matter that the wording is derivative. What matters is a vital congruence with the occasion—and by congruence I do not mean a particular point or fitness which the author deliberately brings out, but an existential integration with the matter at hand. It is because of this inevitable incidence that the expression acquires its unique reverberation. In this sense Hamlet's "To be, or not to be" is strongly original; and no less so, for instance, Achilles' "I sit a vain burden on earth."

Look at the Homeric epithets in this light. Take the phrase πολύτλας δῖος Ὀδυσσεύς. Whoever first composed it, Homer made it his own. It stands out in full effectiveness. It realizes the centrality of the hero's image in instance after instance. If it is impressed on our mind, this is because the instances of the hero's presence, and his exposure in these instances, are concrete, convincing, forcible. We must not be misled here by the great number of occurrences: what underlies our strong impression is a qualitative value which remains one and the same as much in a single instance as in many. We thus see πολύτλας δῖος Ὀδυσσεύς standing, lying, moving, rejoicing, perceiving—and yet not casually but almost always fully existent, strongly visualized or imagined where he is, at once a character and a concrete shape—whether as an agent on his own account or as recipient of whatever happens to him. We might thus say that the many instances of the phrase make up one supreme instance. It is as if the whole poem grew around Odysseus' name and his epithets.

What constitutes originality in a single expression may thus equally appear in an indefinite number of expressions. We have here a value which is naturally expansive. It cannot be appropriated by any one instance and excluded from others. The same pulse thus may run through a poet's whole work and yet no single part can be said to have provided the model. Moreover, this sense of realization, this constitutive principle of originality can be communicated to others. It is no esoteric formula, no private property of an individual genius. Any genuine feeling or thought is capable of moving others just as it moved the person who had it first. The words which express it naturally spread abroad. What cannot be faked is the authenticity of the realization. Where this is lacking, the words ring hollow; where it is present, we find originality in every instance.

We may thus say that Homer's style is eminently original. The recurring phrases are original because they constantly rise to the occasion of what is genuinely perceived in its essential recurring outlines. Hence no idle mannerism: the patterns of expression are patterns descried in the nature of things. There is one given occurrence of a given kind which comprehends its many recurrences. Hector has the same way of rising to speak or moving to battle as Ajax or Achilles; in the same way the light step of the figures on the Parthenon frieze is pursued through the whole length, each instance as original as the other.

Are we any closer to knowing what originality really means? It is easier, perhaps, to say what it is not: it is not in the nature of anything rare, singular, peculiar; or else any freakish thing would be highly original. Nor, obviously, can it lie in any spiritless copy of something else. Whatever it is, it must be a question of values intrinsic to the expression—a fresh resonance, perhaps, that comes from keenly apprehended meaning. And here the problem of derivation or the existence of a model is a consideration which is quite secondary. Thus Dante's "conosco i segni dell'antica fiamma" is no less original than Virgil's "agnosco veteris vestigia flammae." Why? Because it comes where it comes, because it fills with its truth the moment in which it is said, and thus bears the same native quality. As Coleridge put it:

He who can catch the spirit of an original, has it already. It will not be by dates that posterity will judge of the originality of a poem; but by the original spirit itself. This is to be found neither in a tale, however interesting, which is but the canvas; no, nor yet in the fancy or the imagery, which are but forms and colours. It is a subtle spirit, all in each part, reconciling and unifying all. Passion and imagination are its most appropriate names; but even these say little—for it must be not merely passion but poetic passion, poetic imagination. [9]

Notion of heroic

Parry appeals to what is termed "heroic" as a mainspring of poetic thought. In his chapter "Meaning of the Epithet in Epic Poetry" he writes about Homer,

For him and for his audience alike, the fixed epithet did not so much adorn a single line or even a single poem, as it did the entirety of heroic song. These epithets constituted for him one of the familiar elements of poetry, elements which we of a later age find it so difficult to appreciate, but the importance of which, for both poet and audience, is shown by everything in Homer: by the story, by the characters, by the style. In this respect, fixed epithets were just like the other familiar elements of poetry. The audience would have been infinitely surprised if a bard had left them out; his always putting them in hardly drew their attention. Epic lines without epithets would have seemed to them like a heroic character without his traditional attributes.[10]

The emphasis is on "epic," "heroic." Elsewhere in the same chapter Parry says the epithet emphasizes "the heroic quality of a person or thing," that it is "an element ennobling the style"; he mentions in this connection "a tone of grandeur and ceremony and respect."

We do not find here any serious attempt to explain what the term *heroic* really means, quite apart from what we obviously associate with it; and this in spite of the fact that the term is imputed with a notion of expressive value. What is, we may ask, the heroic way of expressing a thing? How is it that "hollow ship," "long-shadowed spear," "deep-eddying river" are heroic ways of expressing these things? The only reply that Parry could give us is: heroic because occurring in heroic poetry. But this is an intolerable *petitio principii*. The trouble lies in the fact that the term "heroic" is transferred *tout court* from the designation of a genre to that of a style, and hence to the very thought which prompts the use of a certain word, even though the word's meaning may not have anything heroic about it. A term which should be merely descriptive is thus given an aesthetic and philosophical status.

I submit that, in order to do justice to the poetic (and real) meaning of words, we must look at them in pure terms of expression. We must give up for a moment the conventional classifications of genre, save to return to them at a later time. We must study the operations of a certain expressive principle which remains the same in the most disparate semantic fields. Thus, as regards the epithets, we must realize that two such different images as "swift-footed Achilles" and "taper-leaved olive" both pursue the same expressive principle; and thus it is the same poetry which calls a hero δαΐφρων and wine μελίφρων, a king διοτρεφής and ἁλιοτρεφής a seal. Compare pp. 133–34 above.

It is in the nature of aesthetic perceptions to resolve all manner of things into values of form. Everything tends to become an image. Any kind of poetry thus naturally strives to eliminate from its subject matter those elements which jar with this image-making process. What emerges to a greater or lesser degree is a sense of form—or of pure being, function, quality— which is intrinsic to the thing itself. This means, for instance, that conventions must give way. Thus in Dante's *Inferno* we are made to sympathize with the doomed as pure human images, in spite of the poet's dogmatic beliefs. Equally so in Homer, in a context which could not be more different. The alien features of the epic matter yield to the Homeric perspective of existence. Nice conventional discriminations of dignity or degree thus fall into the background. This is why Homer's epithets are so expressive of reality, and yet so indifferent to relative merit or importance. The great issues of good and evil are otherwise expressed in the poems; what matters here is a sense of sheer existence.

This is true even in the case of the chief heroes. Their epithets should not be looked upon as particularly "heroic," as particularly expressive of social or personal distinctions. This, at least, is not their chief function. They rather serve to portray, in its various aspects, the full-bodied image of a man. The heroic notion is here superimposed. Where Parry tells us that the characteristics described by such epithets all refer to five qualities: courage, strength, fame, royalty, and that heroic but vague concept, "divinity," we should observe that even these qualities are not the main point. Presented in this conceptual way, they give us only the conventional idea of the epic hero. The point is, rather, that these qualities are such as stand out in the concrete form of a man, and in instances of concrete exposure. They are part and parcel of the living organism (compare pp. 127–28 above). Thus the attributes of strength and courage are ascribed not only to heroes but to any strong animal; fame is attributed to anything that is heard of from far away; divinity is attributed also to the elements of nature.

We commonly speak of "epic," "tragic," "lyric" poetry; we commonly transfer the same qualifications to the diction and to the thought itself; but we seldom ask ourselves why it is so. Is there any deeper notion that underlies these classifications—not in reference to subject matter or performance, but to the form of thought and expression? Lacking an answer, we should rather concentrate on the poetic act itself and see how all-inclusive it is. Homer is epic, tragic, lyric at the same time. Rather than saying that Homer's epithets are heroic, we might thus observe that they represent a lyric element in the epic story in that they let things stand out for their own sake in a purely contemplative, nonnarrative moment.

Facility of versification

Homer's use of the epithet, we saw, is categorically ascribed by Parry to metrical convenience. Facility of versification plays an essential part in his system: formulas are needed for the purpose of instant performance. This is a basic assumption. It amounts to an aesthetic principle.

The hard work is here transferred from the poet to the nameless process which produced the poetic tradition. Parry appeals to the long efforts of many poets, which he assumes to have been the work of centuries.[11] To this achievement the contribution of any individual poet must be minimal, so as not to impair this indispensable facility.

We may wonder how the "oral poet" actually *becomes* a poet. Does this cost him no effort? Does he passively assimilate? Or, rather, is there a stage of intense training after which he is capable of automatically composing and performing any required song? But, if so, can we take so static a view of his activity? Can his work be so taken for granted? Is there no progress, no decline?

Homer himself, of course, gives us no help here. His relation to the Muse, like that of his Phemius and Demodocus, is such as might apply to any later poet as well. Other evidence was necessary. Hence the inquiry into the Yugoslav singers, these latter-day "oral poets" and alleged descendants of Homer. We must here turn to A. B. Lord, who accompanied Parry in Yugoslavia and expounded the records. This is how Šećo Kolić reported his apprenticeship as a poet:

> When I was a shepherd boy, they used to come for an evening to my house.
> ... Then a singer would pick up the gusle, and I would listen to the song.
> The next day when I was with the flock, I would put the song together, word
> for word, without the gusle, but I would sing it from memory, word for
> word, just as the singer had sung it. . . . Then I learned gradually to finger
> the instrument and to fit the fingering to the words, and my fingers obeyed
> better and better. . . . I didn't sing among the men until I had perfected
> the song, but only among the young fellows in my circle, not in front of my
> elders and betters.[12]

Lord here notes the first difficulty which the young singer must overcome—that of adapting words to the fairly rigid rhythmical form. To the obvious objection that this might also apply to the literary poet, Lord replies:

> There are two factors in oral composition which are not present in a
> written tradition. We must remember that the oral poet has no idea of a
> fixed model text to serve him as a guide. . . . Secondly, there is a factor
> of time. The literate poet has leisure to compose at any rate he pleases. The
> oral poet must keep singing. His composition, by its very nature, must be
> rapid.[13]

And here, again, the need of facility in versification, the formulas that come to the rescue like a deus ex machina.

I find here no difference such as might justify a new aesthetics. The "literate poet" hardly uses a written text to serve him as a guide; the knowledge of other poems revolves indefinitely in his mind as a poetic impulse or influence, just as songs once heard must have fermented in the mind of Šećo

Kolić. The whole matter again comes down to the alleged facility of versification.

But this facility is an illusion. Lord looks at the phases of apprenticeship
and performance quite generally. He does not take into account the individual predicament. He hardly does justice to the situation. Consider, rather,
the matter as a moment of experience; and complexities will arise, whatever the circumstances. What a "literate poet" may achieve with the aid of
ink and paper, the "oral poet" achieves by listening to himself. It is, of
course, quite possible that the latter may be far more richly endowed with
the gift of a creative memory, but the process of thought is essentially
no other. We may imagine him, before a performance, repeating his song to
himself, rehearsing the action, identifying with the characters, bringing
out or suppressing this or that detail according to his likes and dislikes, enhancing a shape, stressing a mood. A continually revolving theme haunts
his mind. Let us not belittle his mental effort by making it fictitiously easy.
Here is soul-searching work. It is, as Norman Austin put it, a "memoriz-
ing from within, when the process of creation, with constant meditation on
alterations, additions, and revisions, lays its mnemonic patterns in the
brain." [14]

Lord himself, in pointing to versions of the same story, brings out significant
individual strains—for example, a "moral quality," a "personal sensitivity to
human relations," a "sense of heroic ethic." We might wish that Lord had
spent more time in exploring these inner complications. For here are basic
dispositions, preferences, ideals, values whose roots must have lain deep in
the nature of any one singer. How did they take form and emerge into verbal
expression? How did they fit into the composition? We must suppose a
complex, arduous process— something not very different from what happens,
say, to a dramatist who has long been brooding on some important thought
up to that happy moment in which he can integrate that thought into an actual
scene, in a play whose subject matter he derives from some distant source.
The terms "facility," "difficulty" are hardly relevant here. A poem is both
difficult and easy—difficult in that it requires a complex preliminary process,
easy in that the final felicity of expression seems to come by itself in a spontaneous flow. The same applies to any detail. Even a noun-epithet phrase,
easy as it may seem, comes where it comes through an extremely delicate and
refined sense of representational balance.

These are matters which concern the more intimate aspects of composition.
They lie outside the scope of Parry and Lord, who looked at poetry as primarily an aspect of culture and civilization. To them the environment was all-
important. They went to Yugoslavia as anthropologists rather than critics.
What is more, they went to test upon the singers a preconceived theory. In his
foreword to *Cor Huso: A Study of Southslavic Song*, Parry writes:

Those who consult these volumes should fully understand with what end in mind I gathered my material. It was least of all for the material itself that I planned the study. What I wished to learn was in general what an oral poetry was, and in particular what the Southslavic poetry was.[15]

Or:

The purpose of the present collection of oral texts has been made not with the thought of adding to the already vast collections of that poetry, but of obtaining evidence on the basis of which could be drawn a series of generalities applicable to all oral poetries. . . .[16]

The conversations with the singers are thus designed to further the investigation. They cannot but be superficial from the viewpoint of the singer. There is an ulterior motive. There is a malicious questioning. Would Parry have questioned in the same way, say, Robert Frost in trying to find out who influenced him? He writes for instance:

The seeker after information will himself be at fault here unless he is careful. For instance, it is clear from the conversation in general of Salih Ugljan at Novi Pazar that he was himself unable to remember in a great many of the cases where, and from whom, he had learnt a certain song. Nevertheless, since he was asked in each case where he had learnt a song he felt it incumbent upon himself to give an answer, which was in many cases far from consistent with what he had said elsewhere. In the case of Nikola self-interest is and has been very much at stake. It was only gradually and by circumstance arising here and there which naturally put him to the proof that I learned the smallness of his repertory and the fact that in the case of a good number of the songs of that repertory he did not know them to the end.[17]

The quoted conversations, accordingly, all turn on external facts: what is the source of a certain song? how long did it take to learn the song? is it repeated word by word? It is as though a witness were being examined. The same applies to biographical details: they take the form of a dossier. Hence no attempt to reconstrue the singer's aesthetic experience or to penetrate into the complexities of a single thought. What songs did a singer prefer? Why did he choose one theme instead of another? Why did he omit, or enhance, a certain detail? What common ground might be found in any of these choices and preferences? Did he ever change in this respect? What was the development of his art? Or, again, what was his view of the audience? How was he affected by success or failure? What influence did this have on the composition of the poems? Any such question might have opened a new perspective in the inquiry; the response might have brought out the difficulties which are intrinsic to any serious work. But, as it is, the poetic act lay shrouded in its environment; what emerged were episodes, habits, customs, or a local color.

The twofold view of poetry

Parry identified two quite different kinds of poetry, "oral" and "literary"; two different aesthetics, one for each kind: how did this strange view come about?

Let us look first at Parry. He certainly did not feel the need of an "oral" aesthetics when in his master's thesis he wrote,

> The first impression which this use of ornamental words makes upon the reader is one of utter loveliness. They flow unceasingly through the changing moods of the poetry, inobtrusively blending with it, and yet, by their indifference to the story, giving a permanent, unchanging sense of strength and beauty. They are like a rhythmic motive in the accompaniment of a musical composition, strong and lovely, regularly recurring while the theme may change to a tone of passion or quiet, of discontent, of gladness or grandeur.[18]

Here is a sense of beauty which has universal application. This true and fresh intuition must have given Parry the initial impulse to pursue his studies in Homeric diction. Later, after the system of formulae had been built up, something of the same charm remained, but weakened and displaced:

> We can see what a marvellous thing the bards succeeded in creating. In allowing themselves to be guided by the material elements of the hexameter and by the metrical values of the words they used, and in constantly looking for facility in the making of verse, they created a style which conformed in the highest degree with the rules of thought. The clarity of the sentences in epic poetry is born from the very difficulty of rendering them in the rhythm of the hexameter line.[19]

The "rules of thought," the "clarity of the sentences" are here precious insights applicable to all poetry, but they are checked by the idea of facility in versification.

Elsewhere Parry notes that the influence of analogy on the diction "was entirely subordinate to the taste of the poets";[20] the weak idea of taste hardly suffices to account for the quality of the expression.

That initial sense of loveliness thus lost its first impact. It was taken for granted; or else it might have led Parry to pursue the "rules of thought" beside those of epic technique. As his formulaic system grew in dimension, it seemed to impose its own laws. It had its own raison d'être. Hence the appeal for a new aesthetics applicable to Homer and "oral poetry" in general:

187

In the light of so many compelling proofs, what do we do with the aesthetic principles which Lucian put forth, and which critics like Boileau and Voltaire analysed and taught, the guiding principles still of our own literature? We must eschew them entirely when we study Homer. When we read the *Iliad* and the *Odyssey* we should not have them in our minds at all; we should rather conceive that here is a poet who marked his works with genius not because he was able to model the words on his own thoughts, but because he was able to make use of traditional words and expressions. [21]

Here tradition entirely supplants thought; and, as a consequence, thought is interpreted most narrowly—as aspect of a poet's idiosyncrasy. But a real aesthetics should be a philosophy of perception, reaching beyond any peculiarity of style. It is significant that Parry should here appeal to Boileau and Voltaire, thus ignoring so much speculation which since the Romantic age has thrown light on the relations between word and thought.

Parry seldom wanders off into theory. For further light on the specificity of "oral poetry" we must again turn to Lord—to the idea of *theme* rather than *formula*. [22]

Lord tells us how Avdo Mededovic listened to Mumin Vlahovljak singing a song of several thousand lines quite unknown to him and then, right on the spot, sang it himself but imparted to it a new quality by enriching the "assembly theme." Avdo was not re-creating out of whole cloth, Lord explains, but the inherited technique of building themes made possible what seemed on the surface an impossible feat. [23]

What stands out is the effect of such a theme on the poet's mind. An assembly (or any other of those "recurrent elements of narration and description") is so thought of that it becomes associated with the pertinent imagery. The theme is thus a pattern which has a virtuality of its own. Episodes and characters are forms of ornamentation summoned up by it.

But is it not perverse so to separate the theme from everything else—to pass off as "ornamentation" such things as characterization of people and actions?

If, on the other hand, we were to conceive an aesthetics based on themes, we should so broaden the idea as to make it relevant to all literature. For the themes which Lord mentions are as universally pertinent as can be. Life is indeed made up of assemblies and dispersions, departures and arrivals. But why are they so important? Because they are central occasions of experience. Here is the joy of recognition, the thoughtfulness of solitude, the passionate exchange of a meeting. Here are high moments of life. What mattered to the singers were these inherent values rather than the juncture itself or the theme per se; and if they found these themes indispensable, it is simply that human characters cannot be represented in a vacuum.

Lord thus writes about Avdo and his themes:

Avdo began and as he sang, the song lengthened, the ornamentation and richness accumulated, and the human touches of character, touches that distinguished Avdo from other singers, imparted a depth of feeling which had been missing in Mumin's version.[24]

What Lord calls "ornamentation" is really the most important element from an aesthetic point of view. Thus the wrath of Achilles, or that of Lear, quite outshadows the assembly theme.

There is no need here for a new, narrower brand of aesthetics. The contrary is the case. Aesthetic theory should grow broader and more philosophical, inquiring into the way in which existential conditions (the object of Lord's themes) are translated into poetry. For it lies in the nature of art to essentialize the form of events, where this form may appear concealed by the elusive spectacle of life.

A stronger case for a poetry *sui generis* might perhaps be made for what may be called "submerged" themes. These are not at all obvious. Like archetypes, they exist independently of any particular story, and yet they filter into it by strength of association, even if they are not required by the narrative: a recognition theme, for instance, is associated with a hero's return and it occurs in some form or other (not necessarily touching the hero himself), even though the actual return may not be the point of the song.

We thus have a poetic element quite apart from the poet's intent. Lord speaks in this respect of a habit which is hidden but felt, coming to the surface from the depth of the tradition. "Without such an awareness," he remarks, "the overtones from the past, which give to the tradition the richness of diapason of full organ, cannot be sensed by the reader of oral epic."[25]

Thus, for instance, the four occasions in which Odysseus is struck by the suitors are multiforms of a theme in which the resurrected god in disguise is rejected by the unrecognizing evildoers. In this way the *Iliad* and the *Odyssey*

are both the story of an absence that causes havoc to the beloved of the absentee and of his return to set matters aright. Both tales involve the loss of someone dear to the hero (Patroclus and Odysseus' companions); both contain the element of disguise (the armor of the *Iliad*); in both is the return associated with contests and games and followed by remarriage (Achilles with Briseis, Odysseus with Penelope). . . .[26]

Even if truly there, these are wholly unconscious elements. From an aesthetic point of view they seem to be no more than a mythical sediment, a dead matter which the actuality of poetic expression continually tends to expunge. If given undue prominence, they blind us to what in a poem is most intimately pertinent. What clings to the ancient material like a birthmark can have no room in the really creative process.

Are then these "submerged" or "vestigial" elements *overtones,* as Lord calls them? Overtones of history, perhaps, or of myth or of folklore. For we may decipher, in this sense, an iconographical relic. But this is not so in a truly aesthetic sense. Here an overtone must be an inward implicitness, a penumbra around what we actually see, an infinite fringe of meaning surrounding a clearly realized poetic core. There can be no overtone without a tone to which it is intimately related.

Another attempt to define "oral poetry" is that of M. N. Nagler. We have thematic ideas rather than themes, and these may be suggested even by associations of one word or sound.

A case in point is κρήδεμνον, "veil," as symbolic of chastity. But Nagler warns us against any facile symbolism: "No simple equation 'veil-chastity' will get us very far. . . ." We are dealing with an active symbolic idea that can be realized with a great variety of nuances and which should enable us to get more deeply into the subtlety and expressive power of Homer's techniques." [27]

We thus have Penelope holding up her veil before her suitors to signify that she is impregnable (*Od.* 1.334, etc.); Andromache dashing her veil to the ground in token of her womanhood crushed when learning of Hector's death (*Il.* 22.470); Nausicaa dropping hers in a disguised sign of temptation (*Od.* 6.110). The most striking instance is the sea-nymph Leucothea giving her veil to ship-wrecked Odysseus as an amulet: her self-surrender is only hinted at, for she plunges back, and the dark wave covers her. The wave (κῦμα, whose assonance with κάλυμμα, "cover," is noted) is, in Nagler's language, an allomorph of the same token—a poetic substitute countering the giving of the veil and saving the goddess from a compromising situation.

Are such interpretations revealing of poetry? Indeed a woman's veil has its inherent significance. The fact of holding it up or dashing it to the ground is full of implications. But these implications are all contained within the instant representation. We cannot break up its integrity. It is a mystification so to invest a detail with esoteric importance above all the rest. This is most glaring in the Leucothea passage. Why not mention as a source of poetry the image of an encompassing wave, of a vanishing body—so striking a feature of Homeric poetry (cp. *Il.* 21.268, 326, 202, *Od.* 5.366, 11.243-44, etc.)? In any case it is the sense of nature which stands supreme. Even if Nagler's symbolism is correct, what should be pointed out is Homer's freedom: how he left behind him the traditional figment, how he transformed mythical belief into sheer representation.

It is far worse when the same approach is applied to the very conception of the poems. What we then find is mere construction. Old conventional ideas of adaptation, conflation, and external composition are presented in a new complex form—transferred now from any alleged author to the operations of myth or tradition. We miss the feeling for any vision or for any assimilating force that has its own center.

Thus Lord attributes the brief but concentrated action of the *Iliad* to a conflation of themes: Patroclus is the dying god who should normally wander for a long time before he returns, but Patroclus is here a human substitute, really killed; thus time is cut short, and the lack of the time dimension is compensated for by fitting the story of Patroclus into that of the protracted Trojan War:

> The emphasis on the death of the substitute, Patroclus, in the *Iliad*, in the framework of a story of absence and return, has deprived the story of the element of the length of absence. Yet the element is kept vestigial. It belongs to the story of the war, and hence events are told that we should expect to find at the beginning of the war and not in its tenth year; it belongs to the story of Achilles' absence, the duration of which, together with the duration of the war, has been telescoped into a much shorter period of time.[28]

How could this theory of conflation, if taken as it is, find any room in a philosophy of aesthetic perception? Even if we accept this conflation as a fact, we should suppose it as something accounted for and concluded long before the poem was conceived; for we should otherwise have to make the incredible assumption that a thing so intrinsic to Homer as his sense of time was forced upon him by the necessity of external composition.

No, the facts of the narrative are to be seen in the light of a certain perceptive principle, and not the reverse. We should thus see in the Homeric treatment of time a characteristic way of perceiving events. Homer draws many threads into one moment of human experience, he resolves a long-drawn-out tale into immediate drama. In the same way, he brings up single acts, allotting to each the time-span of its concrete duration. Hence the representation of moments which are witnessed visually, tangibly. Hence the full-rounded phrase which gives us so satisfying a sense of any fleeting but lingering act. Hence the epithets.

APPENDIX

Additional Evidence on the Presence and Absence of the Epithet with Ship[1]

1. Ship as place

The ship image is weakened and there is normally no epithet in the following instances:

a. There is a sense of locality (or topography) rather than of any act taking place at the ships: *Il.* 16.396-97, "between the ships and the river"; cp. *Il.* 8.213, 490, 533, 9.232, 10.336, 347, 12.118, 273, 411, 418, 13.675, 14.28, 46, 15.348, 655-56, 670, 16.395, 17.432, 18.14, 256, 279, 23.365. We may add παρὰ νῆας (*Il.* 1.347, 10.54, 11.805, 9.657) as a specification of place rather than an actual scene of motion. Exceptions are few: *Il.* 17.403, *Od.* 12.354.

b. Such a phrase as in *Il.* 1.487, κατὰ κλισίας τε νέας τε, "in the tents and the ships," a sort of hendiadys which means no more than "in the camp of the Achaeans"; cp. 13.723, 14.146, 16.45, etc. Exceptions are few: *Il.* 1.306, *Od.* 4.255.

c. The meaning is no more than "embark," "disembark," "load," "unload": *Od.* 2.416, "Telemachus went on the ship, and Athena led the way"; cp. *Od.* 3.12, 9.157, 177, 11.534, 636-37, 12.144-45, 306-07, 13.281, 317, 15.547, *Il.* 13.665, 19.194, 23.259; "fall from the ship": *Od.* 10.51, 12.417, 14.307, *Il.* 15.435; "take on ship": *Od.* 15.452. In *Il.* 16.748, "dive from the ship," irony detracts from the image of ship.

Exceptions point more closely to the occasion: *Od.* 13.116-17; cp. 8.500, 9.101, 548, 13.283, 15.284, *Il.* 8.197. Note especially the visual sense in *Od.* 12.100, 245. Hence the full-bodied image in *Od.* 4.708-09, "to embark on seafaring ships which are steeds of the waves."

d. There is narrative looseness in *Od.* 13.272, "going at once to the ships I begged the bright Phoenicians . . . "—a condensed expression, with the

Phoenicians and their ship unmentioned beforehand. Or there is indefinite-
ness: *Il.* 19.59, "would that at the ships Artemis had slain her." Cp. *Od.*
11.399. In *Il.* 18.305, "if Achilles be risen [that is, if he has given up his wrath]
by the ships."

2. Ship as a means of transport

Other instances of lack of epithet through weakening of the ship image:

a. The destination is expanded upon, as in "let us return with the ships to
the dear native land" (*Il.* 2.140, 9.47, 428, 691, 15.499; cp. *Od.* 23.340).
Contrast this with the simpler "to return in the curved ships" (*Il.* 1.170, 2.74,
3.283. An exception in 2.236). But the same thing is fully and freely expressed as idea in *Il.* 2.453-54, 11.13-14, "to them, war was sweeter than to
return in the hollow ships to the dear native land."

b. Circumstance is added: *Od.* 2.226, "going away with the ships he gave
him the house in trust"; *Od.* 10.140, "with the ships we landed in silence."
Cp. 14.298.

c. The meaning "ship" is joined with that of "crew," as in "here I have come
with my ships and my friends" (*Od.* 1.182; cp. 3.323, 9.173, 11.161, *Il.* 1.183).

d. The bodily sense of ship is also weakened in the following:

Il. 2.794, "waiting for the moment when the Achaeans might sail away in
the ships." Expectation blurs actuality.

Il. 11.21-22, "he learnt that the Achaeans were going to sail in the ships."
The action is a theme of hearsay.

Od. 14.188, "on what ship did you come?"; *Od.* 16.24 (cp. *Od.* 16.142,
4.656), "since you left for Pylus on the ship." There is conversational looseness.

Il. 23.829, "the molten iron which Achilles brought in the ships along with
other possessions." This is mere information.

3. Rest or action within the ship

We find the epithet for simple rest *in* the ship: *Od.* 8.445, 13.134, 16.229;
cp. 12.264, 17.160.

Similarly, where an act is self-contained and not impinged upon by other
factors. We thus have *Od.* 4.578, "we laid down the mast and the sails in the
well-balanced ships" (cp. 4.781, 8.52, 11.3, 12.171, *Il.* 1.433), but in *Od.*
9.72, "and we laid down the sails in the ship, fearing death."

The same act may thus be rendered in different ways according to whether
there is an epithet or not: the simple and self-contained "to tie in the hollow
ship" (*Od.* 2.430, 9.99, 10.23, 12.50, 14.345; cp. 10.571), but descriptively
in *Od.* 12.178-79, "they tied me in the ship hand and foot. . . . " Or there are
different degrees of realization: ἰαύω in *Il.* 18.259 and 19.71.

The same reasoning applies to the idea that something *is* in the ship. We
have in *Od.* 12.320, "in the swift ship there is food and drink" (10.176, cp.

12.358), but in *Od.* 9.163, "not yet from the ship the red wine had been wasted, but there still it was." The idea of possession and loss works against the epithet. Cp. 9.348, 12.329.

"To put in the ship": the simple concrete sense requires the epithet in *Od.* 2.414, 12.171, 13.71, 216, 14.295, 18.84, 20.382, 21.19, 24.419; cp. 17.249. So "take from": 13.283. But at times the shipped object has the epithet, the ship being left out of focus without epithet: *Od.* 9.469-70; cp. *Il.* 16.221-24.

Other instances without epithet:

a. We have a general activity: *Od.* 11.9, "to be busy about the ship." Or a general state: 8.232, "no comfort was there for me on the ship"; so 12.110; cp. 10.505. Or the situation is not essential to the ship as such: *Od.* 12.206, "going across the ship I encouraged my friends"; 10.53, "covered up (in sorrow) I lay down in the ship"; cp. *Il.* 2.688. *Od.* 15.456 seems exceptional; *Il.* 13.381 perverse.

b. The act is in a pressing sequence: *Od.* 12.420-21, "and through the ship did I pace until the flood unstuck the keel on both sides." Cp. 228-31, 13.21-22.

4. Ship as object

a. There is normally no epithet with such general meaning as "make a ship ready": *Od.* 1.280, 2.307-08, 14.247-48 (exception: 2.287); "repair a ship": *Od.* 14.383; "to pile the ship": *Il.* 9.358; cp. 9.137, *Od.* 14.87; "to take possession of a ship": *Od.* 4.634; "the shore holds the ships": *Il.* 14.34. On the other hand, in "to give [receive, lose] a ship," we find the epithet, ship being apparently treated as a concrete object: *Od.* 2.212, 4.646-47, 669, 19.274, 24.428; cp. 2.387, 15.269.

b. Ship as object of seeing. There is focalization with the epithet: *Od.* 12.247-48, "looking at the swift ship and my friends, I saw . . . "; 16.472, "I descried the swift ship coming in"; 7.43, "Odysseus wondered at the well-balanced ships." There is casualness, on the other hand, in *Od.* 16.351-52, "Amphino-mous, turning, saw the ship"; cp. 16.356-57; *Il.* 9.359-61, "you will see . . . my ships sailing" is equivalent to "you will see me leave." Lack of focus also in *Il.* 10.14, 11.82; cp. 13.14, where the ships are part of a general view.

c. Ship as a theme of discourse, "to tell about the ships," naturally has no epithet: *Il.* 2.493; cp. 16.113, *Od.* 10.15.

5. Ship as subject

There are some interesting variations of value according to whether there is an epithet or not:

Od. 15.446, "When the ship is all filled with livelihood": this is merely informative, equivalent to "the ship is full" (cp. *Od.* 3.392, and see also 4a above, "pile the ship"); but 15.457, "when the hollow ship was weighed down [ἤχθετο] " makes us much more aware of the ship's body.

Od. 12.66, 69, "no ship did ever escape there . . . only one seafaring ship sailed by." The idea of escape detracts from the ship image, while the simple act of sailing presents it in full.

Od. 24.299, "where is the swift ship?"; 24.308, "the ship is beached in the field near the city": descriptive detail works against the epithet.

6. Ship in the genitive

We often find the epithet when the part and whole are conceived all at once as object or term of an immediate act: *Od.* 7.252, "seizing the keel of the side-curved ship"; cp. 3.10, 10.127, 12.218, 13.74, 14.311, 15.283. Or the part is in the nominative as subject standing in immediate focus or relevance: *Od.* 21.390, 9.322.

Without epithet, there is often a specification: *Il.* 2.154, "they took away the supports of the ships" (or "from beneath the ships"); cp. 9.241, 15.382; cp. 24.443. So *Od.* 15.551-52, "he took from the ship's deck the strong spear" (where, accordingly, it is the spear which bears the stress). We similarly have a mere explanation or information in "they lay down along the ship's cables" (*Od.* 12.32, *Il.* 1.476).

There are variations of concrete evidence. We have in *Il.* 19.43, "those whose task it was to hold the ship's rudder" but *Od.* 12.218, "you are wielding the rudder of the hollow ship" (cp. 3.281); with "ship's deck" the epithet marks focus: contrast *Od.* 15.283, 13.74 with 3.353, *Il.* 15.676.

7. Idea of ship

The epithet gives concreteness to the idea in *Od.* 11.124, 23.271, "those who know not the red-cheeked ships." Cp. 4.559, 5.16, 141, 6.271, 7.34-36, 9.125, 127, 14.224, 17.145. More generally: *Od.* 17.288, "hunger for whose sake the well-benched ships are equipped"; cp. 4.708-09, 2.390. In *Il.* 2.293 the sailor whom the storm keeps from home "pines with his many-benched ship." In such connections the idea of ship, however general, is in full focus and it takes familiarity of form. So in *Od.* 13.156-57, a rock "similar to a swift ship."

Horse [2]

1. Horse as subject

We find the epithet with the concrete idea that the horses *are* in a certain place (even if detail is added): *Il.* 10. 520, "the place where the swift horses were standing"; cp. 10.474, 568-69, 23.279, 550, 3.327; an exception in

8.564. *Il.* 2.775, 20.221: no epithet, since the horses are modified ("each horse," "three thousand horses").

Stress on a certain point works against the epithet: *Il.* 10.407, "where are *his* horses?"; 10.477, "*these* are the horses"; cp. 10.558.

2. Horses as objects of yoking, unyoking

This simple concrete meaning appears to require the epithet: *Il.* 8.433, 503, 10.498, 16.148, 18.244, 23.7, 27, 294, 301, 24.14, *Od.* 3.475, 478, 4.28, 15.46.

The epithet is omitted through supervening circumstance:

a. The act is closely joined with other acts: *Il.* 8.440-41, "the horses he un-yoked, the chariot he leaned on the stand" (where the acts make up one close sequence, unlike 8.433). Cp. 10.480 (one act opposed to another), 19. 392 (generally descriptive), *Od.* 3.492=15.145, 190 (close τε . . . τε coordination).

b. In an object clause governed by a verb of command: *Il.* 15.119, 16.145, 23.131.

c. The horses themselves are modified: *Il.* 8.543=*Od.* 4.39, "the sweating horses"; 11.620, "the old man's horses"; cp. 23.291, 24.279-80.

3. Horse without epithet as object of other acts

a. "To give [or receive] a horse in one's possession": *Il.* 23.540, 577, 591-92, 596-97, 609-10, 612-13, *Od.* 4.601; cp. *Il.* 5.165, 10.545, 557. So *Il.* 5.651, "to give horses in payment" (exceptions: *Il.* 10.305, 392, 11.738. Elsewhere we find no epithet but a pointed attribute of excellence: *Il.* 9.123-24, 23.265-66; cp. 11.680-81; in 5.358, 363 the gold-filleted horses of gods). Hence in *Il.* 19.281, "the horses they drove to the herd"; i.e., "took away," "took as gifts"; compare in *Il.* 5.25, 165 the captured horses which Diomedes bids be brought to the ships.

Why no epithet? The act of giving is not intrinsically pertinent to "horse." A horse is not like a man-made object, which is normally given or received and often has, in such cases, an epithet.

Hence also *Il.* 23.584, "touching the horse now swear . . . ": the horse as object of oath-taking.

b. "To see the horses": *Il.* 23.448-49, 450, 453, 458, 495-96, 498. Why no epithet? Because the interest centers on the race, not the horse; epithets would detract from the spectator's viewpoint. The horses are watched with a purpose. Cp. *Il.* 5.183.

c. *Il.* 5.775, "there did she halt the horses, the goddess white-armed Hera." The stress falls heavily on the divine charioteer. Cp. 5.368, 8.49, 13.34.

4. Other instances of horse without epithet

Il. 13.385, "came in front of the horses." Cp. 13.392, 8.134, 23.582, 24. 286. Contrast the rich use of epithets with ship in the same function (see chap. 9, sec. 1). Why is there a difference? Because "in front of the horse" implies deliberate position or some pointed effect, while the inanimate ship is visualized at once in its local connection with what takes place beside it.

Horse=chariot. *Il.* 5.19, "pushed him from the horses," i.e., "from the chariot." This is very frequent: *Il.* 5.13, 46, etc. There is no epithet since the horse's identity is lost. Exceptions are very few: *Il.* 17.504, 8.128-29; 7.15 doubtful, 18.531-32, meaning perhaps "on horseback."

"Horses and chariot" (*Il.* 4.226, 297, *Il.* 5.192, etc.), "horses and people" (*Il.* 8.214, 10.338, 18.153, etc.), "horses and mules" (*Il.* 24.350), "horse and bridle" (*Il.* 5.230), etc. We often have here a kind of hendiadys, similar to "tents and ships." The meaning "horse" is thus merged with others, losing its concrete identity. Rare exceptions: *Il.* 23.545.

Hence normally no epithet of horse as a possessive genitive: *Il.* 5.851, 8.83, etc.

Persons[3]

1. Field of vision

We have seen (p. 90) the verse end of the type αὐτὰρ Ἀχιλλεύς marking a narrative transition, wherein the proper name rightly has no epithet. Now it is interesting to notice, by way of contrast, other instances in which αὐτάρ starts a new verse and the name follows with its epithet, as in *Il.* 19.40, "then along the seashore he walked, divine Achilles"; cp. 18.203, 19.51, *Od.* 6.224, 7.139, 19.51, 20.1. In these instances the shift of narrative interest is hardly so strong; it is much weaker than, say, in *Il.* 1.247, 20.75, 21.520. No, we have, rather, juxtaposition marked by the name with its epithet. Thus in *Il.* 19.40 we see, on the one hand, Thetis tending Patroclus and, on the other, Achilles walking along the seashore. This shows the importance of visualization in Homer. In other poets we should rather find a new verse marking a new step in the narrative.

Following are other instances in which the presence or absence of the epithet marks different degrees of visualization with corresponding difference of meaning:

a. *Il.* 9.657, "along the ships they returned, and Odysseus was leading (ἦρχε δ' Ὀδυσσεύς)." Cp. 15.306, 17.107, 262, 23.12, *Od.* 2.416, 3.12, 23.370, 24.501. No epithet occurs in such a phrase as ἦρχε δ' Ὀδυσσεύς, which merely modifies the action and might be translated with a passive "led by Odysseus." We have, on the other hand, ἡγεῖτο δὲ δῖος Ὀδυσσεύς in *Il.* 9.192: here Odysseus is seen leading the way. Cp. *Il.* 1.311, 24.95–96, 14.384. Similarly we find the epithet where a character stands out against a vaguer background: *Il.* 16. 166, 18.234, 19.364, 2.446, 477, *Od.* 2.173, 19.430.

b. In *Od.* 6.106 Artemis and her nymphs gambol in their mountain haunts, "and Leto rejoices at heart (γέγηθε δὲ φρένα Λητώ)." Anything like πότνια Λητώ would be jarring: Leto's delight is not at all intrusive; it simply enhances the beauty of the scenery and gives it indefinite extension. Compare *Il.* 20. 155, and similarly in *Il.* 1.473, Apollo, unmentioned, listening to the paean; in *Od.* 3.345, Athena receiving the sacrifice.

Thus, often a god has no epithet when, in the background, he favors or thwarts the efforts of a man; the solitary name comes at the end of the line as a distant influence: *Il.* 8.311, 15.326, 360, 21.6, 304, 5.290, 20.443, 23.865.

2. Genitive

Take the first line of the *Iliad*. The wrath and its specification, "of Pelides Achilles," constitute one single, compact idea placed in focus, as if the words "of Pelides Achilles" were an epithet of "wrath." Compare similar expressions in *Il.* 1.75, 203, 5.444, 13.624, *Od.* 17.581.

Take now a few lines below (*Il.* 1.5), " and the counsel of Zeus was accomplished." The genitive without epithet stresses mere possession or relation. This is an explanatory sentence which gives us a cause and tells us that the counsel was *of* Zeus. Compare similar expressions in *Il.* 5.34, 15.593, 24.570, 20.15, *Od.* 13.127, 14.283, 328.

Here are the same trends which we have seen all along: the epithet tends to bring out a concrete, compact meaning, the lack of epithet a relation. On this basis let us look at a few significant instances:

a. "Son of . . . ," as *Il.* 2.23, Ἀτρέος υἱὲ δαΐφρονος ἱπποδάμοιο. Cp. 157, 205, etc. This is most common with nouns of kinship, friendship, attendance. The person's image is all one with these associations.

There is often no epithet, however, when such a noun is predicative or emphatic, as in *Od.* 1.207, "you *are* the son of Odysseus": *Il.* 6.460, 13.428, 17.271, 20.107, 21.95, *Od.* 2.274, 4.232, 569, 18.424; cp. *Il.* 4.354, 5.43–44, 60, 6.300, 13.519. Exceptions: *Il.* 5.813, 11.138, 24.406, *Od.* 6.196, 11.236-37.

b. "House of . . . ," as in *Od.* 2.394, βῆ δ᾽ ἴμεναι πρὸς δώματ᾽ Ὀδυσσῆος θείοιο. Cp. *Il.* 1.322, 2.9, etc. This is most common. A dwelling (house, tent, temple, etc.) makes one image with its owner as a point of arrival in full focus (see also p. 38).

There is no epithet, however, when there is particular emphasis, as in *Od.* 20.265, "this is not a public house, it is the house of Odysseus"; cp. 17.264. Nor where there is a pointed connection: *Il.* 9.147, *Od.* 2.52–54, 7.22–23, 19.571–72.

c. *Il.* 7.60 (cp. 5.693), ἐξέσθην . . . φηγῷ ἐφ᾽ ὑψηλῇ πατρὸς Διὸς αἰγιόχοιο. The epithet of Zeus confers to the oak its self-contained identity in the moment the gods alight upon it. In the same way is expressed anything similarly associated with a name and instantly presented as a vantage point to any act: cp. *Il.* 10.415, 11.372, 12.373, 24.789.

Contrast this with a loose indication of the way in *Od.* 6.291, "you will find Athena's lovely grove by the road."

d. "Shield [sword, spear, etc.] of. . . . " The possessive name-epithet phrase confers centrality, definiteness, distinctness on the object, quite apart from the need of specifying to whom the object belongs. A weapon is thus centralized over and above the warrior himself, who may lack the epithet as subject in the same passage: *Il.* 13.605-07, "Menelaus missed his blow, his spear turned aside; but Pisander struck on the shield-of-Menelaus-the-brave." Cp. *Il.* 13.159 and 164, 13.189 and 195, 20.263 (267) and 278, 20.323 and 325 (327).

Without epithet, on the other hand, there often is narrative or descriptive interest (besides the need to specify): *Il.* 13.565, "part of his spear, like a burnt stake, remained stuck on the shield of Antilochus"; cp. 17.600, 20.174, 13.504 (=16.614), 5.281-82, 13.646-47.

e. Related to the above is the function of the genitive phrase to remove all casualness, to present a thing as definitely pertinent to a certain person and conspicuously presented as such: Ajax's shield (*Il.* 8.267, 18.193), the arms of Achilles (16.134, 140, 17.195, 214), his horses (10.392, 402, 17.76, 486), the bow of Odysseus (*Od.* 21.74), the oxen of the Sun (1.8). Compare *Il.* 1.14, "holding in the hands the fillets-of-far-shooting-Apollo." Cp. 3.64, 130-31, 8.70-71.

Hence we find similarly expressed anything which the poems make intimately pertinent to a certain character. Significant in this respect are the phrases Ὀδυσσῆος ταλασίφρονος, Ὀδυσῆος ἀμύμονος, occurring only in the genitive and almost always with things which touch upon his character or his role: his return (*Od.* 1.87, 5.31; cp. 3.84), his contests (4.241), his vital strength (4.270), his distinctive voice (*Il.* 11.466), his hearth (*Od.* 14.159, 17.156, 19.304), his famous wound (19.456), or his dog Argos (17.292).

f. "The mind of Zeus." In *Il.* 15.242, επεί μιν ἔγειρε Διὸς νόος αἰγιόχοιο, the epithet makes the idea both self-contained and concrete; the mind of Zeus is here Zeus himself thinking, acting.[4] A similar self-contained concreteness is in *Il.* 14.160, 252, *Od.* 5.103 (=137); cp. *Il.* 17.409.

Without epithet, on the other hand, Zeus's mind is put in relation with narrative circumstances; it tends to become a plan, a design: *Il.* 13.524, "Ares held there by the designs of Zeus." Cp. 15.593, 24.570 (=586). Similarly the agency of other gods: *Il.* 15.412, 10.497, 15.71. A clumsy epithet is in 5.509.

g. What has just been said about Zeus might be said quite generally. Ἕκ-τορος . . . μένος ἱπποδάμοιο (*Il.* 7.38) is Hector himself in his strength. In *Il.* 17.638, Ἕκτορος ἀνδροφόνοιο μένος καὶ χεῖρας ἀάπτους is Hector advancing, his image unaffected by the construction of the surrounding clauses. There is no epithet when μένος takes a particular sense fitted to the context: *Il.* 5.892; cp. *Od.* 2.279. The epithet thus helps keep the whole phrase together, preventing the constituent words from being drawn away into the construction of the surrounding sentence. In the same way compare "the heart-of-patient-minded-Odysseus" in *Od.* 4.270 with 17.216, *Il.* 14.139.

h. "Word of . . . " In "applauding the word of godlike Odysseus" (*Il.* 2.335; cp. 7.404, 9.51, 20.295, 12.109) there is quite a different value than in "let us accept the word of Telemachus, grievous though it is" (*Od.* 20.272) or in "listen to Alexander's word [i.e., his proposal]" (*Il.* 3.87). Whereas in the latter instances the narrative restricts the meaning to a narrow, specific sense, the first one gives us the speaker himself—his actual word enclosed in the finality of the noun-epithet phrase.

3. Dative

The epithet is rarer in the dative than the genitive, since this case, more than the others, conveys intention, purpose, point. We find the epithet when the dative is intrinsic to the nature of the act expressed in the governing verb, that is, existentially pertinent to the meaning of the verb. Consider the following:

a. "Pray [make offerings] to a god." The epithet is here very frequent: *Il.* 1.36, 438, etc.

b. "Deliver a message . . . ": *Il.* 7.373, 15.158, 17.701, *Od.* 14.497, 15.41, 151, 314, 16.329, 458.

c. "Fight against . . . ": *Il.* 3.434, 7.42, 75, 112, 169, 9.356, 13.80, 21.193.

d. "Generate [beget to . . .]": of a woman to a man: *Il.* 2.515, 6.22, 196, 16.176, 20.384, *Od.* 12.133.

e. "Resemble . . . ": this is very frequent in the epiphanies of a god in the shape of a man or woman whose image stands out: *Il.* 2.20-21, 3.386, 4.87, etc.

The epithet, on the other hand, tends to be absent in the "dative of interest": a character sinks into the background as recipient or witness of whatever may occur. We have a relation rather than direct action passing from subject to object:

Od. 4.166, "to Telemachus [that is to say, "in the eyes of Telemachus," "in relation to Telemachus"] away he is gone." Cp. 4.215, 664, 13.35, 16.347, 372, 421, 24.309.

"Woe to . . . , pride to . . .": *Il.* 15.110, 2.160, 176, 304, 4.28, 173; "safety to . . .": *Il.* 8.283, 18.102. "Better for . . . ": 19.63. "To grant glory or victory to . . . ": *Il.* 12.174, 255 (=15.327, 16.730), 15.644, 18.456, 19.414, 22.58, 24.110, 13.347, 21.472; cp. 1.159, 24.57, *Od.* 3.57, 4.209 (a clumsy epithet in *Il.* 14.365, 15.597, 12.438).

"Make a bed for . . . ": *Il.* 9.621, *Od.* 13.73; "a warm bath for . . . ": *Il.* 22. 444; "build ships for . . . ": *Il.* 5.62. Cp. 24.279, *Od.* 3.475.

The meaning of the verb may imply an ulterior motive, as "to wink at . . . ": *Il.* 9.180, 223; cp. 10.476, 19.83; "promise . . . ": *Il.* 5.715, 832, 19.194 (exception in 13.376); "fear for . . . ": 21.328, 23.822; "pay to . . . ": *Od.* 2.133; "propose to . . . ": 2.194.

"To help (ἀμύνω, "ward off for . . .)": *Il.* 11.589, 17.564, 18.171, *Od.* 21.195 and 197. "Relent . . . ": *Il.* 1.283, *Od.* 21.378.

To the objection that in many of these instances the person's name is at the beginning of the line (thus favoring the lack of epithet), we may reply that the position is due to the thrust of the sentence.

The dative without epithet also conveys a relation which is intimate but which outweighs the person, who again sinks into the background. Thus *Il.* 1.188, "grief came to Achilles"; cp. 7.216, 12.392, 24.585. In 5.493, "to Hector the word bit the mind"; cp. 22.78, 10.367, 12.80, 16.656. We find the epithet, however, in *Il.* 14.459=13.418, 14.487, 17.123. See also p. 88. In *Il.* 1.24, ἀλλ᾽ οὐκ Ἀτρεΐδῃ Ἀγαμέμνονι ἥνδανε θυμῷ, Agamemnon is virtually the subject; cp. 15.674.

"To give to . . . " or "hand over to. . . . " There is usually no epithet (if there is an epithet, it is mostly of the giver or of the given object): *Il.* 22.277, 5.272, 10.255, 260, 529, 23.296, 565, 16.381, 18.84, *Od.* 8.254, 262, 478, 13.57, 18.292, 295, 297. But we find the epithet in *Il.* 2.103-06, 5.1, *Od.* 14.447, 21.379; cp. 18.159—instances in which the moment of receiving particularly stands out.

"To send to . . . ": no epithet in *Il.* 9.253, 439, 11.766, *Od.* 14.336; but contrast these instances with *Il.* 24.117.

"To do a favor for (χαρίζομαι) . . . ": no epithet in *Il.* 15.449, 17.291; but an epithet with the more concrete "bring pleasure to" (φέρων χάριν): *Il.* 5.211, 1.572.

"To plan for [devise] . . . ": no epithet in *Od.* 4.843, 16.372, 421; but in *Od.* 6.14 (cp. 8.9, 5.233) we have Athena "planning the return for great-hearted Odysseus." The epithet is justified by the intimate association of the return with Odysseus' name. See p. 200.

We may mention here the meaning "go to . . . " with a person as accusative of direction. There is no epithet most often: *Il.* 6.280, 8.272, 13.279, 459, 469, 15.402, 22.214, 24.338, *Od.* 20.372, 23.314. Usage wavers, however: cp. *Il.* 2.18, 7.312, 10.54, 73, 150, *Od.* 5.149. In fact Homer generally tends to avoid this form of expression. He usually mentions "house of . . . ," "tent of . . . " as a term of direction: *Il.* 1.323, 426, etc.; "the spot where": 4.210,

24.472, *Od.* 6.15, 17.68; or, very frequently, the person as object of finding, visiting: *Il.* 1.498, 3.125, 4.89, etc. See also pp. 87 and 199. This is again a proof of Homer's concreteness: "going to . . ." is most pertinently joined to a sense of place; and the epithet marks this concrete connection.

Epithets in the Genitive

An important function of the epithet, we have seen, is to highlight a thing in immediate connection with an act, so that the act itself (along with the sentence) acquires a weight of its own.

This is true also of epithets in the genitive, but with a difference. The noun-epithet phrase is here often governed by another noun, and it is the whole expression (noun + noun-epithet phrase) which thus gives its weight to a single act. In *Od.* 14.311, for instance, "and Zeus . . . put in my hands the-mast-impregnable-of-the-blue-prowed-ship," the sudden and instant happening takes its full dimension in the full, rounded phrase (cp. 7.252); and we must read in the same way any such sentence, whatever the field of meaning—e.g., *Il.* 13. 606, "he struck on the-shield-of-Menelaus-the-brave."

As a result, the strongest intimacy of relation binds the genitive noun-epithet phrase to the governing noun. The whole expression is one single idea. The force of the epithet spreads over the whole. Thus the reality of the "blue-prowed ship" gives significance to "mast"; or, again, in "shore-of-the-wide-roaring-sea" it is the shore as well as the sea that resounds; in "fulfillment-of-blossoming-marriage" it is the fulfillment as well as the idea of marriage which gives a sense of bloom.

Thus we cannot parse these sentences word by word. These genitives cannot be described merely as "possessive." It might be truer to say that we have here genitives of the whole encompassing the part. The idea of the whole sea is intrinsic to that of shore, the idea of the whole ship to that of the mast; and the shield may be seen as an extension of Menelaus himself. Hence the integrity of this imagery. The close-knit syntax of these phrases cannot be broken up, can hardly be affected by narrative ramifications.

"Beautiful" [5]

The ordinary word for "beautiful," καλός, is not an epithet on the basis of our definition: it is often used with emphasis as a comparative or superlative, as a predicate, or as a neuter abstract, adverbially. But it is used neither casually nor arbitrarily. It has a frame of reference which is natural to it, and thus throws light on the same principle of concreteness as the epithets.

Consider, first of all, certain ways in which καλός is *not* used:

a. It is not referred to qualities or intangibles such as "virtue," "youth," "life." We find it, at the most, with "voice" (*Od.* 5.61, 12.192, 24.60) or "wind" (*Od.* 11.640, 14.253, 299).

b. It is not referred to countries, places, cities. The only passages in which we find it so used are in the *Shield of Achilles: Il.* 18.490-91, "and in it he fashioned two beautiful cities of men"; 18.588, "in it he fashioned a pasture in a beautiful glen"; for these cities and glen are works of art, not actual scenery. A negligible exception is *Il.* 9.152, καλήν τ' Αἴπειαν—a city offered by Agamemnon to Achilles as if it were an object. Homer uses ἐραννός, etc. in this sense: see p. 120.

c. It is not normally an epithet with names of persons, except in mythical or genealogical passages, which are less characteristically Homeric: *Il.* 5.389, 8.305, 9.556, 16.175, *Od.* 11.271, 281, 321. The only real exception seems to be *Od.* 3.464, καλὴ Πολυκάστη; elsewhere it is emphatic as a superlative or with superlative meaning (*Il.* 2.673, 3.169, etc.); joined with other adjectives, especially καλός τε μέγας τε (*Il.* 21.108, *Od.* 1.301); with such appellatives as "girl," "daughter" (*Il.* 22.155, *Od.* 8.320; cp. 6.108).

Consider, on the other hand, what things are most often qualified by καλός:

a. Man-made objects. Basket (*Il.* 9.217, etc.); cups of different kinds (*Od.* 1.137, *Il.* 24.429, etc.); mantle or tunic (*Il.* 24.588, *Od.* 8.441, etc.); table (*Od.* 8.69), and so forth. Especially frequent are the neuter plurals εἵματα, τεύχεα, δώματα—garments, arms, house visualized as one whole (*Od.* 6.111, *Il.* 3.328, 11.77, etc.).

b. Parts of the human body. Neck (*Il.* 3.396), ankles (*Il.* 4.147), hair (*Il.* 14.177), skin (*Il.* 11.352, etc.), face (*Il.* 19.285, etc.), eyes (*Il.* 23.66, etc.).

c. Natural objects, elements of nature. The pure flowing water of a river (*Od.* 6.87; cp. 85), Scamander's current (*Il.* 21.238, etc.), a tree (*Il.* 2.307, 5.693, 17.55). When the view extends to a larger landscape there must be the additional idea of luxuriance, fertility. So we find in *Il.* 6.195, 20.185 (cp. 12.314) τέμενος . . . καλὸν φυταλιῆς καὶ ἀρούρης. Compare Laertes's beautiful cultivated field in *Od.* 24.206, and in 7.114 (if the reading καλά is right) Alcinous's orchard, where the beauty of a mass of trees is coupled with that of their bloom.

In *Od.* 12.318, "the beautiful dancing-places of the nymphs" and *Il.* 20.8, "beautiful groves," the sense of beauty is accompanied by that of religiousness; cp. *Od.* 6.266.

These instances show how καλός applies mostly to what is distinctly perceived as a self-contained form. We thus find it with parts of the body rather than with the whole person; not with a whole land, but at the most with an orchard or grove; not with a city, but a house or a wall (*Il.* 21.447), a battlement (*Il.* 22.3), a harbor (*Od.* 6.263). Similarly it is never said of a river, but of its water or current. Consequently we never find it, for instance, referred to mountains, sky, earth, sea.

Most characteristic of Homer appears the connection of καλός with man-made objects whose clear and solid form is as satisfying to the eye as it is appropriate to practical use. Especially interesting in this respect is the occurrence of καλός in emphatic position at the beginning of a line and immediately followed by epithets or by a relative sentence which more nearly portrays the nature and configuration of the object in question. Thus in *Il.* 11.628-29, "she laid before them a table/beautiful, enamel-footed, well-polished"; cp. *Il.* 2.43, 3.331 (=11.18, 16.132, cp. 18.459), 5.194, 731, 9.187, 11.33, 12.295, cp. 13.611, 14.185, 15.705, 16.222, 18.390, 612, 19.380, 22.154, 314, 23.268, cp. 807, 24.266, *Od.* 1.131, 137 (=4.53, etc.), 5.232, 14.7, 21.7.

These instances tell us a great deal about the perception of beauty. What the epithets bring out as a distinctive feature is gathered by καλός into a diffusive quality. On the one hand, the positive, material identity of each particular thing and, on the other, a more general appeal which springs from it, often emphasized for its own sake. We have two intimately related values. They continually suggest each other so as to blend into one. Aesthetic appreciation arises spontaneously, but enveloped in a strong feeling for the structure and function of the material. And the inverse is also true: structure and function inevitably suggest beauty. Compare my remarks on the scarceness of Homeric epithets that express mere utility (see p. 120).

The Epithets of the Suitors in the *Odyssey* [6]

The suitors (who are, as far as this is possible in Homer, the villains of the piece) have the epithets ἀγανός, ἀγήνωρ, ἀντίθεος insofar as they are objectively seen, met, accounted for. Consider the following:

Od. 1.106, εὖρε δ' ἄρα μνηστῆρας ἀγήνορας. Cp. 17.325, 21.58. What matters is the actuality of the suitors in that they are found to be there. See p. 87.

Od. 1.144, ἐς δ' ἦλθον μνηστῆρες ἀγήνορες. Cp. 17.105. We again have the suitors themselves—their coming, their presence. They have a similarly positive epithet when fully visualized performing a certain act: *Od.* 14.18, 180, 17.65, 18.99, 21.174, 232; and this is so even if their act is a wicked one: *Od.* 2.235. See p. 86.

Od. 23.8, μνηστῆρας δ' ἔκτεινεν ἀγήνορας. Cp. 2.247, 19.488, 496, 21.213, 18.346: the suitors visualized as sufferers, victims. For this function of the epithet, see p. 87. It is typical of Homer to say "Odysseus slew the brave suitors" and not, for example, "the shameless suitors." Notice that in many cases ἀναιδέας could have replaced ἀγήνορας with little trouble.

A derogatory epithet would have been out of place in any of the above instances. Think how un-Homeric the effect would be if the suitors were always called scoundrels.

We do find, on the other hand, the attributes "overweening," "shameless" (ὑπερφίαλος, ἀναιδής). But these are normally used in a different way. "Do not consort with the overweening suitors," (*Od.* 18.167) says Penelope to Telemachus. Similar expressions on the lips of Odysseus: *Od.* 15.315, 16.271; cp. 4.766, 2.266. Or again, Penelope is pictured anxiously wondering whether her son "might be subdued by the overweening suitors" (*Od.* 4.790). Cp. 13.373, 376, 14.27, 20.12, 29, 4.766.

The attributes "overweening" and "shameless" are obviously justified in these instances. Whether in direct speech or not, they are used from the viewpoint of the characters that oppose the suitors. For instance, *Od.* 20.29, "pondering how he might lay hands on the shameless suitors"; 14.27, "he sent . . . perforce a boar to the overweening suitors."

This contrast in expression is remarkably well sustained throughout the poem. Exceptions are negligible: *Od.* 20.291, "he spoke amongst the overweening suitors" and the verse (2.324, etc.) ὧδε δέ τις εἴπεσκε νέων ὑπερηνορεόντων. But is ὑπερηνορεόντων really derogatory? In a pejorative sense we find the adverb κακῶς (*Od.* 2.266, 4.766).

This use of epithets on the one hand and of derogatory attributes on the other is quite in tune with Homer's general picture of the suitors. As presented by the poet to our view, they are essentially a band of banqueting and sporting young men: *Od.* 1.106-12, 144-52, 4.624-26, 16.407-08, etc. We never see them doing any specific outrageous deeds as part of their normal behavior; such deeds are normally attributed to them by their opponents, as when Odysseus says to Eumaeus (*Od.* 16.106-09), "I would rather be dead than have this sight ever before me—strangers being beaten and women shamelessly dragged through the halls. . . ." So 20.317-19, cp. 1.225-29, and in 15. 329, 17.565 the strong statement, "whose outrage and violence reaches up to the sky." In any case, it is most remarkable that the wrongdoing of the suitors is only implied, that it is never made by the poet into a specific narrative theme, as might be expected in any other epic or story.

No, we gain our first impression of the suitors from μνηστῆρες ἀγήνορες (*Od.* 1.144), and ἀγήνωρ is in Homer also the epithet of a strong heart. We cannot translate these Homeric epithets with our own narrowly qualifying adjectives. They conjure up a person's image before the complications of the plot draw out a character. Here is a basic form of identity—as innocent as a name, as vital as a way of being.

What else could the suitors be but ἀνήνορες, ἀγαυοί, ἀντίθεοι, as we see them by themselves, in the prime of life, wooing a woman? "None others would anyone choose, collecting the best in the city," says Agamemnon, seeing their ghosts arriving in Hades (*Od.* 24.107-08). Nothing perturbs them up to their last days. Their glorious epithets, just like those of cup or krater, solidify the imagery of a charmed life. But at the same time, we are made to feel from the beginning that they are guilty, driven by their very role to intolerable encroachment; and they go to their ruin, caught up in the catastrophe of Odysseus' return. This is not the usual story of villains struck down by a hero: it is, rather, a state of things and an existential condition which contains within itself the source of doom.

NOTES

Chapter 1

1. Ralph Waldo Emerson, *Journal* 54 (1863).
2. Max Eastman, *Enjoyment of Poetry* (New York, 1913), p. 49.
3. Ibid., p. 51.
4. James Scully, ed., *Modern Poets on Modern Poetry* (London, 1966), p. 197.

Chapter 3

1. Compare the use of similar terms (though with different assumptions) in Cedric Whitman, *Homer and the Heroic Tradition* (New York, 1965), p. 105.

Chapter 7

1. The word ῥέθεα used here and in 22.68 must mean something different from merely "body" or "limbs." It recurs later in the meaning "countenance," "face." Cp. M. Leumann, *Homerische Wörter* (Basel, 1950), p. 218-22, and P. Vivante, "Sulla designazione del corpo in Omero," *Archivio Glottologico Italiano* (1955), p. 41.
2. Walter Arend, *Die typischen Scenen bei Homer* (Berlin, 1933), pp. 9-27.
3. For instance, Bernard Fenik, *Typical Battle Scenes in the Iliad* (Wiesbaden, 1968).

Chapter 9

1. Epithets of ship: ἀμφιέλισσα, γλαφυρή, δολιχήρετμος, ἐίση, εὐεργής, εὔζυγος, εὔπρυμνος, ἐύσσελμος, θοή, κοίλη, κορωνίς, κυανόπρωρος -εως, μεγακήτης, μέλαινα, μιλτοπάρῃος, ὀρθοκραίρη, πολύζυγος, πολύκληις, ποντοπόρος, φοινικοπάρῃος, ὠκύαλος, ὠκύπορος, ὠκύς.
2. An exception in *Il.* 10.509-10, *Od.* 4.172-73, where the action noun νόστος has a special verbal force: cp. *Od.* 1.78. So in *Il.* 14.410, θοάων ἔχματα νηῶν, "what holds the swift ships."
3. For further evidence on the presence and absence of the epithet with "ship," see the Appendix.

Chapter 10

1. Epithets of horse: ἀερσίπους, ἐριαύχην, ἐρυσάρματες, εὔθριξ, εὔσκαρθμος, καλλίθριξ, κεντρηνεκής, κρατερῶνυξ, μώνυχες, ποδώκης, ταχύς, ὑψηχής, ὠκύπος, ὠκύς.
2. For further evidence on the presence and absence of epithet with "horse," see Appendix.

Chapter 11

1. Epithets of sea: ἀπείρων, ἀτρύγετος, βαθύς, δῖος, εὐρύπορος, εὐρύς, ἠεροειδής, ἠχήεις, ἰοειδής, ἰχθυόεις, κυμαίνων, μαρμάρεος, μεγακήτης, μέλας, οἶνοψ, πολιός, πολύκλυστος, πολύφλοισβος, πορφύρεος. Also such phrases as: εὐρέα νῶτα θαλάσσης, θαλάσσης εὐρέα κόλπον, μέγα λαῖτμα θαλάσσης, ὑγρὰ κέλευθα.
2. Contrast the lack of epithet with παρὰ νῆας, along the ships"; see p. 193 above. While the ships are in this function an intentional indication of place, the line of the seashore is instead a natural boundary.
3. In the same passage (*Od.* 11.124, 23.271), "those who know not the red-cheeked ships"; cp. p. 196 below. Ships are thought of and known in human terms, as something to be used and handled; not so the sea.
4. γλαυκὴ δέ σε τίκτε θάλασσα. Patroclus says to Achilles, "Not Thetis is your mother, but the gray sea gave you birth." Or γλαυκή (cp. Leaf *a.l.*) means "gleaming," but gleaming in a terrific way. Notice how easily πολιή could have been used. Add here *Il.* 21.58–59, οὐδέ μιν ἔσχε πόντος ἁλὸς πολιῆς, an unusual phrase, perhaps perversely ironical; cp. p. 195 above.
5. In *Od.* 7.273, ἀθέσφατον is no proper epithet of the sea.
6. Epithets of the earth: ἀπείρων, ἀπειρεσίη, βωτιάνειρα, ἐρίβωλος, εὐρεῖα, εὐρυοδείη, ζείδωρος, μέλαινα, πολυφόρβη, πουλυβότειρα, φυσίζοος.
7. An exception appears in *Il.* 21.426, which is mock-heroic.
8. In *Il.* 16.384, ὡς δ᾽ ὑπὸ λαίλαπι πᾶσα κελαινὴ βέβριθε χθὼν, the adjective has a pointed meaning: "dark with the clouds that cover it" (Leaf). κελαινή is not used as an epithet of earth. In *Od.* 12.243, "beneath, the earth showed black with sand," we have a descriptive predicate.
9. Epithets of sky: ἀστερόεις, εὐρύς, μέγας, πολύχαλκος, σιδήρεος, χάλκεος.
10. There is a notable exception in the phrase Ζεὺς . . . ἐρίγδουπος πόσις Ἥρης, "Zeus . . . thunderous husband of Hera," as in *Il.* 7.411, "of the oaths let Zeus be the witness, the thunderous husband of Hera" or *Od.* 8.465, "may Zeus bring this about, the thunderous husband of Hera." Cp. *Il.* 10.329, *Od.* 15.112, 180. But the phrase may here have a reason; or at least we may trace its origin: Zeus always thunders, giving a sign of things to be. So in *Il.* 15.377, "loudly thundered wise Zeus, hearing Nestor's prayer." Cp. 8.75, 170, etc.

Chapter 12

1. *Il.* 11.482 (*Od.* 3.163, etc.), ἀμφ᾽ Ὀδυσῆα δαΐφρονα ποικιλομήτην; *Il.* 11.419, ἀμφ᾽ Ὀδυσῆα Διὶ φίλον; 18.69, ταχὺν ἀμφ᾽ Ἀχιλῆα. 11.475, ἀμφ᾽ ἔλαφον κεραὸν. Cp. 4.252, 295–96, 6.436–37, 9.81–82, 11.57–60,

12.414, 13.790-91, 15.301-02, etc. That meaning is here relevant to the epithet is shown by the variety of instances.
2. For further evidence (including cases other than the nominative), see the Appendix.

Chapter 13

1. Cp. Charles P. Segal, "Bacchylides Reconsidered: Epithets and the Dynamics of Lyric Narrative," *Quaderni Urbinati di Cultura Classica* 22 (1976):105.
2. William James, *The Principles of Psychology* (London, 1918), vol. 1, p. 243.

Chapter 14

1. Cp. J. Wackernagel, *Vorlesungen ueber Syntax* (Basel, 1928), vol. 2, p. 65.
2. "Poetry and Language in Homer," *Ramus* 2 (1973): 147-49.
3. θρασύς occurs, however, with a pointed meaning in *Od.* 10.436, σὺν δ᾽ ὁ θρασὺς εἵπετ᾽ Ὀδυσσεύς, the article foreshadowing a later usage. The article with the epithet posits a problem, as in *Il.* 2.278, where we might read δέ instead of δ᾽ ὁ.
4. Note here *Od.* 8.38, θοὴν ἀλεγύνετε δαῖτα, "quickly prepare the meal." I would not call this "proleptic epithet meaning." We see, rather, the epithet's inability to be a predicate of the same meaning. It lacks nimbleness. When predicative, it becomes virtually an adverb. Cp. *Il.* 19.276, λῦσεν δ᾽ ἀγορὴν αἰψηρήν.
5. This active force comes up later in ἀλάστωρ. The development of meaning would be "unforgetting," "relentless," "pursuing." For both active and passive meaning, cp. ἄπυστος (*Od.* 4.675 and 1.242) and see Wackernagel, *Vorlesungen ueber Syntax*, vol. 1, p. 136.
   Chapman renders "thou . . . pestilence . . . to my sere spirits."
6. For a different view of these passages, cp. Anne Amory Parry, *Blameless Aegisthus* (Leiden, 1973), pp. 105, 107, 110-12. I think it is essential to stress here the rare predicative function.
7. Cp. Norman Austin, *Archery at the Dark of the Moon, Poetic Problems in Homer's* Odyssey (University of California Press, 1975), pp. 74ff. both on the connection with speech and on the meaning of the word.
8. It might be objected that in the vocative we find name and epithet unconnected with any verb; but even here a verb is implicit: we may understand the act of hearing, listening.

Chapter 15

1. An epithet used instead of the noun is frequent in the case of gods (γλαυκῶπις, ἑκάεργος, etc.). For heroes, cp. διογενής, διοτρεφής, *Il.* 21.17, 75, etc. At times it is doubtful which is the name and which the epithet: Δῖον Ἀγαυόν in *Il.* 24.251, cp. 13.693, 15.340. This is quite natural where the person's name has a transparent meaning. Common nouns: κυνοραϊστέων (*Od.* 17.300); ὀλοοίτροχος (*Il.* 13.137); ἐᾱνός, I take it, from ἔᾱνος. What stands out is the substantive sense of the epithet.

There is nothing riddlelike such as has been (perhaps wrongly) found in Hesiod's ἀνόστεος (*Op.* 524; cp. 529, 571, 695).

2. I give the main synonyms with their main terms of reference. ταχύς, ὠκύς (which are convenient metrical variants) have generally the same frame of reference—to heroes, horses, deer; ὠκύς, also of birds; ταχύς, frequently of feet. ποδάρκης, only Achilles; ποδώκης, Achilles, horses; ὠκύπους, only horses; ἀργός, ἀργίπους, only dogs; ποδήνεμος, ἀελλόπος, only Iris; κραιπνός, feet, storm, wind; καρπάλιμος, only feet; ἐλαφρός, nimble limbs; θοός, ships; ὠκυπόρος; ὠκύαλος, only ships. Compare Vivante, "Poetry and Language in Homer," p. 161.

3. This is, of course, not to say that Homer ignores the abstract antithesis of opposites. He knows it as well as we do. Cp. *Od.* 8.329, κιχάνει τοι βραδὺς ὠκύν, 8.310-11. So *Il.* 5.801, 13.278, 9.320, 12.446-47. But it is the way of poetry, and of Homer in particular, to go to the essence of things rather than to their relative qualities. The epithets are a constant reminder of this. They necessarily eschew the distinction of more or less. Hence they are rarely used as comparatives.

Chapter 16

1. We might expect βαρείη instead of παχείη at *Il.* 17.296, where the sense is doubtful, and 21.424 (mock-heroic battle of gods). In 21.590 the inferior reading παχείης for βαρείης.
2. On Penelope's hand, see further p. 12*n*, below.
3. Cp. *Il.* 17.296 (doubtful sense), 21.424 (mock-heroic): 21.590 (with the inferior reading παχείης for βαρείης).
4. With or without some slight alteration (such as ἐς for εἰς or the insertion of *ν* -movable) αἰπύν could often replace μακρόν: cp. *Il.* 1.402, 2.48, 8.410, 18.142, *Od.* 20.73. Nevertheless, we find μακρόν fourteen times against two (*Il.* 5.367=868, 15.84).
5. Compare the different nuance of snow covering ὑψηλῶν ὀρέων κορυφὰς (*Il.* 12.282), but people inhabiting ὀρέων αἰπεινὰ κάρηνα (*Od.* 6.123; cp. *Il.* 2.869). Hence ὑψηλός of a wave-smitten promontory (*Il.* 2.395), a riverbank hit by a spear (*Il.* 21.171), a peak upon which two birds are fighting (*Il.* 16.429). On the other hand, we never find anything like ὑψηλὸν ἵκανεν Ὄλυμπον.
6. Note the meaning of ῥηγμῖν: broken sea between rocks.
7. While πυκνός referring to mind is in Homer suggestive of wisdom, λεπτός "tenuous," "subtle," is instead synonymous with foolish: *Il.* 10.226, 23.590. This is the opposite of Latin *subtilis*, English *subtle*, etc. Even in Classical Greek λεπτός means "refined," "sophisticated."
8. Philip Buttman, *Lexilogus,* trans. J. R. Fishlake (London, 1836), pp. 32-37. So Leaf (on *Il.* 2.87) gives an alternative chain of meanings.
9. A possible exception in *Od.* 19.494.
10. A horse's glossy mane (*Il.* 17.439); thighs (*Il.* 15.113); fat (*Od.* 8.476); young men, a young husband or wife (*Il.* 3.26, 53, 6.430, etc.); and marriage (*Od.* 6.66), seen as fruition, ripeness, fulfillment.
11. The same feeling in θῆλυς ἐέρση, τεθαλυῖα τ᾽ ἐέρση (*Od.* 5.467, 13.245).
12. See Leaf on *Il.* 3.142. Comparing Latin *teres*, he discards the meaning "tender" in that it is not suited to the flesh of stalwart warriors. But we

must not be misled by the connotations of modern words. In Homer "tender," "soft," "blossoming," "sappy" all merge into one meaning which fits the nature of a full, sensitive material. In this sense a warrior's is no different from a child's. It would be un-Homeric to adapt the epithet to a character's appearance. Cp. Penelope's "thick hand" in *Od.* 21.6.

13. On the meaning of λειριόεις, see Leumann, *Homerische Wörter*, p. 27.

14. Eustathius in his commentary brings out well the common trait which the elders share with the cicadas: continuity of speech, uninterrupted hum, flowing quality of sound, clarity. On Homer's cicadas and the Greek perception of sound, see W. B. Stanford, "The Lily Voice of the Cicadas" (*Il.* 3.152), *Phoenix* 23 (1969): 3–8.

15. Leumann (*Homerische Wörter*, pp. 27–28) arrives at the following conclusion about λειριόεις: "A common meaning cannot be determined, we only have a twofold Homeric usage in reference to skin (or part of the body) and to voice. Neither can we derive one usage from the other in any normal way, nor can both of them be significantly grouped around a single core of meaning or an original λείριος, -ον. The problem is insoluble because we lack certain irrecoverable phases between the two meanings." This is, again, the kind of approach we must avoid in this case. We should try to realize the meaning from a Homeric or poetic point of view rather than give up because our abstract categories yield no result.

16. The "accusative of relation" has in Homer a concrete significance in expressing the part along with the whole. On the linguistic facts, see E. Schwyzer, *Griechische Grammatik* (Munich, 1950), vol. 2, pp. 84–86; P. Chantraine, *Grammaire Homérique* (Paris, 1963), vol. 2, pp. 46–48. On the poetic implications, see Vivante, "Sull' espressione della parte e del tutto in Omero," *Accademia toscana di scienze e lettere "La Colombaria"* (Florence, 1955).

17. We thus need not explain with Leaf (*a.l.*), "not plain, but adorned." The use of τετυγμένος in *Od.* 9.223 (in the island of the Cyclops) seems to exclude any idea of decoration.

18. See also the Appendix on καλός.

19. Color in Homer has been much studied. A starting point is W. E. Gladstone, *Studies in Homer and the Homeric Age* (Oxford, 1858), vol. 3, pp. 457–99, and "The Colour Sense," *The Nineteenth Century* 2 (1877): 366–88. Gladstone saw that the sense of light and darkness prevails in Homer over that of color; and he thus points to a quantitative rather than qualitative sense of the differences of color, based on the degree of light and shade. Cp. M. Platnauer, "Greek Colour Perception," *Classical Quarterly* 15 (1921): 153–62. I find in Gladstone the important statement that "colours were in Homer not facts but images" ("The Colour Sense," p. 386). But the assumption of primitive insensitivity to color provoked a series of rebuttals: cp. A. de Keersmacker, *Le sens de la couleur chez Homère* (Bruges, 1885); E. Veckenstedt, *Geschichte der Griechischen Farbenlehre* (Paderborn, 1888); F. E. Wallace, "Color in Homer and in Ancient Art," *Smith College Classical Studies* 9 (1927): 1–53. The trouble with these studies is that they aim to give abstract definitions of color and to find exact modern equivalents of the ancient terms. The vital relation between color and the substance of things comes up, on the

other hand, in Eleanor Irwin, *Colour Terms in Greek Poetry* (Toronto, 1974). See the latter, pp. 13–17, for a bibliographical discussion.
20. I can find only χλαῖναν . . . φοινικόεσσαν (*Il.* 10.133, *Od.* 14.500, 21. 118), χλαῖναν πορφυρέην (*Od.* 4.115, 154, 19.225), σφαῖραν . . . πορφυρέην (*Od.* 8.372–73). There is no apparent reason why these things should have such colors.
21. Thus Zenodotus conventionally reads ἡρώων for κυάνεαι in *Il.* 4.282.
22. Cp. Leaf on *Il.* 5.770.

Chapter 17

1. Compare Ὑπερήνωρ, ὑπερηνορέων, on the one hand, and ὑπέρθυμος on the other, where the endings -ήνωρ and -θυμος correspond to each other. Another common trait is that the epithets μεγαλήτωρ and ἀγήνωρ are both used with θυμός.
    We have the positive idea of ἀγαπάω ("to be well" in *Od.* 21.289) particularized in the form of a man rather than the meaning "man-loving" or "loving manliness." Compare the name Βιήνωρ.
2. On the sense of glory in Homer, compare P. Vivante *Homeric Imagination* (Bloomington, Indiana, 1970), pp. 124–27.
3. On Odysseus' epithets, cp. John H. Finley, *Homer's Odyssey* (Cambridge, 1978), pp. 34–36.
4. We do find, of course, an instance such as Κυκλώπων δ' ἐς γαίαν ὑπερφιάλων ἀθεμίστων (*Od.* 9.106); but ὑπερφίαλος, ἀθέμιστος are not epithets. Especially when used in reference to persons, epithets differ from ordinary adjectives in that the latter are used (1) with emphasis, (2) as predicates, (3) with appellatives ("man," "woman," etc.) rather than with a proper name. Compare the use of ἀτάσθαλος, ὀβριμοεργός, κακομήχανος, ἀΐδηλος.
5. The suitors of the *Odyssey* provide another, more sustained, example of how the concrete meaning of the epithet obviates any moralistic preoccupation. A survey of the instances shows that they have such epithets as ἀγήνωρ, ἀγανός, ἀντίθεος insofar as they are objectively seen, met, accounted for, while they are given derogatory attributes (ἀναιδής, ὑπερφίαλος) either in direct speech by their opponents or in strict connection with some opposing plan or thought. This is almost always the case: for a full discussion, see Appendix.

Chapter 18

1. Cp. Simone Weil, "L' 'Iliade' ou le poème de la force," in *La source grecque* (Paris, 1953), pp. 15–17.
2. John Ruskin, *Modern Painters,* pt. IV, chap. XII.
3. Matthew Arnold, *On Translating Homer*, section I.
4. Milman Parry, *The Making of Homeric Verse* (Oxford, 1971), p. 125.
5. With φυσίζοος αἶα in *Il.* 3.243 compare γῆ φυσίζοος in 21.63, where the sentence itself gives the epithet a grim significance. Similarly ἠριγένεια in *Od.* 22.197.

Chapter 19

1. Cp. M. C. and N. K. Chadwick, *The Growth of Literature* (Cambridge, 1932), vol. 1, pp. 22-23, 31, 44, 59, 62, vol. 2, pp. 71, 74, 340, 480-81, vol. 3, pp. 42-43, 753. On the epithets, cp. C. M. Bowra, *Heroic Poetry* (London, 1966), pp. 233-34. On the number of days, cp. G. Finsler, *Homer* (Leipzig, 1924), vol. 1, pp. 243-44; S. E. Bassett, *The Poetry of Homer* (Berkeley, 1938), pp. 42-43 and passim. See also Vivante, *Homeric Imagination*, pp. 129-33.
2. Chadwicks, *Growth of Literature*, vol. 1, p. 23.

Chapter 20

1. On early classifications of the parts of speech, see H. Steinthal, *Geschichte der Sprachwissenschaft der Griechen und Römer* (Berlin, 1891), vol. 2, pp. 209-61; J. Wackernagel, *Vorlesungen über Syntax* (Basel, 1928), vol. 1, pp. 12-26.
2. Dionysius Thrax, *Ars Grammatica,* ed. G. Uhlig (Lipsiae, 1883), pp. 636, 19.
3. See the περί ὀνομάτων in Apollonius, *Works and Fragments,* ed. R. Schneider and G. Uhlig (Leipzig, 1910), vol. 3, pp. 48-54.
4. Steinthal, *Geschichte der Sprachwissenschaft,* pp. 251-52. For a modern statement of the same principle, see Louis Hjelmslev, *Sur l'indépendance de l'épithète* (Copenhagen, 1956), p. 8.
5. Apollonius, *Works and Fragments,* vol. 3, p. 38.
6. Apollonius Dyscolus, *De Syntaxi,* 19.7. Cp. Steinthal, *Geschichte der Sprachwissenschaft,* vol. 2, p. 239.
7. It is significant that in Apollonius the Greek ὑπαρκτικόν (from which *substantivum* is translated) is not applied to the noun but the the verb *to be,* and this is the meaning of *substantivum* in Priscianus.
8. Cp. F. Brunot, *La pensée et la langue* (Paris, 1953), p. 599.
9. See, for instance, Diomedes, *Ars Grammatica,* 1:323 and 459, and Donatus, *Ars Grammatica,* 4:374 and 400, both in H. Keil's *Grammatici Latini.*
10. See *Thesaurus Linguae Latinae* (Lipsiae, 1900), s.v. *epitheton.*
11. H. Meylan-Faure, *Les épithètes dans Homère* (Lausanne, 1899), pp. 14-16.
12. H. Düntzer, *Homerische Abhandlungen* (Leipzig, 1872), pp. 509-11.
13. L. Bergson, *L'épithète ornamentale dans Eschyle, Sophocle et Euripide* (Lund, 1956), pp. 17-18.
14. Parry, *Making of Homeric Verse,* p. 15.
15. See Parry, *Making of Homeric Verse,* p. 153. Parry adopts Brunot's definition of epithets as words or phrases which are attributes of a noun without the intermediary of the copula. This, however, is not correct: the copula is not necessary for a predicate adjective. For instances in Greek, see E. Schwyzer and A. Debrunner, *Griechische Grammatik* (Munich, 1950), vol. 2, p. 623: for the general principles, see A. Meillet, "La phrase nominale en indo-europeen," *Mémoires de la société de linguistique de Paris* 14 (1906-08): 1-26, and *Linguistique historique et linguistique générale* (Paris, 1936), vol. 2, pp. 1-18.
16. Parry, *Making of Homeric Verse,* p. 22. Cp. pp. 118, 130, 141.

Chapter 21

1. *The Odyssey of Homer,* ed. W. B. Stanford (London, 1965). For other instances besides *Od.* 6.1, see Stanford's comments on *Od.* 6.26–27, 18.5, 20.160.

2. I quote from *Scholia Graeca,* ed. H. Erbse, vols. 1–5 (Berlin, 1969–77); *Scholia Graeca in Homeri Odysseam,* ed. W. Dindorf, vols. 1–2 (Oxford, 1855).

3. For "illogical" in this sense, see Parry, *Making of Homeric Verse,* p. 123.

4. This is essentially the position of A. Amory Parry, *Blameless Aegisthus,* cp. pp. 9–10, 102.

5. Parry, *Making of Homeric Verse,* p. 391.

6. See the literature in Erbse's note, *Scholia Graeca,* vol. 2, pp. 388–89.

7. Erbse, *Scholia Graeca,* vol. 1, pp. 420–21 (on *Il.* 3.352).

8. Düntzer, *Homerische Abhandlungen,* pp. 510, 513.

9. Parry, *Making of Homeric Verse,* p. 124.

10. So, for instance, Carolus Franke, *De nominum propriorum epithetis homericis* (Gryphiswaldiae, 1887).

11. See, A. Schuster, *Untersuchungen über die homerischen stabilen Beiwörter* (Stade, 1866). Schuster strains the differences of meaning between the epithets of night (pp. 22–28); remarks that no bloody epithet of Ares is found in the scene of the god's loves with Aphrodite in *Od.* 8.266–366 (pp. 15–18); tells us that all the epithets are relevant to the epic subject matter.

12. Parry, *Making of Homeric Verse,* p. 22.

13. Ibid., p. 44, n.

14. Ibid., pp. 72–73.

15. Ibid., p. 138.

16. For epithets in oblique cases, see pp. 199–203 above.

17. Austin, p. 29. See also passim.

18. J. B. Hainsworth, *The Flexibility of the Homeric Formula* (Oxford, 1968); A. Hoekstra, *Modifications of Formulaic Prototypes* (Amsterdam, 1964). For their thoughts on the poet's originality, see Hainsworth, pp. 14, 30, 31, 57, 113; Hoekstra, p. 7. Further criticism of the idea of formula in W. Minton, "The Fallacy of the Structural Formula," *Transactions of the American Philological Association* 96 (1965): 241–53; T. G. Rosenmeyer, "The Formula in Early Greek Poetry," *Arion* 4 (1965): 295–311.

19. A. Severyns, *Homère, le poète et son oeuvre* (Bruxelles, 1946), vol. 2, p. 50.

20. Hoekstra, *Formulaic Prototypes,* p. 48.

21. Parry, *Making of Homeric Verse,* p. 60. Parry says here that these phrases are not declined because they are not equally useful in all cases. But why are they not useful? Significantly enough, he does not take the next step.

22. Important contributions in this sense: James I. Armstrong, "The Arming Motif in the Iliad," *American Journal of Philology* 79 (1958): 337–53; Joseph A. Russo, "Homer against the Tradition," *Arion* 7 (1968): 275–95; Charles P. Segal, "Andromache's Anagnorisis: Formulaic Artistry in *Iliad* 22.437–476," *Harvard Studies in Classical Philology* 75 (1971): 33–57.

23. Rosenmeyer, "Formula in Greek Poetry," p. 297.
24. E.g., Whitman, *Homer and the Heroic Tradition,* p. 110; Austin, *Archery at the Dark of the Moon,* pp. 67–69.
25. D. H. F. Gray, "Homeric Epithets for Things," *Classical Quarterly* 61 (1974): 109–21; Denys Page, *History and the Homeric* Iliad (Berkeley, 1959), pp. 224–32. The failure of formulas in so interpreting may be seen in Gray's assumption that τετράφαλος of Achilles' helmet in *Il.* 22.315 vaguely means "fabulous" on the grounds that the epithet is there "inorganic" (i.e., nonformulaic) while it is elsewhere associated with formulas describing the "miraculous" helmets of Athena and Agamemnon The whole idea of a miraculous helmet in the *Iliad* appears gratuitous.
26. William Whallon, "The Homeric Epithets," *Yale Classical Studies* 17 (1961): 102, 109–10, 115, passim; cp. Page, *History and the Homeric* Iliad, p. 160; G. S. Kirk, *The Songs of Homer* (Cambridge, 1962), p. 81.
27. Mark W. Edwards, "Some Features of Homeric Craftsmanship," *Transactions of the American Philological Association* 97 (1966): 165, 253. Parry never uses such terms as *fillers* and *padding* when expounding his own theory.
28. Whallon, "The Homeric Epithets," p. 119; cp. 107–08, 112. Such interpretations cannot be refuted on their own ground. They prove, if anything, how suggestive the Homeric epithets can be in so prompting the human mind.
29. J. T. Sheppard, "Zeus-loved Achilles," *Journal of Hellenic Studies* 55 (1935): 113. See also Sheppard, "Great-hearted Odysseus," *Journal of Hellenic Studies* 56 (1936): 36–47.
30. On the general acceptance of Parry's theory, see, for instance, Hainsworth, *Flexibility of Homeric Formula,* p. 1.
31. C. M. Bowra, *Heroic Poetry* (London, 1966), pp. 233–34; C. M. Bowra, *Homer* (London, 1972), pp. 18–19.
32. C. M. Bowra, "Essay on Style," in *A Companion to Homer,* ed. A. J. B. Wace and F. H. Stubbings (London, 1952), p. 34.
33. Bowra, *Heroic Poetry,* pp. 225–26.
34. E.g., G. Finsler, *Homer* (Leipzig and Berlin, 1924), vol. 1, p. 2, p. 249.
35. Parry, *Making of Homeric Verse,* pp. 126–29.
36. R. Kühner and B. Gerth, *Ausführliche Grammatik der Griechischen Sprache* (Hanover and Leipzig, 1904), vol. 4, p. 587.
37. S. E. Bassett, *The Poetry of Homer* (Berkeley, 1938), p. 162.
38. G. Santayana, *The Sense of Beauty* (New York, 1896), p. 178.
39. Erich Auerbach, *Mimesis,* trans. Willard R. Trask (Princeton, 1968).
40. J. Ruskin, *The Elements of Drawing,* Letter 1.
41. F. Dornseiff, *Pindars Stil* (Berlin, 1921), p. 36.
42. Hugo von Hofmannsthal, "Ein deutscher Homer von heute," *Inselalmanach* 14 (1913): 73. See also *Gesammelte Werke,* Prosa III (Fischer Verlag, 1952), p. 95.
43. K. Meister, *Homerische Kunstsprache* (Leipzig, 1921), p. 12.

Chapter 22

1. I grant for the argument's sake that Homer was an "oral poet," as supposed by Parry. Whether he wrote or not is not relevant to my thesis.

2. Parry, *Making of Homeric Verse*, p. 2.
3. Albert Béguin, *Création et Destinée* (Paris, 1973), p. 129.
4. Northrop Frye, *Fables of Identity* (New York, 1963), p. 10.
5. Parry, *Making of Homeric Verse*, p. 324.
6. Ibid., p. 334.
7. Ibid., pp. 82–83.
8. Cp. ibid., p. 166. Here Parry opposes Pindar to Homer: in the opening of Pythian IV, for instance, the noun-epithet phrase "Cyrene-rich-in-horses" is, unlike what we find in Homer, connected with the purpose of the poem celebrating Arcesilas victorious in the chariot race. Had he looked further, he would have found instances of the same indifference to the context as in Homer: e.g., "thin-winged dolphins," "bronze-jawed anchor."
9. From "A letter by Coleridge on plagiarism." See Samuel Taylor Coleridge, *Shakespearean Criticism* (Everyman's Edition, 1960), vol. 2, p. 191.
10. Parry, *Making of Homeric Verse*, p. 137.
11. Ibid., p. 267.
12. Albert B. Lord, *The Singer of Tales* (New York, 1965), p. 21.
13. Ibid., p. 22.
14. Austin, *Archery at the Dark of the Moon*, p. 21.
15. Parry, *Making of Homeric Verse*, p. 439.
16. Ibid., p. 440.
17. Ibid., p. 447.
18. Ibid., p. 427.
19. Ibid., p. 164.
20. Ibid., p. 73.
21. Ibid., p. 144.
22. Albert B. Lord, "Composition by Theme in Homer and Southslavic Epos," *Transactions of the American Philological Association* 82 (1951): 73.
23. Lord, *The Singer of Tales*, p. 81.
24. Ibid., p. 78.
25. Ibid., p. 97.
26. Ibid., p. 186.
27. M. N. Nagler, *Spontaneity and Tradition, A Study in the Oral Art of Homer* (Berkeley, 1974), p. 46. This book is an important attempt to establish a system of expressive values on Parryist premises. But when it comes to the creative act, Nagler's theory is applicable to modern poetry also: the *Gestalt* breaking into a variety of *allomorphs* may be taken as a poetic idea branching off into image-making analogies of its own qualitative identity. Cp. pp. 9–10 above. For a sympathetic appreciation of Nagler's book, see Norman Austin, "Dynamic Homer," *Arion*, n.s. 3/2 (1976): 220–31.
28. Lord, *The Singer of Tales*, p. 187.

Appendix

1. See pp. 65–71 above.
2. See pp. 72–74 above.
3. See pp. 86–93 above.
4. There is ambiguity in *Il.* 17.176, ἀλλ᾽αἰεί τε Διὸς κρείσσων νόος αἰγιόχοιο compared with *Il.*16.688, ἀλλ᾽ αἰεί τε Διὸς κρείσσων νόος ἠέ περ ἀνδρῶν.

The term of comparison undermines the self-contained idea of Zeus's mind (*νόος* refers to *ἀνδρῶν* as well).

5. See p. 120 above.
6. See p. 131 above.

INDEX

Subjects

INDEX

ἔρατος, 121
ἐρίγδουπος, 209
ἐϋκλεής, 103

ἠεροειδής, 122
ἦκα, 124
ἠνεμόεις, 47

θαλερός, 117
θεῖος, 129
θῆλυς, 166
θοός, 105, 210

ἱμερόεις, 121
ἰοειδής, 122

καλός, 132, 203–05
κελαινός, 209
κλυτός (κλειτός, etc.), 129, 103–04
κορυθαίδλος, 92, 129

λειριόεις, 117–18
λεπτός, 211
λευγαλέος, 106
λευκός, 123
λυγρός, 106

μακρός, 114
μεγάθυμος, 92, 127, 129, cp. 47
μεγαλήτωρ, 127
μέλας, 123

οἶνοψ, 122
ὀφρυόεις, 47

παμφανόων, 124
παχύς, 113–14
πεπνυμένος, 108–09
περίφρων, 130
ποδάρκης (ποδώκης, πόδας ὠκύς), 92,
   111, 129–30
πολιός, 122
πολυδάκρυτος, 106
πολύστονος, 106
πορφύρεος, 122
πυκνός, 115–16, 118

σιγαλόεις, 124
σκιόεις, 125
στονόεις, 106

τέρην, 117
τετυγμένος, 120

ὑπερφίαλος, 130, 213
ὑψηλός, 114–15, 211

φαεινός, 124

χάλκεος, of the sky, 97
χλωρός, 125

ὠκύς, 102, 105